The 'Catalan Hermaphrodite' and the Inquisition

The 'Catalan Hermaphrodite' and the Inquisition

Early Modern Sex and Gender on Trial

François Soyer

BLOOMSBURY ACADEMIC
LONDON • NEW YORK • OXFORD • NEW DELHI • SYDNEY

BLOOMSBURY ACADEMIC
Bloomsbury Publishing Plc, 50 Bedford Square, London, WC1B 3DP, UK
Bloomsbury Publishing Inc, 1385 Broadway, New York, NY 10018, USA
Bloomsbury Publishing Ireland, 29 Earlsfort Terrace, Dublin 2, D02 AY28, Ireland

BLOOMSBURY, BLOOMSBURY ACADEMIC and the Diana logo are trademarks of Bloomsbury Publishing Plc

First published in Great Britain 2024
This paperback edition published in 2025

Copyright © François Soyer 2024

François Soyer has asserted his right under the Copyright, Designs and Patents Act, 1988, to be identified as author of this work.

Cover image: Marcantonio Raimondi: Woman with a Dildo, 1500s.
(Photo: Cecilia Heisser, public domain)

All rights reserved. No part of this publication may be: i) reproduced or transmitted in any form, electronic or mechanical, including photocopying, recording or by means of any information storage or retrieval system without prior permission in writing from the publishers; or ii) used or reproduced in any way for the training, development or operation of artificial intelligence (AI) technologies, including generative AI technologies. The rights holders expressly reserve this publication from the text and data mining exception as per Article 4(3) of the Digital Single Market Directive (EU) 2019/790.

Bloomsbury Publishing Plc does not have any control over, or responsibility for, any third-party websites referred to or in this book. All internet addresses given in this book were correct at the time of going to press. The author and publisher regret any inconvenience caused if addresses have changed or sites have ceased to exist, but can accept no responsibility for any such changes.

Every effort has been made to trace the copyright holders and obtain permission to reproduce the copyright material. Please do get in touch with any enquiries or any information relating to such material or the rights holder. We would be pleased to rectify any omissions in subsequent editions of this publication should they be drawn to our attention.

A catalogue record for this book is available from the British Library.

A catalog record for this book is available from the Library of Congress.

ISBN: HB: 978-1-3503-7759-2
PB: 978-1-3503-7763-9
ePDF: 978-1-3503-7760-8
eBook: 978-1-3503-7761-5

Typeset by Newgen KnowledgeWorks Pvt. Ltd., Chennai, India

For product safety related questions contact productsafety@bloomsbury.com.

To find out more about our authors and books visit www.bloomsbury.com and sign up for our newsletters.

In memory of Maria Filomena Lopes de Barros (1958–2021),
Historian, colleague and friend

Contents

Figures

Maps

Acknowledgements

I have benefitted from the insights and assistance of numerous scholars since I first came across Maria Duran's trial in the National Archives of the Torre do Tombo in Lisbon in 2007. I owe debts to Katie Barclay and Sarah Bendall for their insights on various aspects of life and clothing in eighteenth-century Europe. Kathleen Neal kindly invited me to present a paper on Maria Duran's trial at Monash University's Centre for Medieval and Renaissance Studies in 2021, which led to helpful discussions with those present on that occasion. Patrícia Martins Marcos and Ofélia Sequeira kindly undertook research on my behalf in the National Library of Portugal in Lisbon and the Public Library in Évora in 2021 when the Covid-19 pandemic made international travel impossible. Various queries about Portuguese palaeography that I posted on Twitter with the hashtag #twitterstorians drew extremely helpful feedback and suggestions from a huge number of fellow scholars, sadly too many to name here. I would nevertheless like to thank Patrícia Martins Marcos and Pedro Pinto for their help in deciphering some particularly challenging sections of the trial dossier. I owe a debt of gratitude to the staff of the following libraries and archives in Portugal: the Arquivo National da Torre do Tombo in Lisbon, the Biblioteca Nacional in Lisbon and the Biblioteca Pública in Évora. Jaime Sepulcre Samper of the Real Biblioteca de El Escorial in Spain very generously ensured that I had access to a digital copy of a document from that library.

Over the years, I have been able to discuss this case and thereby have gained new insights with the successive cohorts of students that I have been privileged to teach. Most notably, they include the students who stepped out of their comfort zone and chose my year-long special subject *The Spanish and Portuguese Inquisitions* at the University of Southampton in the UK between 2008 and 2017 and those who have enrolled in my postgraduate methodological unit *Understanding History* at the University of New England (Armidale, NSW) in Australia.

Maria Duran and trial number 9,230 of the Inquisition of Lisbon have been a part of my life since 2007. Although various other research and book projects have periodically taken my attention away in the intervening fifteen years, I always remained determined that this fascinating trial should one day become the focus of a book-length study. I wrote the first draft of the manuscript of this book in 2021–2, during the Covid-19 pandemic, hunched over my laptop at my dinner table (for lack of a home office), either very early in the predawn morning hours of a freezing Armidale winter or late at night after a draining day of juggling homeschooling and teaching students online. Since 2007, my beloved Katie has offered constant support and encouragement to pursue this project and our children, Abigail, Chris and Elsa have tolerated my visits to conferences and archives with exemplary patience.

I want to dedicate this book to the memory of my dear friend and colleague Maria Filomena Lopes de Barros (1958–2021), formerly professor of medieval Islamic history at the University of Évora in Portugal. Few historians today can claim to have lifted up an entire subject from obscurity, but Filomena did just that through her pioneering and innovative doctoral thesis on the medieval Muslim minority in the Christian Kingdom of Portugal, which was published by the Fundação Calouste Gulbenkian in 2011 with the title *Tempos e Espaços de Mouros. A Minoria Muçulmana no Reino Português (Séculos XII a XV)*. Filomena was a dear friend, who kindly supported my research before, during and after my PhD at the University of Cambridge. In addition to graciously sharing both her published and unpublished work, Filomena generously offered me and many other scholars visiting Portuguese archives free accommodation in her flat in the Ajuda district of Lisbon. Over the years, and over countless coffees, car trips, lunches and dinners, I frequently had the opportunity to discuss Maria Duran's trial and my publication plans with Filomena, who shared valuable insights from her own research and expressed a keen interest in seeing this book published. Filomena's unexpected and sudden death in March 2021 marks a huge loss to Portuguese historical studies. I can only hope that this book stands as a fitting tribute to Filomena's life and work. *Para Filomena, cara amiga, com saudades dos inúmeros cafés e conversas.*

Armidale, NSW.
January 2023

Chronology of the Life and Trial of Maria Duran

c. 1711: Maria is born in Prullans, bishopric of La Seu d'Urgell, Catalonia (eastern Spain).

c. 1725: Marriage of Maria and Ignacio Sulsona.

c. 1728–9: Birth of Maria's only child, a son who dies nine to ten months later.

c. 1732–3: Maria flees her husband and seeks refuge in Andorra.

1733–4: Dressed in male clothing, Maria travels around southern France.

1734–7: Maria returns to Catalonia, serves in the Spanish army and then moves to Madrid.

1 August 1738: Maria arrives in Lisbon.

August 1738: Maria enters the *recolhimento do Menino Deus.*

Early-mid 1739: Maria enters the *recolhimento* of *Nossa Senhora da Encarnação.*

May 1740: Maria is admitted into the convent of *Nossa Senhora do Paraíso.*

17 February 1741: General Council of the Inquisition approves the arrest of Maria Duran.

23 February 1741: Under escort, Maria Duran arrives at the Inquisitorial Palace in Lisbon and is placed in a cell.

13 March 1741: First Interrogation of Maria Duran.

8 July 1741: Second Interrogation of Maria Duran.

15 July 1741: Interrogation of Maria Duran continued.

29 August 1741: Interrogation of Maria Duran continued.

30 August: Inquisitors write their preliminary report.

2 September 1741: Genealogical Interrogation of Maria Duran.

11 September 1741: Interrogation *In Genere* of Maria Duran.

12 September 1741: Inquisitors of Lisbon write to their colleagues in Barcelona.

23 October 1741: Interrogation *In Specie* of Maria Duran.

7 November 1741: Maria Duran receives her 'admonition' prior to the prosecution presenting its indictment (the *libelo*).

7 November 1741: Correspondence from the Inquisition of Barcelona sent to Lisbon.

8 November 1741: Maria Duran is offered and selects a defence attorney.

15 November 1741: Maria Duran and her attorney prepare and present her defence.

January–April 1742: Defence questions are put to the witnesses in Évora and elsewhere.

18 June 1742: Medical examination of Maria Duran.

11 July 1742: Interrogation of Maria Duran.

12 September 1742: The inquisitors of Lisbon and theologians gather to review the case.

29 October 1743: The General Council of the Inquisition orders the use of torture.

15 April 1744: Maria Duran is tortured.

11 May 1744: The inquisitors of Lisbon review the case. They decide to condemn Maria to abjure her sins in a public *auto-da-fé* and to leave Portugal within fifteen days.

22 May 1744: The General Council of the Inquisition harshens the sentence by adding lashes.

21 June 1744: Maria is publicly condemned at an *auto-da-fé* staged in Lisbon.

22 July 1744: Maria signs the *termo de segredo* and is released.

Abbreviations

AHN	Archivo Histórico Nacional (Madrid)
ANTT	Arquivo Nacional da Torre do Tombo (Lisbon)
BNP	Biblioteca Nacional de Portugal (Lisbon)
BPE	Biblioteca Pública de Évora (Évora)

Maps

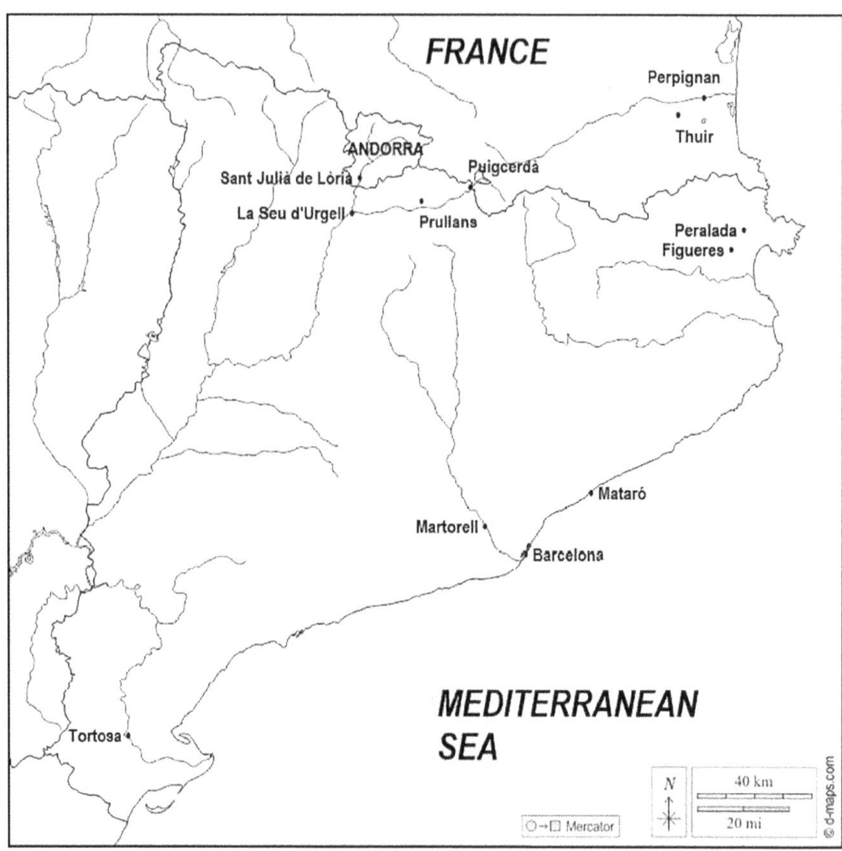

Map 1 A map of the Principality of Catalonia in Eastern Spain, with the towns and villages mentioned in this book (Copyright d-maps.com. Original map: https://d-maps.com/carte.php?num_car=13847&lang=en).

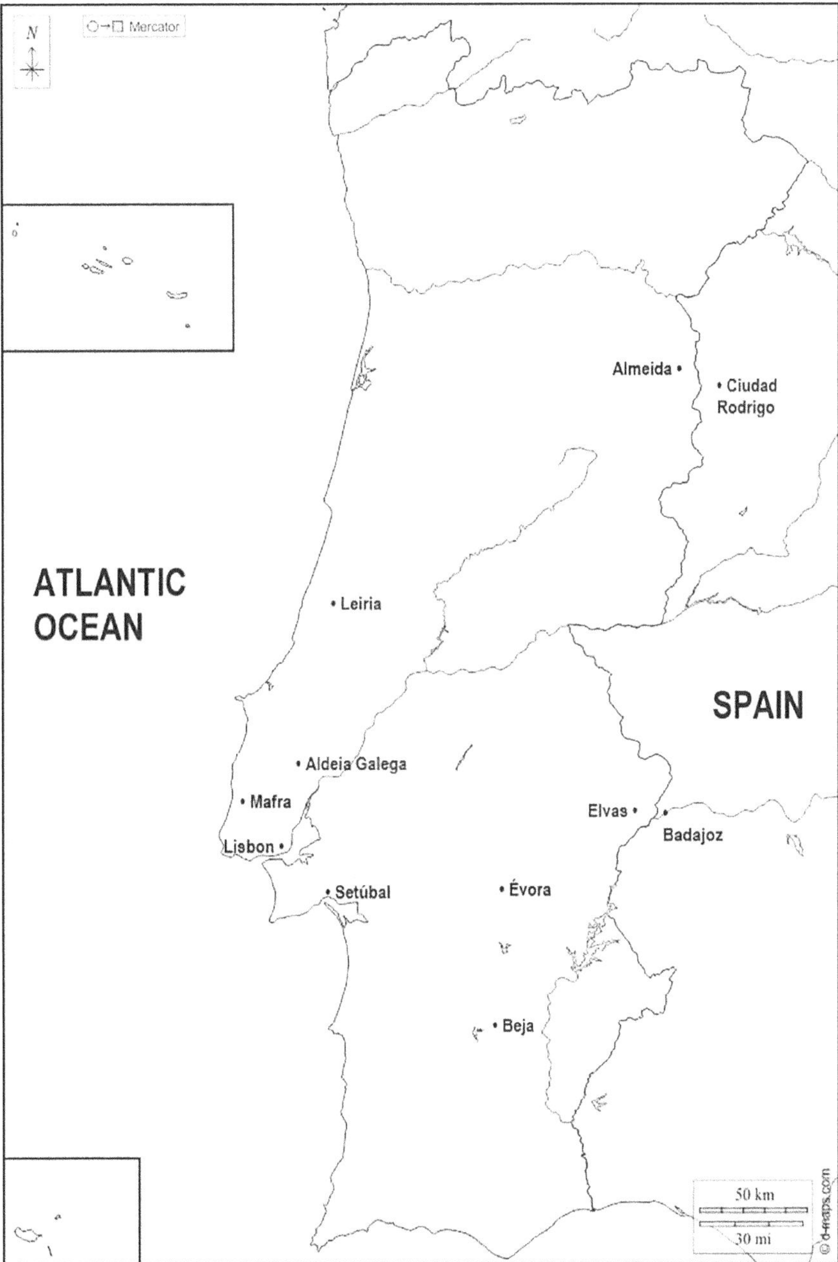

Map 2 A map of Portugal, with the towns and villages mentioned in this book (Copyright d-maps.com. Original map: https://d-maps.com/carte.php?num_car=2499&lang=en).

Introduction

This book is the result of a 'happy accident'. In early 2007, I was conducting research in the *Arquivo Nacional da Torre do Tombo* in Lisbon thanks to a postdoctoral award from the Leverhulme Trust. My project sought to find evidence of collaboration between the Spanish and Portuguese Inquisitions in the archives of the Portuguese Inquisition. The primitive computer catalogue that existed in the archive at the time allowed me to search for surviving trial dossiers that contained documents in languages other than Portuguese. I hoped to find trial dossiers containing letters and documents sent by the inquisitors in Spain to their colleagues in Portugal by typing the word '*castelhano*' (Castilian, i.e. modern Spanish) into the catalogue. One of the numerous trial dossiers identified by the catalogue as containing Spanish language documents was trial dossier number 9,230 of the inquisitorial tribunal of Lisbon. The trial dossier was that of a 31-year-old named Maria Cristina de Escallao e Pinos, identified as a woman and a native of the village of *Prulhanes* (Catalan Prullans) in Catalonia in eastern Spain. The Inquisition prosecuted Maria between 1741 and 1744 and ultimately declared her guilty of making a pact with the Devil.

I duly asked for the sizeable trial dossier – 734 pages long – and began to study it closely. It took me the best part of six months to transcribe the trial dossier but I rapidly realized that the terse description of the trial dossier in the computer catalogue hid an extraordinary story. Maria, whose real name was Maria Duran, had an eventful life involving an escape from her husband and home village in the Pyrenees, cross-dressing, military service in the army of the King of Spain, a journey across the Iberian Peninsula and sexual relations with women in various religious institutions in Portugal. Many of these women accused Maria of being a man possessing a penis and suspected Maria of having made a pact with the Devil. Finally, the dreaded tribunal of the Inquisition in Lisbon arrested Maria and conducted a lengthy investigation and trial to determine if Maria was a man, a woman or a 'hermaphrodite' and whether she had made a pact with the Devil. Maria always claimed to be a 'true woman' but, after three years of imprisonment, was found guilty of having made a pact with the Devil that allowed her to deceive women into believing that she possessed a penis.

The Spanish and Portuguese Inquisitions lie at the heart of Maria Duran's story. The papacy established both inquisitions in 1480 and 1536, respectively, in response to requests from the rulers of the Spanish kingdoms and of Portugal. The inquisitions were law courts staffed by ecclesiastical judges with special investigative powers. Within the first decades of their existence, the Spanish and Portuguese inquisitions divided their respective kingdoms into inquisitorial provinces in which one tribunal was established. Under the supervision of an Inquisitor General appointed by the Crown – the title 'Grand Inquisitor' is a modern invention – each tribunal of the Inquisition ran its own prisons and network of agents (known as 'familiars' and 'commissaries'). Their first aim was to hunt down and prosecute suspected judaizers: those converted to Christianity from Judaism and their descendants who secretly continued to follow their Jewish beliefs. By the eighteenth century, however, the inquisitors had expanded their remit to pursue various other forms of heresy: from 'Lutherans' (a generic term for Protestants) to bigamists and from blasphemers who attacked Catholic dogma to individuals accused of making a pact with the Devil. Inquisitorial trials took place behind closed doors and according to strict inquisitorial procedures that assumed the guilt of the prisoner and forced the prisoner to prove their innocence. In stark contrast to the secrecy surrounding the trial, the sentencing of convicted heretics took place in public. The inquisitors organized public processions of prisoners before reading out an account of their crimes and their sentence in spectacular public sentencings: the *autos-da-fé*.

The Inquisition was a modern judicial bureaucracy. Notaries recorded on paper all court proceedings through detailed transcripts of interrogations and the inquisitors' deliberations. The inquisitors gathered all the material relevant to the trial in a trial dossier and, once the trial ended, they filed it away in the 'secret archives' of an inquisitorial tribunal, which only the inquisitors could access. Each trial dossier provides modern historians with a unique insight into the lives of individuals in Spain and Portugal. Indeed, the seven hundred pages that record Maria Duran's trial offer an excellent opportunity to study not just the life of a single individual – however remarkable that life was – but also to study the wider cultural and social context in which Maria lived. Attitudes towards gender and sexuality as well as ideas about the power of the Devil over the human body and evidence of deeply entrenched cultural norms emerge from both the testimony of witnesses and the questions and deliberations of the inquisitors. In effect, this book is a microhistory that not only focuses on the life and trial of Maria Duran but also shines a light on eighteenth-century Spanish and Portuguese culture and society.

Microhistory has gained popularity since its beginnings in the 1970s and has established an enduring presence in the study of early modern European social and cultural history. Carlo Ginzburg's celebrated *the Cheese and the Worms* (1976) and Natalie Zemon Davis' equally famous *The Return of Martin Guerre* (1983) can be considered the pioneering works of this genre.[1] Through an analysis of an inquisitorial trial dossier, Ginzburg created a window onto popular culture and belief in sixteenth-century Italy. Similarly, Zemon Davis explored a famous and unusual legal case to analyse how individuals created their identities in relation to property and family in southern France during the sixteenth century. Other works that have popularized microhistory include Judith Brown's *Immodest Acts: The Life of a Lesbian Nun in Renaissance Italy* (1986); Richard Kagan's *Lucrecia's Dreams: Politics and Prophecy in Sixteenth-Century Spain* (1990) and even more recently Ulinka Rublack's *The Astronomer and the Witch: Johannes Kepler's Fight for his Mother* (2015).[2]

The trend in these early modern microstudies is obvious: they all examine cases in which an individual was the subject of a legal investigation conducted by the secular or ecclesiastical authorities that policed their society. The rise in judicial bureaucracies during the early modern period has bequeathed a rich body of primary sources to modern historians. Admittedly, these sources and the microhistories that depend on them have a tendency to focus on 'outliers' rather than the life of 'average' individuals. Nevertheless, they still record the voices of those who represent what we could describe as the 'norm' of society. Maria Duran's story, for example, is extraordinary in many ways but the inquisitors did not interrogate Maria alone. Also recorded are the voices of a host of witnesses as well as the inquisitors' own reactions to, and thoughts about, the case.

The first part of this book, entitled The Remarkable Life of Maria Duran, thus seeks to use the legal record of the Inquisition's investigation into the life, deeds and beliefs of Maria Duran as well as other documents to reconstruct the biography of an extraordinary 'ordinary' person. Its ten chapters span from Maria's early childhood in the Catalan Pyrenees to her trial in Lisbon. It begins with Maria's flight from her husband (Chapter 1), cross-dressing and service in the Spanish army (Chapter 2). This is followed by Maria's arrival in Portugal and her time in various establishments for 'helpless women' where Maria conducted love affairs with women before being expelled (Chapters 3 and 4) and Maria's transfer to the convent of *Nossa Senhora do Paraíso* in the town of Évora, where more sexual affairs with nuns and novices occurred (Chapter 5). The first part then examines Maria's arrest by the Inquisition and trial. The trial lasted over three years, during which the inquisitors repeatedly interrogated Maria, ordered medical professionals to conduct a physical examination of Maria's genitals and even determined to have her tortured (Chapters 6, 7 and 8). It concludes with the verdict of the inquisitors and Maria's public sentencing on 21 June 1744 (Chapters 9 and 10). Whenever possible, the information in the trial dossier has been compared to that available from other sources to verify its authenticity. This section also examines points of historical significance that emerge from Maria's life and trial.

Inquisitorial trial dossiers are, by their very nature, potentially problematic sources of information and historians must analyse them with great care. The trial dossiers of the Inquisition were not propaganda documents intended for public consumption. Working in the secrecy ordered by inquisitorial procedure, the inquisitors had no motive to falsify the records or invent evidence. Nevertheless, one must not use such documents uncritically. The perspective offered is always that of the inquisitors rather than the prisoner/defendant or the witnesses. The inquisitorial notaries who wrote the transcripts of interrogations always rendered them in the third person singular and in the past tense: *She was asked … she replied … .* Direct speech, the actual words of the prisoner, rarely entered the written record. Indeed, the only instance in Maria Duran's trial when the notary explicitly wrote down her words was when she was being tortured and he recorded her agonized pleas. Writing about inquisitorial records, the British historian John Arnold has advocated in favour of a heteroglossic approach that recognizes the fact that the testimony of prisoners and witnesses recorded by the Inquisition is a record of numerous and competing discourses and voices of the inquisitors, their officials, the witnesses and the prisoner, which is impossible to disentangle.[3] These different voices are contained in the transcripts of interrogations and they speak within the inquisitorial discourse of dogma/heresy as well as the different positions of the defendant and witnesses. A modern historian must thus tread carefully and endeavour to verify details of witness testimony whenever it is possible by seeking sources of information beyond the trial dossier.

Piecing together and retelling the extraordinary (but often grim) life of Maria Duran is not, however, the sole objective of this work. The second part of this book is entitled The Maria Duran Mystery: Transgressive Sexuality, Transing Gender and Gender Performativity in the Trial of Maria Duran. It tackles the questions that surround Maria's sex, sexuality and gender. The trial of Maria

Duran opens a window onto a world that is rarely recorded in early modern documents: the secretive transgression of gender norms, sexuality and sexual violence in female religious institutions as well as the fears and debates about the power that the Devil could wield over the human body. The inquisitorial trial dossier is a veritable treasure trove of information about gendered cultural norms of masculinity and femininity and social attitudes about men and women. These become apparent in the testimony of the churchmen who sought to enclose Maria in a religious institution to save her soul (and protect the moral order of society), of the women with whom Maria interacted in those institutions as well as the baffled (possibly traumatized) women with whom Maria had sexual relations. Last, but certainly not least, these attitudes are very evident in the questions and deliberations of the puzzled and frustrated inquisitors who judged Maria, as they attempted to make sense of witness evidence that could not be reconciled with medical findings.

Maria Duran's trial coincided with a period in which the medical understanding of sex was gradually changing in Europe and turning against the Galenic 'one-sex' model bequeathed by Greco-Roman Antiquity. Instead, the majority of medical authorities were gradually embracing a new model clearly distinguishing between two sexes and refuting the existence of 'hermaphrodites'.[4] Some of the witnesses who accused Maria Duran of being a man also mooted the possibility that Maria might be a 'hermaphrodite', a being with both male and female sexual organs. Public rumours circulating about Maria soon after her arrest also described her as 'the Catalan hermaphrodite'. Accordingly, the inquisitors gathered a number of doctors, surgeons and even a midwife who conducted a careful examination of Maria's body in general and genitals in particular. When reviewing the case and debating an appropriate verdict, the inquisitors and other theologians discussed the identity of Maria's 'sex' in purely biological terms.

The second part of this book seeks to analyse Maria Duran's story within the wider modern debates about gender and sexuality. There is now a burgeoning scholarly literature on sex and gender in the early modern world. Numerous studies have focused on the move away from the Galenic 'one-sex' model to one that presented male and female as binary opposites. Other scholars have focused on the cultural and social dynamics that shaped attitudes towards, and responses to, sexuality and sexual behaviour perceived to deviate from the norm. Historical debates exist about the potential anachronism of using modern terms like 'lesbian', 'transgender' or even 'intersex' when writing about periods that predate the nineteenth century. Neither Maria nor the inquisitors or the witnesses in the trial, would have understood such terms. Gender as a social construct or product only emerged as an analysis category created by feminists in the 1960s and 1970s and the notion of 'transgender' only appeared in the 1990s. Michel Foucault famously noted in his 1976 work *L'Histoire de la sexualité* that the categories of 'homosexual' and 'heterosexual' as identities ('straight', 'gay', 'lesbian') did not appear until the nineteenth century.[5] Likewise, David Valentine has sounded a warning that 'to imagine historical subjects as "gay", "lesbian" or as "transgender" ignores the radically different understandings of self and the contexts that underpinned the practices and lives of historical subjects'.[6] Notwithstanding these concerns, it is clear from the evidence in the trial that Maria was 'Queer', which is to say that Maria's sexual or gender identity was not straight and cisgender.

To my knowledge, I am the only researcher to have worked on this fascinating historical document/source. I have previously offered only a narrative account of the trial in a short book chapter entitled 'Sister Maria's Secret Penis: The Trial of Maria Duran (1741–1744)', published in my 2012 monograph *Ambiguous Gender in Early Modern Spain and Portugal*.[7] Two years later, I endeavoured to examine Maria Duran's sexuality in a short article that focused exclusively on explaining Maria's behaviour through the prism of female homosexuality.[8] I now recognize that these previous examinations of Maria Duran's life and trial were somewhat uncritical and lacking in depth. Indeed, the story of Maria's life seems to be much more complex and this book draws on new methodological insights to make sense of it. Until writing this book, I had not engaged with the concept of 'trans-ing' gender, which offers a far more useful framework for understanding those individuals like Maria Duran whose past lives did not conform to the biological expectations of their society. Furthermore, since 2014 I have found new documents in the Public Library of Évora (Portugal), the National Library of Portugal and the *Torre do Tombo* archives in Lisbon that help contextualize and shed light on some aspects of Maria Duran life and trial.

Maria Duran's life and trial are probably best explored through the concept of 'transing gender'. In his 2012 work *History in the Making*, the celebrated Iberianist Sir John Huxtable Elliott noted that 'theory is of less importance for the writing of good history than the ability to enter imaginatively into the life of a society remote in time or place, and produce a plausible explanation of why its inhabitants thought and behaved as they did'.[9] The limitations of the primary source evidence nevertheless means that it is impossible to establish conclusively what Maria really thought and why Maria behaved as she did. As such, it is more profitable to turn to a theoretical approach that could help us better understand Maria's behaviour. In 2008, Clare Sear pioneered 'trans-ing analysis', as a methodological approach for studying a wide variety of gender-crossing practices:

> This trans-ing approach centers on the historical production and subsequent operations of the boundary between normative and nonnormative gender. As such, it brings together a range of cross-gender phenomena rarely considered alongside one another – not only people and practices that challenge gender normativity but also cross-gender practices that do not provoke censure, and trans-ing discourses that represent men as feminine, women as masculine, and gender difference as impossible to read.[10]

Likewise, in *Female Husbands: A Trans History* (2020), Jen Manion has offered a fascinating historical survey of various people in Britain and English-speaking North America during the eighteenth, nineteenth and early twentieth centuries who were assigned a female identity at birth but chose to live as men and marry women. For Manion, these people 'transed' gender and Manion uses the concept of 'trans' as a verb since 'to say someone "transed" or was "transing" gender signifies a process or practice without claiming to understand what it meant to that person or asserting any kind of fixed identity on them'.[11] The concept of 'transing gender' thus offers a useful framework for understanding those individuals like Maria Duran whose past lives did not conform to the biological expectations of their society.

Depending on whether we examine it through the prisms of sexuality or gender, two different pictures emerge. Maria may have been a female homosexual who exploited gendered norms prevalent in the eighteenth-century Iberian world to convince reluctant female heterosexual partners to have sex with her.[12] A number of studies focusing on historical cases of female homosexuality in a conventual setting have appeared. Judith Brown's *Immodest Acts: The Life of a Lesbian Nun in Renaissance Italy* (1986) was a ground-breaking study and has been followed by a handful of other microhistories, also based on legal sources. Similarly, Hubert Wolf's *The Nuns of Sant' Ambrogio: The True Story of a Convent in Scandal* reconstructs a story of sexual abuse, bitter feuds and apparently bogus visions behind the walls of the convent of Sant'Ambrogio della Massima in nineteenth-century Rome.[13] In some respects, Maria Duran's story bears striking similarities with these cases and it would be tempting to analyze Maria's story as a case of early modern female homosexuality.

Limiting an analysis of Maria Duran's life and trial to the subject of sexuality as I did in my 2014 article is not satisfactory, given Maria's cross-dressing as well as the testimony concerning Maria's behaviour. There is also the distinct possibility that Maria was an individual born with female sexual organs and assigned a female identity at birth who crossed gender and embraced a male gender identity. In relation to the Iberian Peninsula and Iberian empires, scholars have devoted considerable attention to the life of a number of individuals described, or identified, as 'transgender'. Elena/o de Céspedes, whom the Spanish Inquisition prosecuted in 1587, appears to have been transgender and scholars have extensively studied Elena/o's voluminous inquisitorial trial dossier.[14] Likewise, a great deal of interest has focused on the famous case of the 'Ensign Nun' (*la Monja Alférez*) Catalina de Erauso (1585/1592–1650), a renegade nun who left Spain to serve as a soldier in the Spanish Americas and whose colourful autobiography continues to generate debate about its authenticity.[15] More recently, Thomas A. Abercrombie's *Passing to América. Antonio (Née María) Yta's Transgressive, Transatlantic Life in the Twilight of the Spanish Empire* has shed light on another individual whose gender and sexuality puzzled contemporaries in both Spain and modern-day Bolivia.[16] In the second part of this work, Maria Duran's life and actions are compared to these early modern examples as well as other twentieth-century cases of individuals born female who cross-dressed and took on a male identity and had sexual relations with women.

The second part of this book ends by engaging with Judith Butler's theory of the performativity of gender, which argues that gender is constructed through the 'acts' that mark a person as 'man' or 'woman'. After briefly surveying comparable cases from the sixteenth to the twentieth century and drawing their links with that of Maria Duran, I argue that the case of Maria Duran offers powerful evidence of how the performativity of gender is crucial to the successful transing of gender. Indeed, gendered norms and the male/female binary, paradoxically, greatly facilitate the transing of gender. Social expectations of feminine and masculine behaviour in everyday life, interpersonal relations and sexual relations posit rigid boundaries. Maria was clearly aware that in order to successfully 'trans' gender, to pass as a man, it was necessary to 'perform' or 'act' male. To be accepted by others as male, Maria needed to perform daily acts that would convince her mundane social audience that she was male. The evidence from the trial indicates that, unsurprisingly, Maria took obvious steps like donning male clothing to good effect, binding her breasts and carefully hiding any signs of menstruation when passing as a soldier. This was supplemented by the deliberate adoption of patterns of behaviour that were culturally deemed male, or as Maria put it in her own word 'to imitate male customs', even down to pretending to urinate 'like a man'.

The question of pronouns

The questions surrounding Maria Duran's gender identity raise the important issue of what pronouns (he/him/his, she/her/hers or they/them/their) should be used to describe Maria Duran's person and actions. In the trial dossier, both during Maria Duran's interrogations and in the testimony of the witnesses, Maria is always referred to with the Spanish or Portuguese feminine pronouns: *ella* and *elha*, respectively. Despite using male aliases, deliberately adopting behaviour culturally deemed to be 'male' and crossdressing in male clothing, Maria Duran resolutely claimed to be a 'true woman' (*verdadeira mulher*) and denied being either a man or a 'hermaphrodite', even when subjected to torture. Of course, this could well have been part of a deliberate defence strategy. Maria may have been fearful that any other claim might lead to a severe sentence for having made a pact with the Devil, possibly even a death sentence.

This book thus uses the feminine pronouns that feature in the original documents, albeit sparingly. Some readers may well argue that doing this is a problematic choice if Maria Duran was indeed transgender. The crucial fact, however, is that it will never be possible to know what Maria Duran's sense of identity was. The modern historian cannot, any more than an eighteenth-century inquisitor, get into Maria's mind. This book studies Maria's ability to 'trans' gender without making unprovable assumptions about what this meant for Maria's sense of self.

Part I

The Remarkable Life of Maria Duran

1

The fugitive wife from a small village in the Pyrenees

Located at an altitude of approximately 1,100 metres, the village of Prullans lies on the northern bank of the Segre River valley, approximately halfway between the regional towns of La Seu d'Urgell and Puigcerdà in Catalonia. The area is part of the mountainous historical region of Cerdanya and the inhabitants of Prullans speak Catalan. To the south of the village, across the Segre River, rises the impressive mountain chain of the Serra del Cadí, part of the so-called pre-Pyrenees, whose highest peak (named Vulturó) reaches up to 2,649 metres. Directly to the north of the village, the ground rises extremely steeply and continuously to eventually form a mountainous ridge over 2,000 metres high that extends northwards before joining up with the rest of the Pyrenees. As one walks (or rather climbs) north from the village, the trees of the Segre valley progressively give way to bare rocks and tufts of high-altitude grass that are covered by snow in wintertime. The borders with France and the independent Principality of Andorra both lie only a dozen kilometres to the north of Prullans.

The Ceretani, an Iberian people who populated the valley of the Segre, were conquered by the Romans in the first century before the birth of Christ. Due to its relative isolation in the Pyrenees, the Segre valley may well have been spared the worst depravations that followed the takeover of Spain by the Germanic Visigoths in the wake of the disintegration of the Western Roman Empire and then by the Muslim conquest of Spain in 711. Later, the inhabitants of the Segre valley became part of the early Christian push to conquer (or 'reconquer' as medieval Christian chroniclers would put it) the Muslim territories further south in the Ebro Valley at the start of the twelfth century.

The name of Prullans first appears in the early ninth century in records of the consecration of the cathedral of La Seu d'Urgell, in whose diocese the village was included. A Latin document of 1061 refers to the 'forum de Prullanos', indicating that the settlement had a public market but probably no fortifications since no reference is made to a 'castle' (*castrum*). By 1309, however, there existed a fortified building of some type and the village became the fiefdom of the barons of Prullans. The absence of any major castle at Prullans is probably explained by the presence, since 1050, of an imposing castle located on a rocky outcrop at Sant Martí dels Castells, just over 2 kilometres to the west.[1]

The village itself has little to distinguish it from any other human settlements in the area. The most prominent building is the Church of Sant Esteve (Saint Steven). Like most of the ancient churches in the Segre valley, including the cathedral of La Seu d'Urgell, it is a typical Romanesque church of the twelfth century. The building is simple, built of stone ashlars with a single nave, small windows, a quadrangular bell tower and a rounded, semicircular apse. Situated near the Church of Sant Esteve and next to the main square in the centre of the village is the 'castle' itself. The castle was probably never a sizeable fortification since it is also referred to as a 'tower'. Over the centuries, the successive barons converted it into a residence (the *casa dels barons*) and there is little visible evidence of its former military purpose (see Figure 1). Today, Prullan's main attraction for local and foreign visitors is its location amidst stunning natural

Figure 1 The village of Prullans, looking southwards, with the Church of Sant Esteve (centre) and the massive walls of the *casa dels barons* (left). The Serra del Cadí is visible in the background (Alamy.com Image ID: 2D3EFFY. Reproduced under licence).

mountainous scenery rather than any historical architecture. The present population of the village stands at around 200 to 250 souls.

It was in this mountainous village that a child was born around 1711.[2] Eighteenth-century Prullans was, in demographic terms, no smaller than the modern village and in fact appeared to have been slightly more populated. A 1719 census counted two hundred and fifty inhabitants.[3] The newborn was the daughter of Antonio Duran and his wife Margarida. Thirty years later, when questioned by inquisitors in Portugal, Maria could recall that her father was a humble 'worker' (*lavrador*) and that she was baptized in the parish church of Sant Esteve. Maria also remembered that the first names of her godparents were Martin and Maria. It was a common practice for children to take the first name of the godparent who was of the same sex and thus the child became Maria Duran.

Maria was born at a time of war and disorder for Catalonia and the modern-day serenity of Prullans and the Segre valley contrasts with the bloodshed that the area witnessed in the first decades of the eighteenth century. The Segre valley was a militarily strategic road that led straight from France to the cathedral town of La Seu d'Urgell, whose capture would allow any invading French force to strike far deeper into Catalonia. Following the death in 1700 of the physically and mentally infirm King Carlos II, the last ruler of the Habsburg dynasty in Spain, a succession crisis plunged Spain into a state of civil war. Other European powers, especially France, Britain and Austria, became involved in what became known as the Spanish War of Succession. Whilst Catalonia supported one claimant, a Habsburg, the rest of Spain supported another, a Bourbon. The principality rapidly became a battlefield and the port city of Barcelona was besieged no less than three times. Neither was the Segre valley spared: the citadel of La Seu d'Urgell was besieged and forced to surrender to Bourbon forces in 1713.[4] Eventually, following the fall of Barcelona after a particularly protracted and bitter siege in 1714, the Catalans found themselves on the losing side of the conflict.

Peace did not settle easily on the land. A vengeful Bourbon monarch, Philip V of Spain, imposed a harsh centralizing government on the rebellious Catalans, whom he described to the British ambassador as 'outlaws and scoundrels' (*forajidos y pillastres*). In 1716, the government of Philip V abolished all local Catalan laws and Spanish replaced Catalan as the official language of administration. Unsurprisingly, a Spanish government official commented in 1718 that the Catalans were 'restless' and guerrillas loyal to the defeated Habsburg claimant continued to haunt the principality, led by a charismatic and feared semi-legendary guerrilla leader named Pere Joan Barceló (popularly known as *Carrasquet*, the 'coal burner'). The Bourbon government stationed a large military force of loyal troops in Catalonia to secure its control. Indeed, the military force was so large that the cost of garrisoning Catalonia still represented a third of the Spanish Crown's military expenditure as late as 1725.[5]

Even if Maria was too young to remember the War of the Spanish Succession, she would have been old enough to remember the renewed thunder of guns and tramping of soldiers marching past her village a few years later, when Spain found itself isolated and at war against a powerful European coalition composed of France, Britain, the Holy Roman Empire, the Dutch and the Duchy of Savoy. The conflict, which is the largely forgotten conflict called the War of the Quadruple Alliance, placed Prullans on the frontline between France and Spain. Since the late seventeenth century, the French repeatedly used a well-established overland route to invade Catalonia. Known as 'Noailles' way' (*chemin de Noailles*) and suitable for artillery and horse drawn wagons, the route led from the border town of Puigcerdà straight to Prullans.[6] Aged around eight, Maria would have witnessed the doubtless impressive sight of a French army of 6,000 to 7,000 soldiers, cavalry and artillery marching past Prullans on its way to besiege and capture La Seu d'Urgell. Maria's parents and neighbours would doubtless have been required to contribute resources to accommodate the billeting of French troops in the valley and might have endured the pillaging and destruction that early modern rural communities commonly suffered at the hands of campaigning armies. The following year, however, a young Maria would have watched a Spanish force march past Prullans as it chased the retreating French army back to the border.[7]

Despite these rude interruptions of European politics into the lives of the inhabitants of the Segre valley, Maria's childhood was probably no different from that of other girls in her Pyrenean village. She received no formal education, and even though she was later able to write down her name by herself, her handwriting was shaky and she frequently misspelt her own name. It is thus highly likely that Maria, like a significant part of the villagers she grew up with, was functionally illiterate. Certainly, Maria's parents would have seen little use in formal schooling for their daughter. Instead, she began to assist her parents with domestic chores from an early age. Maria recalled that her parents frequently sent her out to seek firewood for the family hearth and occasionally entrusted her with the minding of sheep grazing in the Segre valley or on the Pyrenean mountainsides.

Maria's childhood, however, came to a crashing halt around 1725 when, at the tender age of fourteen, she married another villager, a shepherd and labourer named Ignacio Sulsona. Contrary to modern stereotypes of medieval and early modern Europe, her young age was quite unusual for a bride. Historians have argued that Western Europe developed a distinctive 'marriage pattern' in the medieval and early modern periods in which couples tended to marry in their twenties. Research on Catalan society in the eighteenth century indicates that the Catalans generally followed this trend with most women who married doing so in their early twenties.[8]

Such an unusually early marriage could have been the result of rape (the marriage of the victim and perpetrator protecting the social reputation of the woman and her family's honour); an unexpected premarital pregnancy or even a poor family's desire to get rid of an extra mouth to feed. There is no evidence to suggest that Maria's marriage was linked to any of these causes. Maria never mentioned any full siblings, only a half-sister fathered by her father, although it is unclear whether this half-sibling was older or younger. Three or four years after her marriage, Maria Duran could not recall exactly, Maria gave birth to a boy named Pedro, again after one of his godparents who was a tailor in Prullans. The infant only lived nine or ten months, however, and the couple produced no other children.

Although Maria gave few details, the marriage to Ignacio Sulsona lasted seven or eight years and appears not to have been a happy one. Maria claims that she left her husband after he became 'very *galicado*'. The expression can literally (if somewhat clumsily) be translated into English as 'very Gallicised' or 'very Frenchified' and it is clear that Maria was referring to his contraction of the venereal disease syphilis. This was a common expression since it was current in Spain, just as in the rest of Europe, to assign blame for venereal diseases to foreigners. Medical practitioners in the Iberian Peninsula commonly described syphilis as the 'French disease' (*Morbo Gallico*).[9] When Ignacio Sulsona began to display the initial symptoms of the disease – skin lesions or chancres on the genitalia within the first few weeks followed by wart-like lesions on the rest of the body a month or two later – the couple sought medical help. The couple called upon the services of a surgeon in the nearby village of Bellver de Cerdanya, four kilometres to the east. The surgeon examined Ignacio and officially diagnosed the disease.

The 'French disease' or syphilis first appeared in Italy during the 1490s. Modern historians still debate its origins. Many argue that it was an American venereal disease brought back to Europe after the first Spanish voyages to the New World but some argue that it was a mutation of a spiral-shaped bacteria (*treponema*) that already existed in medieval Europe.[10] Whatever its true origins, the disease reached epidemic proportions in early modern Europe. Early modern medicine did not properly understand the disease. It was believed to be curable because of its multiple stages and the fact that the early symptoms generally disappeared before the lesions appeared later. A respected Spanish authority on the 'French disease' even argued in a work first published in 1600 and republished as late as 1715 that it was possible for a man to cure himself naturally by infecting a woman (and vice versa).[11] As in the rest of Europe, there existed a flagrant double standard in the way that syphilis affected the social status of men and women in Spain. Whilst men might boast of the 'French disease' as evidence of their amorous prowess, for women it carried a heavy burden of stigma. The surgeon's diagnosis placed Maria in a very difficult position. As a wife, she could not refuse to have sexual intercourse with her husband, who could legally rape her if that was his desire. Moreover, divorce was not an option in an eighteenth-century Catholic society and the birth of a child proved that the marriage had been consummated, thus making it impossible to secure an annulment.[12]

Maria's plan was to flee from the company of her husband 'to avoid infection by such a contagious evil' by moving to the village of Sant Julià de Lòria, a trip of roughly forty kilometres along the main road west from Prullans to the cathedral-city of La Seu d'Urgell and then north toward Andorra. The choice of Sant Julià de Lòria was no accident. It was the first village in the principality of Andorra that Maria could reach. The tiny Pyrenean principality of Andorra was (and remains to this day) something of a political oddity in Europe. Separated from Catalonia, but essentially Catalan in culture, the principality came under the co-rulership of the King of France and the bishop of La Seu d'Urgell from 1607 onward. Maria must have chosen to seek refuge in Andorra and cross a political boundary because she hoped that this offered her potential safety from any legal action that her husband might take to force her to return to Prullans. Maria took with her a donkey, some cloth and some spices (*especiaria*) from her home to sell in order to be able to sustain herself for a while.

Maria stayed in Sant Julià de Lòria for two months but was soon forced to leave her refuge. Her flight from Prullans was a grave injury not just to her husband's reputation and social standing in the village but also to that of her in-laws. She soon met acquaintances from the Segre valley in Andorra who told her that her brothers-in-law had threatened to find and kill her. Such news must have been deeply traumatic for Maria. Whilst she might be safe from any legal action, there was nothing to stop her in-laws from crossing the border and ending her life in an act of premeditated violence. Well aware that word of her presence in Andorra would inevitably make its way back to Prullans, Maria resolved to leave as soon as possible. She therefore sold her donkey and handed over some of her goods to a local official in order to pay for her outstanding debts in Sant Julià de Lòria.

Maria decided that her only option to escape the vengeance of her in-laws and remain safe was to move even further away from Prullans and the Segre valley. She could either head to another part of Catalonia or, alternatively, further north, across the Pyrenees and into the neighbouring kingdom of France. Remaining in Catalonia meant returning to an area under a legal jurisdiction that her in-laws might use against her, so she settled on the second option. Across the mountains lay the region of Languedoc-Roussillon. Roussillon, the southernmost area, was culturally Catalan and this meant that, as a Catalan-speaker, Maria could hope to secure some form of employment with which to sustain herself. Yet even moving to France was perilous. The high peaks of the Pyrenees might not be a barrier to shepherds, travellers and merchants who regularly crisscrossed the Franco-Spanish border but the roads were potentially dangerous to an unaccompanied woman. A young woman, travelling alone on countryside roads, was vulnerable not just to brigands on the prowl for isolated travellers but also to sexual assault. Moreover, a chance unfortunate encounter in France might easily lead to her whereabouts being discovered and to an attempt by her husband's relatives to harm her or abduct and return her to Prullans. It was then that Maria took a momentous decision: to become a man.

To ensure her personal safety, Maria needed an entirely new identity. Even changing her name was not sufficient. People would inevitably ask prying questions about a young Catalan woman who suddenly appeared in the Roussillon: where did she come from in Catalonia? Who were her relatives? Why had she come alone to France? Maria thus decided to become a man, at least in the eyes of those around her. Maria's plan was carefully prepared prior to her departure from Andorra. From the various female clothes she owned, Maria fashioned items of typically male attire: two shirts, a coat and a pair of breeches. She could not start to dress as a man in Sant Julià de Lòria itself without running the risk of attracting attention and being discovered. To ensure her safety, Maria's 'transformation' must remain secret at all costs and, therefore, had to be very carefully timed. Consequently, Maria left Sant Julià de Lòria on the road leading to France dressed as a woman. Once she was alone, she darted into a nearby wood and changed into her male clothing before rejoining the road and heading north, to France and to a new life.

As she walked north of Sant Julià de Lòria, through the narrow valleys of Andorra and then down towards the valleys of the Roussillon, a new world opened up before Maria for which her childhood and early life in the Segre valley had not prepared her. It was the start of a remarkable journey that would lead Maria first into the ranks of the Spanish royal army, then later into a Dominican convent in Portugal and, eventually, before the dreaded judges of the Inquisition.

2

Maria becomes a soldier

Maria entered the province of Roussillon in France in search of a new life. The course of events during the following two years are difficult to reconstruct. The inquisitorial trial dossier includes not only the transcript of Maria's interrogation and the claims she made but also evidence gleaned from witnesses interrogated in Spain. Maria herself later candidly told the inquisitors when they quizzed her about contradictions between the testimony of the witnesses and hers that 'so many events have occurred in her life that it is no great deal if she has made a mistake remembering something'. Notwithstanding their occasional contradictions, these two sources of evidence about Maria's life after fleeing from Prullans are sufficiently in agreement to make it clear that the basic outline of her claims about this remarkable period of her life was correct.[1]

Without a network of friends and family to support her, Maria's existence in France was a difficult one. Dressed in male clothing and with a male identity, Maria erred in Languedoc and Roussillon for the next two years. She recalled 'sometimes sustaining herself through work, and sometimes from things [presumably food and clothes] that she was given' by charitable people. Since Maria had no particular skill or craft, she must have earned some money from whatever agricultural labour she could find, perhaps helping to till the fields and harvest the grapes grown in the Languedoc vineyards in the late summer and early autumn. In her later trial, Maria did not provide much information about this period of her life. We do not know how she found shelter or how, more significantly, she managed to keep her new identity as a man secret or even what male name she used in public. Her successful deception, however, apparently filled her with confidence and she decided to return to the city of Barcelona in Catalonia. As a large urban centre, Maria doubtless hoped to find more stable employment there.

Her departure from France was nonetheless expedited by another unexpected development. Whilst temporarily residing in the house of a widow in the village of Thuir, close by the town of Perpignan, Maria and the widow formed a close relationship that developed into an attachment that went beyond mere friendship. Maria later told the inquisitors that her skill at singing, dancing and playing musical instruments impressed the woman, who fell in love with Maria. It would appear that Maria and the widow, whose name she could not recall over a decade later, did not have sexual intercourse and that the widow did not see through the deception, since she asked Maria to marry her only a month after their first meeting. Marriage was obviously out of the question for Maria since it would inevitably result in the exposure of her sex, cause uproar in the village of Thuir and lead to her arrest by the local French authorities. In the short term, Maria stalled by providing the widow with a written promise of marriage, a legally binding document.

Fortunately, the formalities of church law offered Maria a chance to slip away without causing a scandal and running the risk of arrest. To reduce cases of bigamy and obtain proof of identity in an era without identification cards or documents, the church required prospective spouses who were not a native of the parish in which they intended to wed to present a valid certificate of baptism from their home parish. Pretexting the need to travel to Catalonia to secure such a certificate, Maria abandoned the hapless widow and travelled onwards to Barcelona, crossing the border between Spain and France once more. As time passed and it eventually became clear that Maria was not coming back from Catalonia, the nameless widow must have come to believe that she had been duped and was the victim of another feckless young man avoiding commitment and reneging on his pledge.

When she was asked to elaborate about the manner in which she was able to successfully pass herself off as male, Maria revealed that she had always taken great care to 'blend in' during her social interactions with men and women. Single, unattached men (and especially soldiers) were a rowdy bunch who frequented taverns, drank (often to excess) and engaged in amorous social intercourse with womenfolk. To conspicuously abstain from or avoid such pursuits would have singled Maria out as odd to her comrades and invited unwelcome scrutiny. Maria later told the inquisitors that she was able to escape detection because she deliberately 'played along' and 'joined in' these revelries including communal singing and the telling of 'jokes' (*galhofas*). Sometimes this horseplay brought Maria perilously close to disaster. Although no one discovered that she was a woman, Maria admitted that many men and women had commented that 'she had the face of a woman' or that she must be a 'capon' (i.e. a eunuch). With remarkable *sangfroid*, Maria was able to deflect suspicion by cunningly accepting these provocative quips and 'she herself often proclaimed [to her companions], as a joke, that she was a woman'.

In addition to partaking in raucous male carousing, Maria added that she 'slept with many men in the same beds'. In modern Western culture, two individuals sharing a bed are assumed to be in a heterosexual or homosexual sexual relationship and the very expression 'to sleep with' has become a common euphemism for sexual intercourse. The situation was somewhat different in medieval or early modern Europe. Same-sex bed sharing had no sexual overtones. The limited living quarters of many dwellings meant that it was common for young, unmarried men to become 'bedfellows'.[2] Given her public identity as an unmarried male, Maria would have been expected to sleep on the same mattresses as other men. Her acceptance as a bedfellow by her male companions marked another critical stage in her successful deception. Maria's ability to sleep next to men undetected suggest that most men did not sleep naked but wearing some form of underwear or flowing robes that enabled Maria to conceal any physical traits that might have otherwise betrayed her secret.

The widespread practice of bed sharing by individuals of the same sex should not be taken as evidence that early modern European society was in any way so relaxed about same-sex relations as to be 'innocent' and unaware of male homosexuality. In the thirteenth century, King Alfonso X of Castile had ordered that male homosexuals guilty of anal penetration must undergo castration followed by death by stoning since such sexual acts were 'contrary to nature' and threatened to bring God's wrath upon the kingdom. A later law passed by Queen Isabel the Catholic in 1497 associated male homosexuality and bestiality. It ordered that anyone convicted of such offences must be burned at the stake in the town or village where they had committed their crime so that their deaths could serve as a warning to others. The warning was deemed necessary since, it was argued by Queen Isabel's decree, failure to punish homosexuality would bring down God's terrible anger against all Spaniards. In the early modern era, preachers continued to fulminate from their pulpit against the 'unmentionable sin'. One preacher lecturing the masses in the seventeenth century cast aside any notion of Christian mercy when it came to 'sodomites':

> Sodom means treason and Gomorrah means rebellion … . The contagiousness and danger presented by the epidemic [of sodomy] is such that to show any compassion is [in itself] a crime. [God punished Sodom and Gomorrah with a rain of fire and] that is the example [we must follow], fire and utmost rigour, without compassion or mercy! This vice [of sodomy] has afflicted this place with

> such strength that, in order to free even an innocent [person] of it, the violence of many angels is necessary.[3]

Those caught and found guilty could expect either a horrific death at the stake or a slow death as a slave rowing on the galleys of the Spanish navy. Homosexuality remained a death penalty offence in Maria's lifetime and the secular authorities and the Inquisition both tracked down 'sodomites' in different parts of Spain.[4]

It is upon Maria's return to Catalonia that the thread of her story must be reconstructed with great care, due to her inconsistent testimony. Maria initially claimed after her arrest by the Inquisition in Portugal that she had been jailed in Barcelona when she was discovered to be carrying a prohibited weapon. The testimony of Catalan witnesses, however, contradicted this claim and Maria later admitted that this was an honest mistake. In fact, Maria travelled to the coastal town of Mataró, *c.* thirty kilometres northeast of Barcelona. It was there that Maria took her male impersonation to a completely new level by joining the ranks of the Spanish royal army.

Maria never explained the reasons that led her to join the army. It seems likely that, once again, the need to find a reliable source of income may well have been the principal factor. Like all eighteenth-century armies, the Spanish army was chronically short of manpower. Moreover, an unprecedented expansion of the Spanish royal army under the new Bourbon dynasty meant the creation of new regiments and the hurried recruitment of men to fill their ranks. The outfit that Maria joined in Mataró was a regiment of mounted infantry, newly established in July 1734 by a wealthy aristocrat: Coronel Joan Manuel de Sentmenat i d'Oms. The regiment was named the Dragoons of Villaviciosa (*Dragones de Villaviciosa*). The formation of the regiment was completed on 21 May 1735 when its standards were blessed during a solemn religious ceremony held in the church of the Jesuit college of *Nuestra Señora de Belén* in Barcelona.[5] This was not an ordinary regiment of cavalry but rather one of light mounted infantry. Armed with muskets and swords, the dragoons' task during warfare was to scout ahead of the army and skirmish with the enemy. Unlike heavy cavalry units – the cuirassiers – the dragoons wore no armour as their mission was to avoid the close-quarter mêlées of cavalry battles. In peacetime, dragoons were often used as a military police force to hunt down the brigands that plagued the roads and countryside of Spain as well as the guerrillas in Catalonia who still refused to recognize the legitimacy of the Bourbon regime (see Figure 2).

How did Maria achieve the remarkable feat of joining the army without anyone noticing that she was a biological woman dressed as a man? To begin

Figure 2 Uniform of the dragoons of the Regiment of *Villaviciosa* (mid-eighteenth-century). Detail from Biblioteca Nacional de España (Madrid). Anon, *Soldados de diferentes cuerpos de Infantería y Caballería* (no date), DIB/13/6/13. (http://bdh-rd.bne.es/viewer.vm?id=0000183574; CC BY-SA 4.0).

with, her physical appearance seems to have been unremarkable, or at the very least not particularly 'feminine'. Witnesses who had seen her in Spain and who were asked to describe her eight years later agreed that she was fairly tall, sturdily built and that her skin as 'somewhat brown' in colour. She had long black hair, no visible facial hair and her ears had small (doubtless difficult to notice) holes indicating that they had been pierced. On the other hand, Maria was 'flat chested', and one witness recalled that she had a voice that was '*algo abultada*', a Spanish expression that is difficult to translate but which seems to indicate a deep voice that would have been perceived as a distinctively male trait. Finally, Maria bore a noticeable round scar or mark on one of her cheeks.

Beyond the absence of any overtly 'feminine' physical traits, the uniform of the regiment would also have helped Maria 'blend in' among her fellow dragoons. The use of uniforms began to become standard in all western European armies in the late seventeenth and early eighteenth centuries. The dragoons of the Villaviciosa regiment wore a striking yellow uniform, with a black tricorn hat and long riding boots.[6] As the etymology of the word uniform itself makes abundantly clear, military uniforms serve to standardize the appearance of soldiers and erase an individual's identity. One final particularity of the dragoons probably assisted Maria: their distinctive hairstyle. Most dragoons wore their hair long and, to avoid it becoming an encumbrance, it was gathered at the back of their heads in a braided plait or pigtail. As such, Maria's long black hair would not have drawn any particular notice or caused undue suspicion. Indeed, one witness specifically remembered that Maria wore her hair braided 'in the fashion of dragoons'. The capacity of military uniforms and a standardized physical appearance to conceal individuality made the army a logical place for Maria to seek employment.

Maria's ability to pass herself off as male in order to serve as a dragoon did not just rely on the uniform she wore. She had also developed additional, seemingly calculated, strategies with which she could deceive men into thinking she was physically male. Maria later described these strategies to the inquisitors, and it is worth quoting her in full:

> She says that in all things she took great care to imitate male customs and to conceal those that were characteristic of women, to such an extent that she bound her breasts with a strap to hide them. On the front of her breeches, facing the opening, she placed an instrument manufactured from her shirt, or sometimes another instrument [to create a bulge in the area of the crotch that was indicative of male genitals]. When she menstruated, she wore a doubled up piece of cloth in her pants that she washed when it was necessary. When she [particularly needed] to pretend to be a man, she would conceal a gourd [full] of water in her breeches. When she reached a wall, she would open [her fly] with one of her hands and urinate just like a man because, even though she had become accustomed to urinate whilst standing (like many women do), she could not manage it with her breeches fastened.[7]

Presumably, Maria urinated against a wall and facing away from any of her fellow soldiers so that the deception might not be exposed. Maria appears to have perfected these clever techniques of dissimulation during her previous years in France. What is fascinating is not just that Maria knew to take measures to conceal evidence of her 'female body' (breasts and menstruation) but that she also clearly realized the importance of playing to the gendered expectations of society. Maria was acting out her official male identity by playing up to the prevalent stereotypes of masculinity and male behaviour. Urinating against walls was not the only way that Maria 'acted male' to ensure the continued secrecy of her identity. Even before she joined the army, Maria had to conform to expectations about male social behaviour.

To a modern reader, Maria Duran's ability to preserve her secret and successfully pass herself off as a man in a military environment might seem implausible. In fact, Maria's story was far from unique. Incidents of women secretly joining military outfits were far from unknown in early modern Europe and they aroused considerable interest even at that time. A study published in 1989 and focusing on northern Europe counted 119 known cases of women dressing as men between 1550 and 1830. Usually, these women joined the army or became seafarers and they almost all shared a similar background. They were young, from the poorer classes of society and forced to leave their homes and communities because of the death of their parents or a family quarrel. Most of them were single.[8]

Maria Duran fits into this wider European trend perfectly. Some of the women who secretly served as soldiers became celebrities once their biological sex was exposed. Amongst the most famous are the Spaniard Catalina de Erauso (1592–*c.*1650), *La Monja Alférez* (the Lieutenant Nun), a fugitive nun who travelled the Spanish Americas as a soldier and fought the indigenous Mapuche people of Chile. Another case, this time a contemporary of Maria Duran, was Hannah Snell (1723–1792), an Englishwoman who served as a soldier and fought with the British Army in India during the 1740s before reverting to a female identity after returning to England in 1750. Finally, it is interesting to note how, in Holland, Geertruid ter Brugge (who died *c.* 1706) not only performed military service but also earned the nickname of 'La Dragonne' after serving in a regiment of dragoons, exactly like Maria Duran. The surviving representations of these famous cases – paintings and prints – always present them in their military clothing as a way of emphasizing how such clothing assisted their public imposture. Such a remarkable transgression of gender norms – warfare was, after all, perceived as an exclusively masculine activity and women's participation was presented as largely auxiliary – fascinated early modern Europeans. This early modern interest in the stories of individuals born female who 'transed' gender to assume a male identity as soldiers is made clear by the large amount of popular literature that such cases generated. Its legacy endures in the debates of modern historians, who debate whether these individuals were merely opportunist cross-dressers, transvestites or even transgender. Whilst the ancient Greek story of the Amazons may have created a cultural matrix in which female warriors became, in male eyes, exotic objects of fantasy, there was little real toleration for cross-dressing in early modern Europe. Once exposed, the authorities compelled such individuals to revert to female dress in order to restore the perceived 'natural' order of society.[9]

Maria Duran's period of service in the dragoons of Villaciciosa was cut short by events beyond her control. In 1733, Spain had found itself embroiled in yet another eighteenth-century dynastic European conflict that has been largely forgotten by many modern Europeans: the War of the Polish Succession. Spain's involvement in this war was chiefly motivated by a desire to expand into southern Italy at the expense of the Austrians. The Spanish army sent to southern Italy was successful in its Italian campaign but reinforcements were needed. Maria's regiment, which was ready for muster in May 1735, was on the list of units that the Crown ordered to be sent overseas. One witness interrogated by the Inquisition, however, suggested that Maria was transferred to another regiment (the *regimiento de la Reina*) about to be shipped overseas. In either case, the prospect of the perils of war and physical danger in a foreign land doubtless did not appeal to Maria. Whilst the regiment was stationed in the small town of Peralada, near the border with France, Maria revealed her secret to her astonished officers who immediately ordered her to be expelled from the regiment and detained by the local authorities.

Inevitably, news of the 'woman soldier' spread rapidly and Maria attracted a great deal of curiosity. Numerous people came to gaze or gawp at Maria in her jail cell. One of these was a noblewoman from the noble Gayolà family. Moved by pity and a desire to 'reform' the wayward Maria, the woman persuaded Maria to accept her charity and, doubtless using her status and connections, convinced the local authorities to order Maria's release and removal to the town of Figueres, close to the border with France. In the Gayolà family household, Maria found herself once more attired in women's clothing and subject to the reforming attentions of a Jesuit father from the local college of the Society of Jesus. The chief aim of the Jesuit reformer was to ensure that a woman like Maria would no longer dress as a man or endanger her eternal salvation and that of others by putting herself in a situation where she might commit the sin of fornication or turn to prostitution. Accordingly, a plan was put into action to gather sums of money that would enable Maria to have the funds to pay the 'spiritual dowry' necessary for her to enter a Magdalene house or convent. Maria claims that she was unwilling to enter a religious establishment. She later told the inquisitors that her qualms were motivated by the fact that such institutions only accepted 'young maidens' and that, as a married woman (albeit a runaway wife), she was not eligible. Of course, she had a point. As a married woman, not a widow, the sacrament of her marriage was still valid in the eyes of the church and she could hardly legitimately become a 'bride of Christ'. In the face of this complication and her refusal to be 'reformed', her would-be patrons washed their hands of her and Maria once more found herself alone and on the streets.

Maria resumed wearing male clothing and erred on both sides of the Franco-Spanish border for an unspecified period of time until she found a patron in the town of Martorell (roughly twenty-five kilometres east of Barcelona). Some of the witnesses who knew her in Catalonia asserted that Maria managed to ingratiate herself with a local priest in the town of Martorell. In public, Maria adopted the identity of a minor nobleman named Don Antonio Peretada but she confided to the priest that she was really a noblewoman named Doña Christina Bordas, the illegitimate scion of a noble family and sister-in-law of a respected royal official in Puigcerdà (near her native Prullans): Don Josep de Pastor. The precise reason for such an elaborate deception is unclear. Was Maria a conartist hoping to obtain money from the priest? Whatever its aims, her scheme was exposed when the priest wrote to Puigcerdà and the response of the furious Don Josep de Pastor led to Maria's arrest.

The official cause of the arrest was not just Maria's impersonation but also the fact that officers of the law discovered that Maria was carrying a small sword (*espadín*) on her person. In a society where the possession of a sword was a distinguishing sign of nobility, it is not surprising that Maria would have displayed such a weapon to confirm her false identity as the noble Don Antonio Peretada. Moreover, even whilst publicly pretending to be a man, it was a sensible precaution for a commoner travelling the roads like Maria to have a weapon to hand with which to defend herself. Unfortunately, the carrying of a weapon without authorization was not a trifling offence in eighteenth-century Spain. The Spanish authorities had passed laws seeking to restore a modicum of social order to the kingdom after the chaos of the War of the Spanish Succession and to prevent the proliferation of weapons. In 1722, the King had promulgated an edict threatening severe punishments against all those individuals found with daggers, small swords and other bladed weapons (*armas blancas*) without a licence or valid reason to bear them. As a commoner feigning to be a nobleman, Maria fell afoul of this law. Maria later claimed that the penalty was death but it was actually six years of exile to Spain's North African fortified outposts (*presidios*) for noblemen and six years of service as an oarsman in the galleys of the Spanish navy for commoners. In practice, given the dreadful conditions endured by galley oarsmen, death and service in the galleys may well have meant the same thing for many commoners.[10]

Did Maria attempt to present a 'sanitized' version of her 'misdeeds' in Catalonia to the inquisitors after her arrest in 1741? Did she limit her version of events to cross-dressing and pretending to be male? Certainly, the witnesses' claims that Maria sought to deceive a member of the clergy suggest a darker motive behind her cross-dressing deception. Keen to prove to the inquisitors that she would not lie under oath and was willing to reform, Maria might well have decided that it would be injudicious to confess to her lies in Martorell or her repeated refusal to submit to the will of the authorities and society.

Once again, Maria found herself in a difficult position as she was taken to face trial in Barcelona. At first, the Catalan officials who arrested Maria for the illegal possession of a weapon and deception do not appear to have realized that Maria was, in biological terms, a woman. Maria's arrest would have led to her imprisonment on remand in a male prison, where she would struggle to conceal her sex from her inmates in a shared and presumably crowded cell. Understandably, the prospect of sexual assault must have filled Maria with dread. She resorted to the only possible course of action and revealed 'that she was not a man despite her clothes but rather a woman' to the local judge (*merino*). After his initial surprise, the judge of the royal court (*audiencia*) in Catalonia whose responsibility it was to enforce law and order in Barcelona, Antoni de Serra i Portell, ordered Maria's transfer to a female jail. In this jail, two women conducted a physical examination of Maria and confirmed that she was a woman after scrutinizing her genitals. Maria was fortunate that the pious Don Antoni was moved more by pity for her plight than by disgust or anger at her deception. Maria claims that the judge offered her a 'good quantity of money as alms' and ordered her to be placed in the house of a local woman and under the spiritual guidance of a local Dominican friar. Once again, the aim seems to have been to end Maria's cross-dressing peregrinations and 'reform' her. The friar offered Maria a position working in the refectory of a local hospital but she refused it. It was not long before Maria was, once more, on the road and dressed as a man.

Upon leaving Barcelona, Maria claims to have travelled eastwards to the city of Zaragoza, on the banks of the River Ebro. Her experiences in Catalonia did not move her to abandon her by now well-established modus operandi. She began to wear male clothing again and to pass herself off as male. A more surprising development, however, is that she joined another military regiment in Zaragoza, undeterred by her previous experience in the Spanish army.

Maria's second period of service in the Spanish army seems to have been as short-lived as the first. Maria claims that whilst the regiment was stationed in the coastal Catalan town of Tortosa (south of Barcelona), she was exposed when one of her officers ordered her to receive a beating following some unspecified 'misconduct' on her part. To avoid this punishment, Maria ran to the Cathedral of Tortosa to seek the protection of the local bishop to whom she revealed her identity as a woman and pleaded for assistance. Maria did not identify the regiment involved and her claims might well arouse suspicion at first, but Catalan witnesses interrogated during her subsequent inquisitorial trial confirmed this. One witness, a man of the Church, swore on the gospels that he had received a letter from the bishop of Tortosa relating this strange story and that Maria had used the fake surname of Pinos. The bishop took pity on Maria and made yet another attempt to 'reform' her by placing her in the household of a pious priest, presumably as a first step towards directing her to a religious institution. Predictably, like all the others previous attempts, this one failed when Maria left and once more took to the open road.

Whatever really happened after Maria was expelled from the army a second time, she decided to leave Catalonia for good. Her deeds must have been widely discussed in the region, and her notoriety would have made it very difficult for her to remain there and continue to pass as a man. Instead Maria turned her attention westwards and travelled to the capital of the Spanish monarchy and empire. Maria offers no hint of what drew her to Madrid. She certainly did not have any relatives or friends there. Located near the geographical centre of the Iberian Peninsula, the Spanish capital was the largest city in Spain, with a population estimated at between 130,000 and 150,000 in the second quarter of the eighteenth century.[11] The city in which Maria arrived had recently suffered a disastrous loss: the royal palace (the *Real Alcázar de Madrid*) had been destroyed by an accidental fire on Christmas Eve 1734, with the loss of numerous works of art including work by the celebrated master Diego de Velázquez.

Once again, the attraction of the capital for Maria was certainly linked to the prospect of securing some form of employment. The royal court, government offices and the households of the aristocrats and wealthy artisans created an urban economy in which people with few or no skills could hope to rapidly find gainful employment. Maria would have been only one of a multitude of people moving to the capital.[12] In Madrid, Maria could reasonably hope to blend in without attracting any unwanted attention, even though she was now no longer in Catalonia and in a Spanish (Castillian)-speaking environment. Moreover, there was also the relative anonymity afforded by a large urban centre and Maria doubtless hoped that, so far from her native village and land, she would not run into people who might know her and her unusual story.

Maria does not provide much information about her stay in Madrid. She only revealed to the inquisitors that she 'stayed for some eight months in the house of a brigadier of the Royal Guards named Don Antonio Morisco'. Although the inquisitors do not appear to have bothered checking this claim, a near-contemporary document confirms the existence of a Don Antonio Morisco serving with the rank of 'sub-brigadier' in the Spanish royal guard.[13] Beyond this, however, it is impossible to confirm this claim and the vague wording in the inquisitorial trial does not allow us to be certain of the nature of Maria's purported employment, or even whether she dressed as a man or a woman. It is equally plausible that Maria could have served Don Antonio Morisco as a female or male domestic. Whatever her status and employment, Maria did not remain in Madrid for long. She claims that she became 'angry with her work' without specifying if her anger was the result of mistreatment by her employer, her own boredom with the life of a domestic or something else. Rather than staying in Spain, Maria now decided to move further westwards to the neighbouring kingdom of Portugal and to establish herself in another great city of eighteenth-century Europe: Lisbon, the metropolis of Portugal and its empire.

3

Maria Duran travels to Lisbon

Portugal and Spain shared a long land border but also had a long history of conflict by the eighteenth century. Indeed, most recently, the two Iberian kingdoms and empires had been at war between 1735 and 1737 over territories in South America. No fighting took place in Europe but the long border between both kingdoms – well over a thousand kilometres long – was a tense and highly militarized zone with impressive fortresses and officials keeping a close eye on the movement of goods and people. Whilst residing in Madrid, Maria may have heard of the reopening of the border after the peace treaty of 1737 and seen an opportunity to leave Spain. From Madrid, Maria Duran's easiest route to Lisbon would have been to travel to the bridge over the River Guadiana, which itself formed the border between the two kingdoms and separated the towns of Badajoz in Spain and in Portugal. For reasons that she never explained, Maria chose instead to take a more arduous northern route: travelling to Ciudad Rodrigo and entering Portugal via the heavily fortified border town of Almeida. To enter into Portugal, travellers needed to present themselves to the customs and royal officials who would check their passports and goods, keeping an eye out for unwelcome vagrants like Maria. Most likely Maria sought a more remote point of entry in order to avoid officialdom and illegally enter Portugal. What is clear, however, is that Maria left Madrid dressed as a man once more, and having successfully evaded the scrutiny of the authorities at the border, arrived in Lisbon clothed in male attire.[1]

We can pick up the thread of Maria's story once again from the point at which she arrived in Lisbon. The exact date of her arrival is unclear. She later told the inquisitors that she arrived in the Portuguese capital 'on the eve of the jubilee of Porciuncula' but does not specify exactly what year. The jubilee of Porciuncula is an important religious festival that commemorates a miraculous vision that Saint Francis of Assisi experienced in the church of Porciuncula (Porziuncola in the original Italian) in 1216, and it is held on 2 August. Based on this information and claims by witnesses in early 1741 that she had been in Lisbon 'for between two and three years', the likely date of her arrival thus appears to be 1 August 1738.

During the first half of the eighteenth century, the kingdom of Portugal experienced, and benefitted from, a remarkable economic boom. The spice trade and commerce with Asia that had propelled Portugal to prominence in the sixteenth century may have waned, but the kingdom was benefitting from the development of colonial Brazil's plantations and the discovery of considerable mineral wealth in the Brazilian hinterland.

King João (John) V had ascended to the throne in 1706 and reigned as an absolute monarch. To show off his wealth to his subjects and to the other rulers of Europe, the Portuguese monarch spared no expense both as a builder and as a patron of the arts. The construction of a vast and hybrid convent-palace to the north of Lisbon at Mafra, which began in 1717, mobilized thousands of workers. Portuguese ambassadors sent to France and the Holy See amazed their contemporaries through the extravagance of their triumphal entries. Indeed, the Portuguese envoy to Rome arrived in a cortege of stunning golden carriages, decorated with elaborate Baroque statues. The lavish expenditure of King João V was not solely devoted to his palaces or court but also funded a number of urban projects. To meet the desperate need for clean drinking and washing water in Lisbon, the king had ordered the construction of a remarkable structure: the aqueduct of *Águas Livres* ('Free Waters'). This feat of eighteenth-century engineering, with solid arches standing up to 65 meters tall in places, still stands today. Although its construction began in 1731, it would have still been a work in progress when Maria arrived in Lisbon and did not begin to bring fresh drinking water to the inhabitants of Lisbon until 1748. Behind a façade of religious respectability, and despite his public image as a protector of the Catholic Church and moral order in his dominions, King João V was an inveterate womanizer. Aside from his dynastic marriage to the daughter of the Austrian Emperor, who bore him six children, the king had numerous mistresses. Among these paramours, who bore him numerous illegitimate children, were two nuns who resided in a convent just to the north of Lisbon.[2]

Modern visitors to Lisbon cannot help but notice that the old historic centre of the city is characterized by a grid plan that dates from the eighteenth century. The city that Maria arrived in, however, was very different. The present-day grid plan was a later creation, the result of careful planning during the rebuilding of Lisbon after the cataclysmic earthquake of 1755. Prior to 1755, the layout of Lisbon remained that of a medieval city. Stretching along the northern bank of the Tejo River, its centre was a warren of narrow, twisting streets and alleys crammed with shops, houses and churches and contained between two hills to the west and the east. On the hill to the west of the centre were the prominent Carmelite and Franciscan Convents, whose buildings still stand today, albeit only in ruins in the case of the Carmelite convent. Opposite, on the rising ground to the east were the cathedral of Lisbon and the imposing medieval São Jorge Castle (Castle of Saint George), whose ramparts still dominate central Lisbon (see Figure 3). By the standards of the eighteenth century, Lisbon was a large city. An estimation from 1730 reckoned that the city counted 20,000 dwellings, 40 parishes and around 250,000 inhabitants. It was also a multicultural town. Its inhabitants included not only native Portuguese (including the descendants of Jews forced to convert to Christianity in the final decade of the fifteenth century, who were often suspected of secretly remaining Jewish and known as the 'New Christians') but also Black Africans (both enslaved and free) as well as established merchant communities from all over Europe.[3]

The flat ground in the centre of the town featured two squares in the 1740s. On the northern bank of the Tejo River lay the square known today as the *Praça do Comercio* (Commerce Square). In the eighteenth century, the square was known as the *Terreiro do Paço* (Palace Yard). This name came from the presence on its western side of the *Ribeira* Palace complex (in Portuguese *ribeira* literally means 'riverbank'), whose main feature was a monumental rectangular tower dominating the square and overlooking the Tejo. Contemporary paintings suggest that the square was a bustling place: crowded with nobles, ecclesiastics, commoners and slaves going about their business. Indeed, the square was large enough to host bullfights and military parades on special occasions. An embankment bordered the Tejo with two small platforms jutting out into the river and hosting a number of artillery pieces used for ceremonial purposes. Like many early modern European towns, however, Lisbon suffered from poor public sanitation. An English traveller visiting the city in 1701 complained that the banks of the Tejo River were little more than a rubbish dump that stank to high heaven, even just outside the royal palace.[4] A Frenchman complained in 1730 that the inhabitants of the city carelessly threw their waste into the streets and that those streets situated next to the river and the *Terreiro do Paço* were cleaned infrequently and often mud-covered.[5]

North of the *Terreiro do Paço*, away from the Tejo river and more or less in the centre of the town, was located the other great square plaza of the Portuguese capital: the *Rossio*. On the eastern side of the Rossio stood the monumental hospital of All Saints (*Todos-os-Santos*), a huge charitable medical establishment

Figure 3 Map of Lisbon before the 1755 earthquake. George Matthau Seutter, *Lisabona magnificentissima Regia Sedes Portugalliae et florentissimum Emporium* (Aug. Vindel.: s.n., *c.* 1710–50). (B.N.P., E. 528 R, https://purl.pt/27603, CCO 1.0).

created by the Portuguese monarchy at the turn of the fifteenth and sixteenth centuries. With its elaborate façade decorated in the distinctly Portuguese Manueline style, it would have presented an awe-inspiring sight to a new visitor in Lisbon. On the northern side of the *Rossio* square stood the *Estaus* palace. Originally a royal residence and stable, it had become the headquarters of the Lisbon tribunal of the Portuguese Inquisition. Established in the second half of the 1530s, the Portuguese Inquisition was (like the more infamous Spanish Inquisition) essentially a network of special religious tribunals whose task it was to defend the orthodoxy of Catholicism by proactively hunting down and prosecuting any heretics.

The Portuguese Inquisition was created to tackle a 'crisis' perceived to be threatening Portuguese society: the allegedly widespread continued practice of Judaism ('judaizing') by the thousands of Jews forced to convert to Christianity by King Manuel I in 1497 and their descendants. Its official name was the Holy Office of the Inquisition against Heretical Depravity and Apostasy and, despite being a religious tribunal, it was under the authority of a royally appointed Inquisitor-General. The Inquisitor-General headed the General Council of the Inquisition that supervised the activity of the provincial tribunals. Each tribunal counted a number of inquisitors (investigator-judges), other staff members and facilities to jail arrested suspects during their trial. By the eighteenth century, the Portuguese Inquisition counted no less than four such tribunals: three established in Portugal itself (in the towns of Lisbon, Coimbra and Évora) and one located thousands of kilometres away in Portuguese India (Goa). Whilst the Portuguese inquisitors focused most of their energies on remorselessly hunting down supposed judaizers, other crimes also came to fall within their jurisdiction including homosexuality, blasphemy relating to the sacraments of the Church, Protestantism and accusations of having made a pact with the Devil.[6]

Although the Portuguese Inquisition has lived in the shadow of its more notorious Spanish namesake, its mission and methods were essentially the same. Prisoners arrested on suspicion of heresy were jailed and isolated from outside contact by the Inquisition and subjected to a secret (i.e. not public) trial in which the identity of their accusers was not revealed. Those found guilty were generally sentenced in spectacular *autos-da-fé*: public processions and ceremonies designed to humiliate the prisoners and warn the crowd of onlookers about the dangers that awaited all those who challenged the dogmas of the Church. Between the hospital of All Saints and the palace of the *Estaus*, on the northeastern corner of the *Rossio* square, was located the church of Saint Dominic (São Domingo) in which pictures with inscriptions bearing the names and sentences of past heretics were hung to act as lasting reminders and warnings to the Catholic faithful.[7]

Once Maria arrived in the Portuguese metropolis, she faced a familiar problem: how could she sustain herself? Firstly, there was a language barrier since Maria spoke little or no Portuguese. Secondly, she had no support network of family or friends to house and feed her before she could find some form of employment. Finally, Maria was little more than a vagabond and beggar in a country where the authorities and the law took a dim view of vagabonds and beggars, especially those who were foreigners.[8] Moreover, the Portuguese law threatened public floggings, fines and even exile overseas to anyone caught cross-dressing like Maria and offered rewards to those who denounced them.[9]

Like all early modern European cities, Lisbon had a dark side. Alongside the elegant façades of the royal and aristocratic residences, there existed extreme poverty and crime. The poor and precariously employed inhabitants of Lisbon eked out a living in the shadow of the opulent wealth of the Crown and landed aristocratic families, suffering from crime and grumbling at attempts to impose new regulations and taxes upon them. Maintaining order was a perennial cause of concern for the authorities. In 1735, the king ordered the local authorities to deploy armed patrols across the city to apprehend all those aged seven and older who caused disturbances in the streets. The lack of success of such measures is clear from the fact that the Crown issued similar decrees in the following years. Lawlessness could easily lead to more serious and direct threats to the Crown. A riot in January 1737 caused by the imposition of new taxes led an unruly mob to the entrance of the royal palace in Lisbon. Only the presence of a sizeable military force led to their dispersal and the return of an uneasy calm.[10]

After nightfall, the unlit streets of the city were a dangerous place. A foreign resident in Lisbon noted in 1742 that 'the Portuguese, and many foreigners, are so apprehensive of the sinister accidents which often happen at Lisbon in the night-time, especially to a person who ventures out alone, that few are found in the streets of this city at a late hour'.[11] Manuscript newsletters produced in Portugal during the first half of the eighteenth century graphically reveal the anxiety that many Portuguese residents of Lisbon felt about crime rates in the capital. News of violent robberies in the darkened streets and the discovery of corpses at dawn, more general complaints about burglaries and a perceived lawlessness during the nighttime as well as the apparent inability of the authorities to tackle crime effectively, are a recurring theme. One Portuguese writer bemoaned in 1742 that organized gangs of criminals 'every day grow bolder and discover new ideas for their crimes'. Even beggars were not safe. In November 1744, the corpse of a beggar with a wooden leg who played the viola in the street to earn coins from charitable passers-by was discovered at daybreak. Unknown cutthroats had strangled the hapless man to rob him of his few coins. In an eerie echo of Maria's own story, a newsletter recorded that one criminal arrested by the authorities turned out to be 'a woman dressed as a man'.[12]

For an unaccompanied woman, the nights of Lisbon were particularly dangerous and it is not surprising that Maria kept her sex hidden after her arrival in the Portuguese capital. The danger for women residing in Lisbon inevitably extended beyond robbery to include the possibility of sexual assault and murder. Once again, the manuscript newsletters offer horrifically graphic evidence. In 1736, the mutilated corpse of a young woman was brought to the royal hospital. The victim's hand and feet had been bound together, her mouth was sown up, her breasts were cut off and a stick was protruding from her head. The authorities arrested a number of male 'lackeys' in the employment of an aristocrat for the horrendous crime. The account does not mention a motive but the extreme violence of the murder strongly suggests a sexual motive, perhaps even a gang rape followed by murder.[13] The body of another woman was discovered in a vineyard just to the west of Lisbon on a Monday morning in the autumn of 1744 'with a metal instrument inserted in her private parts' the identity of the murderer remained unknown.[14]

Isolated and without friends or funds, Maria appears to have decided to take the only measure available, one that was familiar to her from her days in Catalonia: she sought the help of a charitable churchman. In the stifling heat of the Portuguese summer, Maria proceeded to the Jesuit college of São Antão, built on the site of a former mosque of medieval Islamic Lisbon on the slopes of the hill leading up to the royal castle. She later told the inquisitors that she wanted to receive the special indulgence offered to those who confessed their sins on 'the Jubilee of the Porciuncula'. Whether this was Maria's real intention will never be known but, once she entered the Jesuit church, she sought out a priest named Ignacio Vieira. Despite her lack of fluency in Portuguese, Maria proceeded to reveal 'that she was woman and not a man' during her confession. We can imagine that such a revelation, far from the venial and mortal sins ordinarily confessed by penitent parishioners, must have come as a rude surprise for Father Vieira. After absolving Maria of her sins, the priest spoke to one of his colleagues. Since priests were under a strict prohibition not to break the secret of the sacrament of confession, we must assume that Father did so with Maria's consent. Despite the language barrier, Maria was able to make her plight known to the priests and they were able to find a Catalan priest who could communicate with her more easily.

The Catalan priest in question was Father José Jofreu. Born in Barcelona in 1676, Father Jofreu had been a supporter of the losing side in the War of the Spanish Succession. Expelled from Catalonia in 1714, he lived as a political exile in Portugal from 1718 onward and became a well-respected figure in Lisbon who enjoyed the patronage of King John V.[15] The elderly Father Jofreu, who was in his sixties, headed the nearby Convent of Rilhafoles, a charitable establishment that looked after the education and welfare of poor orphaned girls. Maria's predicament apparently moved him, and he was willing to provide assistance. Was the priest compelled to assist Maria by feelings of compassion for a repentant sinner? Was it the sympathy felt by one exiled Catalan for a compatriot in trouble? It was probably a combination of both of these. Maria herself states that the priest decided to help her because 'she spoke to him and begged for his help, seeing that they were from the same land and she found herself in this city [of Lisbon] without anyone to help her and exposed to the dangers that threaten foreign women [in such situations]'. Maria told the priest that she wanted to devote her life to God and she promised that she would enter a convent. It was agreed, however, that her limited grasp of Portuguese did not make this possible for the moment and that she would have to enter into a *recolhimento* instead.

A *recolhimento* was not a convent but rather a religious house established to serve a congregation of lay sisters. Indeed, an eighteenth-century Portuguese writer defined a *recolhimento* as 'an establishment with a church [attached to it] in which, according to the wishes of its founder, women of differing statuses are gathered together and live cloistered and under the supervision of a regent'.[16] As the historian Laurinda Abreu has noted, *recolhimentos* tended to fall into different groups: the educational, the contemplative and the reforming. The first group sought to prepare their inmates for either a monastic vocation or married life. The second group 'gathered together under the same roof a group of women who had decided to give up living in society and create their own, self-regulated microcosm'. Finally, the third group focused on reforming repentant prostitutes and converting them into 'virtuous' women.[17]

Part of the established poor-relief system in early modern Portugal, the *recolhimentos* of eighteenth-century Lisbon were essentially repositories for girls and women: repentant prostitutes, orphaned girls, young widows without resources, vagrant women or any other 'helpless women' (literally *mulheres desemparadas*). As one seventeenth-century Portuguese churchman put it, such *recolhimentos* aimed to 'reduce free and ill-accustomed people to a life of subjection and virtue'. The situation of these girls and women was deemed to constitute a threat to the religious and social order in Portugal since it was assumed that such women would otherwise inevitably join the ranks of the many prostitutes selling their bodies to survive. Placing these girls and women in a *recolhimento* was a way to ensure the salvation of their souls as well as those of the men who might be tempted to have sinful sexual intercourse with them.[18]

Similar institutions existed throughout Catholic Europe and in the Iberian overseas colonies. There were numerous *recolhimentos* in Portugal and its overseas empire. Some were founded and endowed by the Portuguese Crown. By way of illustration, the *Recolhimento das Órfãs do Castelo* was an institution for orphaned girls situated close to the Castle of Lisbon. Its aim was to provide dowries so that the girls would be married off in Portugal or the colonies and achieve a respectable social status. Private individuals, however, established other *recolhimentos* though charitable bequests of money or property that guaranteed a basic (but often inadequate) income. Sometimes the women – or *recolhidas* – in the smaller institutions depended on alms to survive.[19]

The Portuguese capital counted at least a dozen female *recolhimentos* at the start of the eighteenth century. Beyond 'free and ill-accustomed people', some *recolhimentos* also accepted paying boarders. It was not uncommon for wealthy men travelling overseas to temporarily place wives and daughters into such establishments as paying boarders when, as one English visitor observed in 1701, they were concerned about the safety of their womenfolk and, presumably, also that any sexual impropriety during their absence would besmirch their family's honour.[20] There was an institution in Lisbon that specialized in 'converting' repentant prostitutes named *Casa Pia das Convertidas* and it was colloquially referred to as the *recolhimento de convertidas.* Nevertheless, *recolhimentos* were not straightforward 'Magdalene houses' and it would be wrong to think of them as such. Instead, the word *recolhimento* can be variously translated into English as a 'depositary' or 'shelter' for women and girls with a wide variety of personal situations whose spiritual salvation was deemed to be at risk.

The women cloistered behind the walls of the *recolhimentos*, the *recolhidas*, were expected to conform to the daily routine of a cloistered religious life that shared a great many similarities to that of professed nuns, cut off from the secular world outside. Under the authority of a senior woman known as 'the regent' as well as the supervision of the local (male) ecclesiastical authorities, regulations specified the observance of three daily acts of communal worship, with the first starting at dawn. The communal meals of the *recolhidas* took place in a refectory and they spent a large part of the day in various forms of manual labour performed in silence. Leisure time was kept to a strict minimum, usually no more than two hours a day since idleness was considered a road to perdition. The girls and women received the same, simple clothing and any unnecessary adornments or cosmetics were prohibited. Each *recolhimento* had its own rules, depending on the religious order to which it was affiliated.[21]

Some *recolhidas* would eventually return to life in society as 'respectable' married women. The Portuguese Crown also earmarked some orphaned *recolhidas* for the Portuguese overseas colonies, where there was a dearth of European women, as brides for Portuguese colonists in the hope that they would produce a self-sustaining population of loyal white colonists. The numbers of *recolhidas* who ended up overseas was limited and probably in the hundreds rather than the thousands. Some of the orphaned *recolhidas* in Lisbon were married off to men in exchange for dowries provided by the Crown or desirable jobs in the colonies. Other women, usually those boarders from wealthier families, would live out their lives in religious establishments and some would even become 'brides of Christ' in convents.[22] Likewise, mariners caught in terrible storms out at sea sometimes begged for divine intervention by promising to marry a repentant prostitute if God spared their lives. As one eighteenth-century English visitor to Lisbon remarked: 'It is considered a good deed to turn an indecent woman into an honest one'.[23]

Given the nature of the *recolhimentos*, and the fact that numerous *recolhidas* were not there by choice but rather because of circumstances not linked to any religious vocation, it is not surprising that discipline was sometimes lax, strict enclosure was not always followed and the authority of the regent frequently contested by her subordinates. In such cases, the local ecclesiastical authorities were called upon to intervene. Indeed, not long after Maria's arrival in Lisbon, the Misericórdia *recolhimento* in Lisbon was rocked by a mutiny of the *recolhidas*, led by two boarders whose 'serious scandals' resulted in their expulsion from the institution.[24] Such problems were not just limited to *recolhimentos* but also experienced in some Portuguese convents. Illicit visits to convents by men colloquially known as *freiráticos* or 'nun lovers' caused considerable scandal and led to the promulgation of laws and severe penalties against these men by King João V's government. Newsletters produced in the 1730s frequently mention the arrest and punishment of *freiráticos*. Ironically, the greatest *freirático*, and the greatest hypocrite, was King João V himself. Earlier in his reign, the Portuguese monarch had installed a number of his mistresses in various convents around Lisbon.[25]

It was to one of these establishments that Father José Jofreu destined Maria Duran, doubtless in the hope that Maria might be 'reformed' but at the very least to remove her from the streets of Lisbon. The institution chosen was the *Recolhimento do Menino Deus*. Before Maria's admittance, however, Father José Jofreu decided to make sure that Maria was indeed a woman. Given that Maria had presented herself in male clothing, it is not surprising that Father José wanted to be certain of Maria's sex before acting as her sponsor. Maria was dispatched to the house of a midwife of the palace named Luisa dos Santos, who inspected her genitalia. The midwife wrote a report declaring that Maria was 'a real woman', thus making her admittance possible. It is in the *recolhimentos* of Lisbon, for the *Recolhimento do Menino Deus* was to be only the first of a number of religious institutions through which Maria would transit, that we first get detailed evidence of Maria Duran's transgressive sexuality.

4

Sex and suspicion in the *recolhimentos* of Lisbon

Prior to Maria's entry into a Lisboan *recolhimento*, the inquisitorial trial dossier reveals little that is unusual about her sexuality. Her heterosexual relationship with her husband in Prullans, resulting in the birth of a son who died young, is the only explicit reference to any sexual activity prior to Maria's arrival in Portugal. It is true that her relationship with a widow in southern France could have appeared suspicious. Nevertheless, Maria claimed that the widow believed her to be a man and had proposed marriage under that belief. Maria never claimed that any actual sexual relations had taken place between them and the inquisitors did not push Maria on this point. It is only during her stays in two different institutions for 'helpless women' in Lisbon that Maria's sexuality began to alarm those surrounding her and raised questions about her gender.[1]

Given Maria's previous experience of life in the Spanish army, the regimented communal life inside a *recolhimento* may not have presented too much of a shock. Maria entered the *recolhimento do Menino Deus*, situated in a quiet street just to the east of the walls of Lisbon's castle. King João V founded the institution in 1717, but it only opened its doors in 1737, a year before Maria's arrival in Lisbon. The building was a compact edifice, consisting of a large rectangular church to which was attached a rather diminutive cloister with two floors. Its striking name – the Portuguese *Menino Deus* translates literally as 'Infant God' – derived from the presence in its church of a statue of Jesus Christ as an infant. The *recolhidas* venerated the statue and, according to an eighteenth-century author, it 'was responsible for prodigies that are renowned in this city [of Lisbon]'.[2] The women and orphaned girls admitted into this *recolhimento* were expected to live as Tertiaries, which is to say according to the rule of the Third Order of St. Francis. According to Maria, she was a resident within the walls of the *recolhimento do Menino Deus* for eight or nine months which proved to be extremely eventful.

Upon her entry into the *recolhimento*, Maria changed her name to Christina de Christo Crucificado in accordance with the regulation that ordered new arrivals to choose a religious name to symbolize the new life that they were entering. There is little information about Maria's first few months of communal life in the *recolhimento*, but five months after entering, probably in January 1739, she met another *recolhida* named Agostinha Theresa da Purificação. Agostinha was a native of Lisbon, born Agostinha Maria de São José, and aged between eighteen and twenty. She had been a resident in the *recolhimento* from a very young age. Maria and Agostinha soon became close, sharing the same cell as their sleeping quarters, and Maria embarked upon the first of a number of sexual relationships that eventually came under the intense scrutiny of the inquisitors. Aged around twenty-eight in 1738, Maria was roughly a decade older than Agostinha. Fortunately, we have access to both Maria and Agostinha's account of the relationship. The inquisitors not only recorded Maria's version during her interrogation but also sent an agent to interrogate Agostinha in a convent in the southern Portuguese town of Beja, to which she had subsequently moved after deciding to become a fully professed nun.

Maria confessed to having 'sordid relations' (*comunicação torpe*) with Agostinha but did not elaborate. Agostinha herself, however, offered more details recorded in the transcript of her later interrogation. Immediately guessing why she was being questioned by the Inquisition, Agostinha's account of the relationship is startling. She freely admitted that, during her time in the *recolhimento do Menino Deus*, she engaged in 'many intimacies, filthy touchings and carnal acts' with Maria and she believed Maria 'to be a man like any other, able to father a child', by which she evidently meant that Maria has a penis, was able to have an erection and ejaculate semen. Yet, at the same time, she had 'never [visually] observed her to possess a penis despite the fact that she heard it said that [Maria] did [have one]'. Moreover, Agostinha claimed that Maria told her that she 'possessed both sexual organs but only used the male one'. Other *recolhidas* recalled that Maria later boasted of her sexual relations with Agostinha and even claimed that Agostinha had become pregnant before miscarrying at four months.

Maria's boasts extended to claiming unnatural powers. She told Agostinha that she could convince women to have sexual relations with her 'merely by setting her eyes upon them', suggesting some unnatural power, although Agostinha had never heard Maria utter any magical words to invoke the Devil. Nevertheless, Maria had once told her that the Devil once appeared to her and, speaking Catalan, had said, 'Why are you surprised'? and other words that Agostinha could no longer recall, to which Maria had responded, 'by your shamelessness'. Agostinha remembered that Maria frequently woke up in the mornings with bruises and scratches on her body, from which blood flowed. Agostinha believed that the Devil had frequently physically abused Maria and inflicted these unexplained wounds. This belief was reinforced when the wounds disappeared after being cleansed with holy water.[3]

Agostinha was not the only person to claim that Maria Duran interacted with the Devil. The Franciscan Father Pedro de Santa Clara was responsible for hearing the confessions of the *recolhidas* of the *Recolhimento do Menino Deus*. He recalled that, 'on one occasion soon after entering the *recolhimento*', Maria Duran told him that her body was covered 'with deep scratches over her chest and hidden parts, which the Devil inflicted on her at night because he often persecuted her in bed'. Maria sought to show him the wounds under her clothing, but the embarrassed priest refused to permit this. Instead, Father Pedro decided to perform an impromptu exorcism. He seized Maria's neck and made a sign of the cross, 'ordering the Devil to free her if he was the cause of her illness'. Soon afterwards, Maria 'felt better without needing any other remedy'. Despite this seemingly miraculous recovery, Father Pedro thought that whilst Maria might have been telling the truth, it was also possible that she could have been lying and that her wounds could have healed naturally. Perhaps unsurprisingly, Father Pedro rapidly took a dislike to Maria Duran. Furthermore, he became aware of 'a very close and intimate friendship' between Maria and the 'young and good looking' Agostinha, seemingly preferring to use this euphemism rather than spell out his suspicion of illicit sexual activities. Consequently, Father Pedro told the inquisitors that he 'took all possible measures to ensure she would leave the *recolhimento*, as she did'.[4]

Maria Duran's stay in the *recolhimento do Menino Deus* thus appears to have come to an abrupt end as Father Pedro de Santa Clara contrived to have her expelled. Father José Jofreu nevertheless rapidly arranged for Maria's transfer to another *recolhimento* for 'helpless women'. This second establishment was known alternatively as the *recolhimento* of *Nossa Senhora da Encarnação e Carmo* (Our Lady of the Incarnation and Carmel) or more simply as the *recolhimento de Cienfuegos*. Located on the hill of Sant'Ana, just north of the Rossio square, this *recolhimento* was a relatively recent creation as it had been founded in 1704 by a devout woman named Isabel Francisca. Its founder enjoyed the support and patronage of the Spanish Jesuit and well-respected theologian Juan Álvaro Cienfuegos Villazón (1657–1739). Like Father Jofreu, Cienfuegos was another supporter of the defeated Habsburg pretender to the Spanish throne who was living in political exile in Portugal. From the moment of its foundation, the *recolhimento* struggled to function as it suffered from an acute lack of funds. In 1712, it could only sustain three *recolhidas* out of the sixteen who had initially joined. It does not appear to have had a church attached to it, although, eventually, it gained a small chapel. It was only in 1738 that, thanks to the support of the Jesuit Order, the *recolhimento* had enough funds to purchase the houses it had been renting until then. After incessantly importuning the cardinal patriarch of Lisbon, the prelate granted the *recolhimento* a licence to form a fully cloistered *recolhimento* following the rule of the Third Order of the Carmelite Order, making its inmates lay Carmelites. Yet the establishment that Maria Duran joined remained in a parlous state. A report in 1740 noted that the building was 'damaged and threatened to fall into ruin', with the tiled roof and its supporting timbers needing extensive repairs or replacement.[5]

Maria's stay in this small and ramshackle *recolhimento* lasted only seven to eight weeks but was extremely eventful. Almost immediately, the *recolhidas* treated Maria with suspicion. Indeed, the head or 'regent' of the *recolhimento* of Our Lady of the Incarnation was Josefa Maria Xavier, a 38-year-old native of Lisbon. Desperate to find an establishment that would accept Maria Duran, Father Jofreu appears to have exaggerated Maria's religious zeal. Josefa ruefully told the inquisitors that the priest had insisted that Maria Duran 'was a saint', very repentant about her previous life of sin and given to regularly mortifying her body as a penance. Nonetheless, the regent of the *recolhimento* claimed that she 'always had a poor impression of Maria because her behaviour was always very vulgar and her social status was very low and because it was suspected that she was a man' and she found Maria to possess 'little humility or virtue'. Soon after entering the *recolhimento*, Maria unashamedly told her fellow *recolhidas* about her past experiences 'travelling the world dressed as a man' and 'various stories about dishonest dealings with women' that the regent took to be groundless 'boasting' (*jactância*). The confessor in charge of the *recolhidas*, the Jesuit Father Ignacio Vieira, had ordered the regent to keep a close watch on Maria and 'not to allow her to build friendships with the young girls that they were educating and raising in the *recolhimento*'. Josefa Maria Xavier further revealed that Maria was the subject of frequent conversations about the identity of her sex/gender among the *recolhidas* and she claimed to have dismissed these rumours as 'codswallop' (*parvoíce*) since she was aware that Father Jofreu had ordered an examination of Maria's genitals prior to her admission to the *recolhimento do Menino Deus*. More disturbing still, however, the regent asserted that she had frequently heard Maria claim that she was 'pursued by the Devil at night' and that the Devil had taken her to a place named Val de Cavalheiros and 'other places'. One morning, Maria had shown the regent scratches on her arms, supposedly caused by the Devil during the previous night.[6]

Notwithstanding the hostility and rumours circulating about her in the *recolhimento* of Our Lady of the Incarnation, Maria rapidly had sexual relationships with a number of women during this time. These women all provided detailed and graphic testimony to the Inquisition. Only three days after the arrival of Maria in the *recolhimento*, a *recolhida* named Vitoria Rosa visited Maria's cell. When they were alone, Maria 'began to utter loving words, stared at her intently and embraced her'. Vitoria Rosa claimed that she was taken aback and sought to avoid Maria after this. Nevertheless, during prayers in the chapel of the *recolhimento* on the evening of the same day, Maria used threatening language to intimidate Vitoria Rosa and force her to return to Maria's cell. Once the door was shut, Maria attempted to rape Vitoria. According to her testimony, Maria seized her and then 'took her to the bed, onto which she was thrown'. Maria took off her robes and 'placed herself on top of her, like a man who wants to have carnal relations'. Vitoria remembered that Maria 'touched her shameful parts with a penis'. The rape was only avoided because the *recolhimento*'s gong rang, summoning the *recolhidas* to gather in the refectory for dinner. The respite was only short-lived, however. At five in the morning the following day, Maria used another excuse to lure Vitoria to her cell and raped her. This time, Vitoria remembered and asserted that Maria penetrated her with something that felt like a penis and it seemed that Maria had ejaculated into her vagina, leaving her vagina 'wet'. This sexual assault was followed by 'twelve or thirteen' other acts of sexual intercourse over a period of twenty to twenty-five days during Maria's stay in the *recolhimento*, which occurred in a variety of different positions either in Maria's cell or 'in any other place where Maria could get hold of her by herself'. In all of these sexual acts, Maria had 'ejaculated from her penis' and 'deeply penetrated her vagina'. Maria had ordered Vitoria not to reveal their sexual relations to her confessor, telling Vitoria that the confessor would refuse to absolve her of her sins. Maria also ordered Vitoria to keep taking communion and confess her other sins to avoid arousing suspicion.

The actions of Maria Duran were accompanied by a clear attempt to manipulate Vitoria's confusion and sense of shame. Vitoria stated that, in order to 'persuade her' to have sex, Maria claimed to be 'a man and a woman', that is, a hermaphrodite, and that she possessed 'both sexes, the sex of a woman above and that of a man below'. When Vitoria became visibly upset 'by what was happening to her', Maria sought to comfort her by telling her that their sexual relations were 'normal' heterosexual intercourse since 'she had been deflowered by a man'. Furthermore, Maria had apparently offered to let Vitoria touch and stroke the penis but 'she never wanted to do it'. Maria bragged about her previous sexual exploits in 'many lands where she had sexual relations with many women and girls as young as nine years old and that she had even fathered a son by one of these women'. These boasts extended to claims that Maria had the extraordinary ability to seduce any woman and to persuade that woman to sleep with her through either a mere look or 'some words'. Maria also boasted that she could use this power to seduce 'the mother regent and all the women of the *recolhimento*, whether young or old', if this was her desire. Finally, Maria even promised to marry Vitoria, going so far as to produce a written promise of marriage, signing it in the name of Don Antonio de Escalhão Pinos. The written promise was handed over to Vitoria, who nonetheless destroyed the document 'in order to hide her misery and because she did not want her parents to come to know of it'.

Vitoria was adamant that she always thought that Maria 'was a man'. During an outing from the *recolhimento* with her parents, she was convinced that she had seen Maria dressed as a man in the company of a group of Catalan men. After starting their sexual relations, Maria had shown Vitoria 'a sharp knife that she used to shave off her facial hair every day'. In addition to this, Vitoria saw with her own eyes that Maria possessed male clothing: breeches and stockings as well as long-sleeved shirts that Vitoria had starched for Maria. Maria had taken these clothes with her after her expulsion from the *recolhimento*. The spectre of the Devil and witchcraft also featured in this relationship just as much as it did in Maria's previous affair with Agostinha. Vitoria recounted being disturbed when, upon waking up in the morning, Maria would complain to her about sleeping badly and show Vitoria scratches and large bruises all over her body, except for her arms and face. When Vitoria inquired what these marks were, Maria 'always responded that she had spent the night outside with witches, asking her not to tell anyone else about this'.

Vitoria was not the only *recolhida* to attract the attentions of Maria. Another woman with whom Maria had sexual relations was Veronica Maria. Veronica states in her testimony that Maria, who occupied the cell next to hers, cared for her during a period of illness. One day, Maria got up and followed Veronica back to her cell. There Maria got into Veronica's bed and 'after many caresses' sought to convince her to have sexual relations by claiming that she was a man named Antonio, who possessed both male and female sexes. Despite her 'great repugnance', Veronica consented and felt during intercourse that Maria possessed a penis. Intercourse was not consummated because Maria withdrew her penis before ejaculating, claiming that she wanted to avoid Veronica falling pregnant. Even though Veronica never touched the supposed penis with her hands, she was convinced that Maria 'was a man with a penis like any other, with which Maria penetrated her'. Her certainty was based on the fact that Veronica had felt her vagina being penetrated, she had been a virgin and her hymen had broken on the first occasion, causing her mild pain and a small loss of blood. Moreover, after sex she observed a liquid on her bedsheets that she took to be semen.

The third woman with whom Maria had sexual relations in the *recolhimento* of Our Lady of the Incarnation was the *recolhida* Maria de Jesus, the teacher (*maestra*) of the young girls who were living in the *recolhimento*. One night, fifteen days after her arrival in the *recolhimento*, Maria Duran called Maria de Jesus to her cell. Once they were alone, Maria Duran told Maria de Jesus 'that she loved her very much'. When Maria Duran threw her onto the bed, Maria de Jesus resisted and asked her whether she was 'a man or the Devil', to which Maria Duran responded 'that she might well be a man and a woman'. Maria de Jesus's resistance meant that Maria Duran was not able to penetrate her, but she sensed a 'thing' (*vulto*) that felt like a penis rub against one of her thighs and 'in less time than it takes to recite an Ave Maria', Maria Duran seemed to climax and ejaculate without penetrating her. Although she did not see it with her eyes, Maria de Jesus's notion that Maria Duran had a penis was bolstered when, afterwards, she felt a 'wet' substance on one of her thighs and assumed that it was semen. On a second occasion, not long afterwards, Maria Duran 'bothered her to commit the same filthy deeds.' This time, Maria de Jesus sought to grasp the penis with one of her hands but Maria Duran 'would not consent'.[7]

As the teacher of the *recolhimento*'s girls, Maria de Jesus noted that Maria Duran had a habit of behaving inappropriately with the young girls, 'touching their breasts whenever she could and performing other dishonest actions'. Like Vitoria Rosa, she was adamant that Maria Duran shaved and 'she came to believe that [Maria Duran] was a man not only through the way she behaved but because every day she gave signs on her face of growing a beard. When she touched [Maria Duran's] face [during sexual relations] it felt rough to the touch'. Furthermore, on one occasion, Maria de Jesus asked Maria Duran directly 'if she was a man or not' and the latter evaded the question by responding ambiguously, exclaiming, 'poor me, not even the king knows what I am!'[8]

The testimony of the four women with whom Maria Duran had sexual relations in the Lisbon *recolhimentos* – Agostinha, Vitoria Rosa, Veronica Maria and Maria de Jesus – is consistent and paints a portrait of a predatory individual who used a combination of physical force and psychological manipulation to achieve her desired ends. While Agostinha was a decade younger than Maria Duran, the other three women were aged *c.* twenty-six, thirty and thirty-five in 1740. In all four cases, Maria Duran apparently coerced the object of her affections into having sexual relations. She sought to reassure them that she was a man or a 'hermaphrodite' and that their sexual relations were consequently heterosexual. Maria bragged about previous relationships with women, claimed to have fathered children and to possess extraordinary powers allowing her to seduce any woman to whom she was attracted. Maria Duran told the women that she had dealings with the Devil although these statements were always vague about their exact nature. These claims nevertheless made a big impression upon the *recolhidas*, whom Maria Duran wanted to have sex and seem to have helped intimidate them into compliance.

While Maria did not shy away from boasting about her sexual conquests and the visits that the Devil supposedly paid her within the confines of the *recolhimentos*, it appears that she was aware that such claims would cause her problems if they came to the ears of the male ecclesiastical hierarchy. Maria ordered Vitoria Rosa not to discuss their sexual relations with her confessor, telling Vitoria that the confessor would refuse to absolve her of her sins. To this Maria added a threat, stating that she was a hermaphrodite who could hide her penis so that 'if they examined her they would not be able to find anything except her female sex'. Consequently, anyone who accused her of being a man 'would be accused of being a liar'.

Word of Maria Duran's sexual relations with her fellow *recolhidas*, and of her claims to possess both male and female sexual organs, rapidly came to the attention of the *recolhimento*'s regent Josefa Maria Xavier. The *recolhida* Maria de Jesus, one of Maria Duran's sexual partners, recalled that the *recolhimento* was in a state of turmoil. The frightened *recolhidas* were refusing to sleep in their rooms. Instead, they were all sleeping together in the chapel's choir. The regent duly complained to Father Ignacio Vieira, who took measures to have Maria expelled. Maria, however, did not submit meekly. According to Maria de Jesus, she locked herself in one of the *recolhimento*'s rooms and stayed there for three days without food or water. At the end of those three days, Maria terrified the *recolhidas* by crying out that she would kill anyone who entered.[9] It is not clear whether Maria was forcibly removed from the room, or willingly left it after three days.

Given the circumstances in which Maria Duran was expelled from a *recolhimento* for a second time, Father José Jofreu commissioned a qualified surgeon named Antonio Soares Brandão to conduct a second physical examination of Maria Duran's genitals to confirm whether Maria 'was a man or a true woman'. The 35-year-old Antonio Soares Brandão was a rising star in the field of surgery in Portugal. Appointed as one of the Portuguese royal family's supernumerary surgeons in 1732, he also became an official lay assistant of the Inquisition that same year, making himself available to provide medical assistance to the inquisitors and their prisoners when called upon to do so. By 1740, he was the resident surgeon in the hospital of São Lázaro in Lisbon and the King ennobled him by royal decree. Antonio Soares Brandão would later enjoy the favour and patronage of King João V's successor, King José I, and rise to become the chief surgeon of the Portuguese Crown and Portuguese Army.[10]

When questioned by the inquisitors a couple of years later, Antonio Soares Brandão would remember having conducted a physical examination of 'a foreign woman from Catalonia'. The examination took place in a private house near the *Recolhimento do Menino Deus* and in the presence of 'two or three women', whose names he could not recall. Soares Brandão examined Maria's 'genital hole' (*vazo genital*), by which he meant vagina, and 'found it to be the same as that of any other woman' with no notable differences or abnormalities that could lead someone to doubt that Maria was a woman (at least in physical terms). The examination did not stop there, however. Troubled by the account of events in the *recolhimento* he had heard from Father Ignacio Vieira, presumably Maria's boasts about being a hermaphrodite, Soares Brandão decided to conduct an experiment. The surgeon placed Maria in a tub of hot water 'to see if there was anything retained in the vagina'. By this, the surgeon meant that he wanted to ascertain if Maria had a penis trapped within her body that might emerge if Maria's body temperature was raised. This experiment was directly linked to Galenic theories about the effect of heat and bodily temperatures on the formation of human sexual organs. Soares Brandão could report that he had not witnessed any sign that a penis might be trapped inside Maria's body. Nonetheless, he later claimed to the inquisitors that he retained some suspicions because Maria Duran proved to be uncooperative during the inspection, refusing to allow him to conduct an invasive internal examination of the vagina with his finger. Once his examination was completed, and despite these alleged suspicions, Soares Brandão wrote a report for Father José Jofreu confirming that he had no doubt that Maria was 'a real woman'.[11]

After this unpleasant experience, Maria Duran's life became somewhat chaotic and peripatetic for a while. Father José Jofreu still seems to have harboured doubts and wanted medical practitioners to conduct a second physical examination. When Maria categorically refused to consent, his patience finally snapped. He decided to disown Maria and ordered her to be cast out 'onto the street'. Maria claims to have decided to leave Lisbon and travelled to the small town of Aldeia Galega, situated across the river Tejo from Lisbon, dressed as a man. The hapless Father Jofreu seems to have had a change of heart, or perhaps he was moved by a bad conscience, fearing that he had condemned Maria Duran to eternal damnation. He sent a Catalan man to find Maria. This man brought Maria back to the Portuguese capital, where Father Jofreu arranged (and paid) for her to reside in the man's home, with his wife and children for a few months. Claiming to have been spooked by unknown people searching for her at night, Maria left Lisbon once more. Crossing the Tejo River and travelling to the port town of Setúbal, thirty kilometres to the south. There, Maria confessed her sins to a Franciscan friar named Fray José de Santa Rita. Maria recounted her life story (or at least a version of it) and begged him for his help, blaming Father José Jofreu for her predicament. The Franciscan wrote to Father José Jofreu, who forwarded two coins to help Maria. From Setúbal, Maria travelled inland and eastwards to the city of Évora. In that city, Maria proceeded to the Franciscan convent, where she confessed her sins to a Friar named Joaquim and confided that her desire was to lead a secluded religious life. Impressed by Maria's story, Fray Joaquim directed her to the Jesuit Father José da Silva Vieira who arranged for Maria to be admitted as a novice in the Domincian convent of *Nossa Senhora do Paraizo* in Évora.

Contacting an unknown churchman, gaining his confidence or exploiting his piety and pleading to be admitted into a religious establishment seems to have become Maria Duran's modus operandi in Portugal. Maria Duran's religious piety is certainly open to scepticism and it is more likely that Maria Duran's objective was to find shelter and food. Whatever Maria Duran's true motives, Maria Duran's stay in the Dominican convent in Évora was to prove just as eventful as her time in the Lisboan *recolhimentos* as well as a decisive step on the road to the dark cells of the Inquisition.

5

The nuns and novices of Our Lady of Paradise

'This is a most ancient city …. It is at present an archbishop's see; and there are no less than twenty-five convents in it. The town is large, but it is nearly depopulated, and going to ruin: neither trade nor manufactures prevail; nothing appears, but the gloom of bigotry.'[1] Évora made a distinctly unfavourable impression upon Major William Dalrymple, a British officer garrisoned in Gibraltar, when he visited the town in 1777 during his travels through Spain and Portugal. Anti-Catholic prejudice obviously influenced the Protestant British soldier in his appraisal of the town, but there can be no doubt that the atmosphere of eighteenth-century Évora was a far cry from the bustling and wealthy streets of Lisbon.

The chief city of the Alentejo region of southern Portugal, Évora lies roughly 140 kilometres southeast of the Portuguese capital and sits on a hill in an area of wide inland plains propitious for the cultivation of olives, vines and cork trees. Its Mediterranean climate was influenced by its inland location, resulting in variations of extreme heat in summer and cool winters, with cold, sometimes freezing nights. An ancient town and settlement with a history stretching back millennia, the city probably took its name from the yew trees (*ebura*) that Celtiberian inhabitants found there. The town remained a significant settlement during the Roman period – from which it inherited a prominent temple whose ruins and Corinthian columns still stand in the town centre although it was used as a slaughterhouse in the eighteenth century – and then into the post-Roman Visigothic kingdom and even after the Islamic conquest in the eighth century. Following the Christian 'reconquest' in 1165, Évora became an important religious centre in the medieval and early modern period with a sixteenth-century Jesuit university, multiple monasteries and convents. A fortress-like cathedral whose construction began in the twelfth century was the seat of the archbishop of Évora. By the middle of the eighteenth century, Évora had a population estimated at around 4,000 'hearths' (*fogos*) or households, amounting to *c*. 15,000 inhabitants, making it only a tenth of the size of Lisbon. The town's high point had been in the sixteenth century, and by the 1740s its economic fortunes had begun to suffer a marked decline.[2]

Among the many religious institutions of the town stood the Convent of Our Lady of Paradise (*Nossa Senhora do Paraíso*), a community of nuns who followed the Dominican rule. Consecrated to God, the Dominican nuns dedicated themselves to a cloistered life devoted to secluded worship. They sought to lead a life of prayer, penance, hearing the Word of God and contemplating the mysteries of Salvation. The origin of the convent stretched back to the 1400s, when it was founded as a *recolhimento*. By the end of the fifteenth century, its *recolhidas* were living as tertiaries of the Dominican Order. The formal transformation of the *recolhimento* into a cloistered convent for Dominican nuns took place after the grant of a papal decree authorizing this and with the support of King Manuel I in 1516–17. The convent received some grants of land from the Crown to support it, but it was hardly a particularly wealthy or prestigious institution. Its main claim to fame was the possession of the 'Virgin of Paradise' (*Virgem do Paraíso*): a fourteenth-century ivory sculpture of the Virgin Mary holding the Christ child gifted to it by 'an honourable matron'. The sculpture had given the convent its name. The statue, which survives and is presently conserved in Évora's Museum of Sacred Art, could be opened up to form a triptych with sculpted scenes of the life of Mary. It is part of a type of devotional sculpture known as a *Vierge Ouvrante* (Opening Virgin) meant to be displayed on altars in monasteries, convents and private chapels. According to legend, one of the fingers of the infant Christ held by the Virgin Mary was accidentally broken off, resulting in a miraculous flow of blood. Since then, the sculpture was venerated with great devotion both inside and outside of the convent. It was taken to the beds of those suffering from illness and reputed to bring about miraculous cures among both nuns and lay people in Évora.[3]

An elegant illuminated manuscript produced in 1537 set out in considerable detail the written rules and statutes by which the nuns and novices of the convent were ordered to live an austere existence dedicated to prayer. The rules ordered nuns and novices to wear only 'honest wool habits' and live in silence as much as possible. Infractions to the code of conduct, both 'light' and 'grave', were to be punished by the prioress and the nuns were expected to submit themselves to medicinal bleedings (*sangrias*) four times each year. Moreover, there were strict rules governing the admission of novices into the convent. Postulants had to submit themselves to an interrogation about their 'life and customs' to ensure that they were socially respectable and not married or fleeing an abusive husband. Moreover, they were expected to undergo an examination to ensure that they were not pregnant. If the prioress and nuns could not be certain whether an applicant was pregnant or not, the regulations specified that the applicant must wait 'until there is such evidence', presumably a reference to menstruation. The probation time before a novice could seek to become a nun was set at a minimum of one year. To ensure that the convent was not overcrowded, the rules established a set number of nuns but noted that a separate and lower class of nuns, called 'converse sisters' (*freiras conversas*), could be admitted 'in moderate numbers' to assist the 'choir sisters' (*freiras de coro*) in their duties.[4]

It is difficult to picture the convent that Maria Duran entered in 1740 since the building itself no longer exists. The 1537 rules and statutes mention a single 'strong' door giving onto the street and a chapel in which a grille separated the nuns and novices from the lay faithful who came to attend religious services. The convent was abolished as an institution in November 1897, after the death of the last nun, and the physical edifice of the convent was demolished in 1899–1900. In May 1908, the local authorities in Évora asked for the permission to take over the land as part of their programme to improve 'public hygiene' and the 'salubriousness' of the town. They wanted the terrain to be 'filled with trees and beautified'.[5] This ambition was fulfilled and today the area once occupied by the convent is a pleasant and quiet park in the shape of a triangle: the *Jardim do Bacalhau* (Cod Gardens). Photographs of the exterior of the convent taken just before its demolition show that it was a compact edifice with sun-baked whitewashed walls, squeezed between two streets and sitting on sloping terrain. The building included up to four levels and the elevated part of the building located at the higher, western end of the convent looms like the prow of a large ship (see Figure 4). When the convent was inspected by an official in 1857, he described it as a 'small' edifice, with a diminutive cloister and choir where the nuns held masses, although the choir was nevertheless 'the best and most beautiful of all those of the religious houses in this city not only because of its architecture but also because of the magnificent paintings it contains'.[6]

Maria Duran told the various churchmen she met in Lisbon and Setúbal that she wished to enter a convent and dedicate herself to God. Whatever the truth of such claims, and even though Maria was admitted into the convent of Our Lady of Paradise as a novice, it seems unlikely that Maria could ever have realistically hoped to become a fully professed 'choir nun'. Such an ambition would have required significant patronage, given that novices and their families needed to arrange for the payment of a significant 'dowry' or endowment to the convent. As the distinction between the 'choir sisters' and 'converse sisters' set out in the 1537

Figure 4 Photograph of the Dominican convent of *Nossa Senhora do Paraíso*, Évora, prior to its demolition in1899–1900. Taken from the western side of the convent, at the present junction of the *Rua de Machede* and the *Rua de Mendo Estevens*. Printed with the kind permission of the *Arquivo Fotográfico da Câmara Municipal de Évora* (Ref. PT/AFCME/AF/CME/3038/287).

regulations of the convent showed, there was a pecking order among the women living in Our Lady of Paradise. Even among the professed nuns, there existed further distinctions in status that were indicated by the colour of their veils and the differences in the 'dowries' that were paid (usually by their families) to the convent in order to seal their spiritual marriage to Christ. Two nuns who were to feature prominently during Maria Duran's stay in the convent offer interesting evidence of this. On 8 September 1739, Sister Teresa Maria Evangelista became a professed nun, taking her vows and bringing with her with a dowry of 600,000 *reais* for which she became a nun with a 'black veil' (*de veo preto*). Conversely, Sister Narcisa Teresa do Espirito Santo took her vows on 15 January 1738. Her dowry was smaller at 400,000 *reais* and she became a nun with 'a white veil' (*de veo branco*).[7] Only a nun with a black veil, a fully fledged 'choir sister', was entitled to participate fully in the convent's affairs.

Most likely, Maria entered the convent in May 1740 as a novice who would become a *freira conversa* or, to use an eighteenth-century term employed in Portugal, a *donata*. This term referred to a woman who would live a religious life similar to that of the professed nuns but essentially become a servant in the convent.[8] As a novice, Maria came into the care of a 'teacher' (*maestra*) who was responsible for teaching Maria the regulations that governed her new way of life, especially humility, silence and obedience. In accordance with the rules of the convent, Maria pledged her obedience to the Virgin Mary and Saint Dominic. Despite the heavy emphasis that the rules placed on silence, the convent was a lively community, and Maria did not shy away from freely conversing with other novices and nuns. Maria's behaviour was certainly far from what one might expect of a novice supposedly dedicated to silent prayer.

The inquisitors later asked the most senior nuns of the convent, including the prioress, to describe and assess Maria Duran's behaviour and religious beliefs. While they all considered Maria to be 'a faithful Catholic', their impressions of her religious zeal were far from favourable. Maria attended the daily religious services, confessed her sins and frequently received communion but the senior nuns did not deem her 'life, customs and religious beliefs' to conform to those expected of a 'good Christian'. According to their assessment, Maria was 'insufficiently god-fearing and lacking in the modesty, devotion and attention required by her vocation and during the communal acts of worship'. Indeed, they deemed her behaviour to be frequently nothing short of scandalous. They recalled that Maria was often absent from the choir 'for frivolous reasons'. Worse still, Maria obviously preferred the company of the younger members of the conventual community and would sometimes disturb the choir by staring intently at other women, laughing and making signs at younger nuns and novices gathered in the convent's choir. Her lax performance of spiritual exercises – most notably fasting and the mortification of her body with a cilice (an uncomfortable hairshirt) – similarly did not impress them.[9]

It is worth remembering that the senior nuns' descriptions of Maria's conduct were legal testimony provided under oath only after Maria's arrest. Nevertheless, younger nuns in the convent also confirmed the general tenor of these claims. Maria's manner was described by one younger nun as 'happy, agreeable and playful' and she 'embraced, kissed and said gallant words, but not dishonest ones', to the other novices and nuns, both old and young. Maria told the nuns that she was from Catalonia but completely exaggerated her social status, claiming to be the daughter of a 'very noble and illustrious' aristocratic couple named Don Raymundo Escalhão, the Count of Pinos, and his wife Teresa. Moreover, Maria did not shy away from talking to other nuns and novices about her earlier physical examinations by midwives and Antonio Soares in Lisbon. Regarding this story, however, Maria claimed that this was the result of false accusations that she had impregnated another woman.

Maria remained in the convent until her expulsion and arrest by the Inquisition in February 1741. During the nine preceding months, Maria had sexual relations with at least three of the nuns: Sister Teresa Maria Evangelista, Sister Iria Joachina and Sister Isabel Elena dos Anjos. Of these women, the first two were aged in their mid-twenties whilst Sister Isabel Elena was aged forty-five 'more or less'. The nature of these sexual relations, revealed during their interrogation under oath by the Inquisition, was very similar to those described by the *recolhidas* in Lisbon.

Sister Teresa Maria Evangelista, for instance, recalled that she developed a close friendship with Maria, which led to 'many fondlings and embraces between them' between June and August 1740. Sister Teresa remembered three occasions when Maria 'convinced her to have carnal copulation': once on her bed, the second time 'in a chapel connected to the first-floor balcony' and the third time 'in her cell but not on the bed'. During these seemingly consensual instances of sexual intercourse, Maria touched Teresa's genitals 'like a man' and Teresa sensed that the 'thing' (*cousa*) that 'touched' her was 'warm' and 'animated', which is to say erect like an aroused penis. Sister Teresa was convinced that Maria 'was a man with a penis' although she did not see or touch either the alleged penis or Maria's naked crotch. Teresa acted in accordance with this belief, taking care to avoid being penetrated and a possible pregnancy. She initially claimed that Maria had ejaculated on the bed, but later retracted this claim. Teresa claimed that she ended the relationship and that a resentful Maria treated her coldly afterwards.[10]

The much older Sister Isabel Elena dos Anjos had sexual relations with Maria at least five times, either on her bed or on Maria's. On these occasions, she remembered that she would lie down on a bed facing up with Maria lying on top of her. She felt that her vagina was 'touched by something similar to a penis, albeit small, but gentle and erect that touched but did not penetrate her vagina, causing her pleasure'. She did not see any evidence that Maria had ejaculated 'since she focused on her own pleasure and these acts took place in a great rush and fear, so that no one might become aware of their illicit friendship'. When pressed for more details by the inquisitors, Sister Isabel Elena went further, however, by claiming that she did not believe that Maria was anything but a woman using an 'instrument' to simulate a penis, apparently a dildo. During their 'filthy acts', Sister Isabel noticed that Maria Duran always had one of her hands on Isabel's vagina. She could not remember whether it was the right or the left hand but Sister Isabel assumed that Maria used this hand to 'prepare and handle' the dildo.[11]

Beyond Sister Teresa and Sister Isabel, Maria Duran also engaged in sexual intimacy with a Sister Iria Joachina. This nun's sexual relations with Maria were apparently limited to enjoying 'various venereal pleasures' in which Maria used one of her hands to masturbate Sister Iria and the other hand to masturbate herself whilst they were sitting next to one another. Sister Iria was very clear, however, that this was the limit of their relations and that Maria did not lie on top of her or attempt to penetrate her in any way. Sister Iria reported rumours circulating in the convent that three other nuns – Sister Maria Jacinta, Sister Ignacia Candida and Sister Narcisa Teresa – had engaged in sexual relations with Maria Duran. When interrogated, however, none of these women confessed and they claimed not to know why the Inquisition was questioning them.[12]

Regarding Maria Duran's identity as a man, a woman or a hermaphrodite, the two nuns who described their sexual relations with Maria Duran in graphic detail offered contradictory testimony. Sister Teresa insisted that Maria had sought to persuade her that she was a hermaphrodite 'born with the sexes of a man and a woman'. Yet she claimed that Maria 'only used the male sex' and 'urinated with the posture of a man', clearly a reference to passing water whilst standing up. Moreover, she had never seen any evidence that Maria menstruated. Sister Isabel, on the other hand, claimed that Maria 'gave the external appearance of having a female sex', urinating 'with the same posture as other women' which is to say squatting or sitting down, and she had witnessed traces of blood on her clothing indicating that Maria menstruated. Sister Isabel had also heard Sister Josefa da Assumpção, who had cared for Maria during an illness, say that she had only seen Maria's vagina but no penis. When questioned, the 56-year-old Josefa da Assumpção confirmed the information stating that she had observed and even touched Maria Duran's 'venereal parts' when applying a remedy and had seen stains on her clothing that was evidence that Maria Duran menstruated. Sister Josefa had shared a cell with Maria Duran for a period of three months and 'never witnessed any action indicating that [Maria Duran] possessed a penis'. Similarly, Sister Iria, who claimed that Maria Duran had masturbated her, was clear that she believed Maria to be a woman 'who does not possess and does not use a penis, either a normal one or one conjured by means of diabolic arts'. At the same time, however, Sister Iria noted that Maria Duran acted suspiciously since Maria would not allow her to touch her groin. She had only heard rumours that Maria 'had both sexes and hid the male sex [organ] after having sexual relations'.[13]

The greatest contrast between the evidence of the *recolhidas* in Lisbon and the nuns in Évora relates to the claims that Maria Duran had made a demonic pact. None of the nuns of the convent of Our Lady of Paradise thought that Maria had made a pact with the Devil or claimed to have heard Maria utter such a claim. Unlike the *recolhidas*, they could not remember Maria ever making claims about having supernatural powers of seduction or as the inquisitorial scribe recorded it: 'being able to convince a person to commit disgusting acts with a mere look'. None of the nuns had heard Maria invoke the Devil or verbally abuse or misuse sacred objects. During their sexual trysts with Maria, Sisters Teresa and Isabel did not notice any suspicious signs such as peals of thunder or 'observe things that normally do not happen'. The only reference to magic that Maria had made was during a curious incident described by Sister Isabel Elena. According to Sister Isabel, the nuns found out that Maria could play the rebec – a bowed stringed musical instrument – and pressed her to play it for them. Maria refused, however, pleading that 'she did not play it because a sorcerer had taught her to do so and her confessors had forbidden her to play'. No further details about this odd tale emerged and none of the other nuns remembered hearing it.[14]

The breakup between Maria Duran and Sister Teresa resulted in jealousies that disturbed the nuns' communal life. Sister Josefa da Assumpção and Sister Isabel remembered a heated exchange between Maria and Sister Teresa on the first floor balcony of the convent in which the two 'insulted each other with words' although they did not hear the exact words exchanged. Maria Duran was distraught and went to ask the prioress to allow her to leave the convent but the latter refused. A month later, Sister Josefa witnessed Maria pick up a stick. When it became clear that Maria intended to ambush and attack Sister Teresa 'in a dark part of the [convent's] infirmary', Josefa and four other nuns decided to intervene. They went to find Maria in order to 'dissuade her from her bad intentions' but, despite their arguments, it was only with 'great violence' that they were able to physically restrain Maria and bring her to the cell of Sister Josefa to calm down. Afterwards, Maria Duran and Sister Teresa never spoke to each other, but fellow nuns heard both of them plotting revenge against one another.

After nine months, Maria Duran's antics had disturbed the communal life of the nuns to such an extent that the prioress wrote to her superiors in the Dominican order to plead for help and authorize her expulsion from the convent. Fray Bernardo do Evangelista, the archdeacon (*vigário*) responsible for supervising the spiritual life of the nuns of the convent, was informed, and he appealed to his own superiors for advice. Eventually, the matter fell into the hands of Fray Pedro de Santo Tomás, the prior of the monastery of São Domingos in Lisbon and a doctor in theology. Fray Pedro was also an 'advisor' (*consultor*) on theological matters for the Inquisition and it may well have been this role that convinced him to hand the matter to the inquisitors in Lisbon. On 28 January 1741, Fray Pedro wrote a letter providing the inquisitors with a brief summary of Maria Duran's time in Lisbon and Évora and noting the physical examination that Maria underwent after her expulsion from the *recolhimento* of Our Lady of the Incarnation. Moreover, Fray Pedro stressed how 'to the ruination of the convent and great scandal of Reason she is using a penis'. In his opinion, this seemed to strongly suggest that Maria had made a pact with the Devil 'who would be able to conceal any sign of the penis, even under the examination of the most expert surgeons'. Since it was reasonable to suspect that Maria had made a pact with the Devil and had a demon familiar, Fray Pedro concluded his letter by urging the inquisitors to act 'without delay since there is great danger and this demon must be expelled as soon as possible from the convent [of Our Lady of Paradise]'.[15]

Fray Pedro de Santo Tomás's letter was written in a hurry and betrays the bafflement and alarm that Maria Duran's case caused among the Dominican churchmen who were responsible for the convent in Évora. The use of the expression 'to the great scandal of Reason' (*mayor escandalo da Razão*), deliberately spelling Reason with a capital R, is particularly interesting. Homosexual activity between women in convents was far from unknown and there were procedures for dealing with such '*actos torpes*' but this case did not conform to such a scenario. Claims that Maria Duran possessed a penis clashed with the evidence from her previous physical examination. A demonic pact seemed to be the only possible, indeed reasonable, explanation. It is therefore hardly surprising that Fray Pedro drew such a matter to the attention of the Inquisition, within whose jurisdiction cases of alleged demonic pacts fell. For Fray Pedro, this was an extraordinary case beyond his theological competence that required extraordinary measures.

In agreement with the head of the Dominican Order in Portugal, José da França, Fray Pedro de Santo Tomás concluded his letter by stating that he was making an official denunciation to the Inquisition. This deliberate action effectively triggered the intervention of that feared institution. The letter would have been taken by a domestic the fifty meters or so from the Church of São Domingos to the doors of the *Estaus* palace, the seat of the Inquisition in Lisbon. Maria Duran was formally expelled from the convent of Our Lady of Paradise and conveyed to the Inquisition in Lisbon. Interestingly, there existed a fully functioning inquisitorial tribunal in the town of Évora that should have handled the case since the convent was within its territorial jurisdiction. The reason for this transfer of the case to Lisbon is never explained in the trial dossier but it may be surmised that the inquisitors felt that such an unusual case might be better handled in the Portuguese capital. Moreover, the fact that many witnesses were present in the Lisbon *recolhimentos* probably also factored in the decision. Maria was arrested on the order of the Inquisition in Évora on Tuesday 14 February 1741. The man entrusted with apprehending Maria and conveying her from Évora to Lisbon was apparently the Count of Soure.[16] For Maria, the scene was set for a confrontation with a fearsome judicial machine that would last over three years, during which the inquisitors would exert themselves to extract the 'truth' about her gender, sexuality and supposed ties with the Prince of Darkness.

6

Enter the Inquisition

The Inquisition – or to give it its official name, the Holy Office of the Inquisition against Heretical Depravity and Apostasy – was established in Portugal by the papacy at the request of the Portuguese Crown in 1536. Its function was to act as a special ecclesiastical court, and its mission was to protect the religious orthodoxy of the kingdom by actively tracking down religious beliefs and behaviours that endangered it. The inquisitors were both judges and active investigators and, by the eighteenth century, there existed three tribunals in Portugal. Based in Coimbra, Lisbon and Évora, these tribunals divided up Portugal into three inquisitorial districts roughly equivalent to the north, centre and south of the country. In each one of these districts, a network of lay and ecclesiastical agents – known as familiars and commissaries – assisted the inquisitors in such tasks as the collection of denunciations and evidence or the arrest of prisoners. A General Council of the Inquisition based in the Portuguese capital and presided over by the Inquisitor-General oversaw the work of the tribunals.[1]

The Inquisition had been established to hunt down the descendants of converted Jews, known as 'New Christians', who were suspected of continuing to secretly practice Judaism. The fear that secret Jews were working to undermine the church and monarchy became an obsession in certain sections of the Portuguese society. In the sixteenth century, various institutions adopted statutes barring anyone with impure 'Jewish blood' in their veins. In contrast to the situation in Spain, where the Spanish Inquisition eventually turned its attention to other heretical groups (such as Protestants, secret Muslims and those who uttered heretical blasphemies), the Portuguese Inquisition consistently focused on alleged secret Jews well into the eighteenth century, and the majority of trials concerned 'judaizers'.[2] Critics of the Inquisition claimed that its procedures, designed to extract confessions, forced genuine Christians, whose only crime was to be descended from Jews, to make false confessions. One Portuguese nobleman grumbled in 1737 that the Inquisition 'turned Christians into Jews' just as the royal mint in Lisbon turned metal into coins.[3] Soon after her arrival in Lisbon, Maria Duran may well have heard discussions about the Inquisition's recent arrest of groups of 'New Christians' in the city, including António José da Silva. One of Portugal's leading playwrights in the eighteenth century, António José da Silva, was prosecuted and convicted as a 'judaizer' before being garrotted and burnt at the stake in Lisbon in October 1739.[4]

The intervention of the Inquisition plunged Maria into a new world that must have been bewildering. The Portuguese Inquisition was a formidable judicial machine that followed rules and procedures carefully set out in remarkable detail in a series of books of regulations, the *regimentos* printed and updated in 1552, 1570, 1613 and 1640.[5] Unlike other secular or ecclesiastical courts, the trials of the Inquisition took place behind closed doors. Inquisitors, inquisitorial officials and prisoners were sworn to secrecy, and severe punishments threatened those who discussed details of the trials outside of the walls of the Inquisition's tribunals. Prisoners were held in isolation and allowed no contact with the outside world. Guilt was assumed, and prisoners bore the burden of proving their innocence without having access to the full evidence possessed by the inquisitors. For most prisoners, an inquisitorial trial meant financial ruin (prisoners paid for the costs of their imprisonment and their trial), social stigma, psychological and sometimes even physical torment (torture) and possibly even death. The only public part of the Inquisition's procedures was its spectacular, highly choreographed public sentencing ceremonies: the *autos-da-fé*. Designed to humiliate the guilty and highlight the danger of heresy to the watching masses, the *autos* included a grand procession, a sermon and the reading out of sentences before those prisoners deemed to be unrepentant or second time offenders were conveyed to a place of execution. Protestant propagandists in northern Europe rapidly seized upon the secretive procedures of the Inquisition as polemical ammunition in their anti-Catholic works. The total number of executions carried out, however, was limited. The number of defendants condemned to death either in person or in effigy by the three inquisitorial tribunals in Portugal between 1536 and 1767 (the date of the last execution) was 6 per cent overall although the number of death sentences was in decline in the eighteenth century after culminating in the seventeenth.[6] The Inquisition certainly used torture but this was far from unique to that institution. Furthermore, the inquisitors used torture only in specific circumstances outlined by the regulations of the Inquisition.

Despite its seeming preoccupation with the hunting and punishment of secret Jews, witchcraft and demonic possession also fell within the jurisdiction of the

Portuguese Inquisition. A section of the 1640 regulations of the Portuguese Inquisition dealt with the subject of how to sentence 'wizards, sorcerers, diviners and those who invoke the Devil or have concluded a pact with him or use the art of judiciary astrology'. Only cases deemed 'manifestly heretical' would fall to the inquisitors, with lesser cases of superstitious beliefs left for the local bishop's courts to deal with.[7] Compared with the overall number of prosecutions, inquisitorial prosecutions of witches and sorcerers were limited. Portugal was spared the brutal witch-hunts that took place elsewhere in early modern Europe, and there was only a single execution for the offence in the seventeenth century. A modest spike in witchcraft prosecutions did occur between 1700 and 1760, but historians have not been able to explain the causes underpinning it.[8] In common with the rest of Europe, however, such accusations tended to disproportionately affect women in Portugal. Indeed, an exhaustive study of witchcraft and sorcery cases in Portugal between 1600 and 1774 revealed that 83 per cent of the defendants were female.[9] In the early eighteenth century, the inquisitorial tribunal in Lisbon prosecuted a small number of individuals accused of practising sorcery with the aid of the Devil.[10] While the specific nature of the charges against Maria may have been unusual, the inquisitors thus had some experience of prosecuting individuals accused of making a demonic pact.

The first document in Maria Duran's trial dossier is the official act of remand (*auto de entrega*), which records that Maria Duran arrived with her escort at the doors of the Lisbon Inquisition on 23 February 1741. The officer in charge searched her but found no personal possessions on her person to record and impound. He then led Maria to a cell. The *Estaus* palace of the Inquisition in central Lisbon had been a royal residence in the Middle Ages, but it was transformed into a tribunal and prison after it was handed to the Inquisition in the sixteenth century.[11] The Inquisition commissioned a remarkably detailed plan of the building, which had four levels, in 1634. The 1755 earthquake that devastated Lisbon destroyed the edifice, but it was largely unaltered in the 1740s. The plan shows that the part of the building closest to the Rossio Square included large rooms that served the administrative needs of the Inquisition, including as interrogation rooms. Further back and concentrated inside the centre of the building were multiple rows of apparently windowless cells (see Figure 5).[12]

Unsurprisingly, the inquisitorial documents do not offer Maria's perspective on, or reaction to, being imprisoned by the notorious Inquisition with no idea of how long the trial would take or how it would end. A rare and near contemporaneous prisoner's account does exist, however. John Coustos, a Swiss

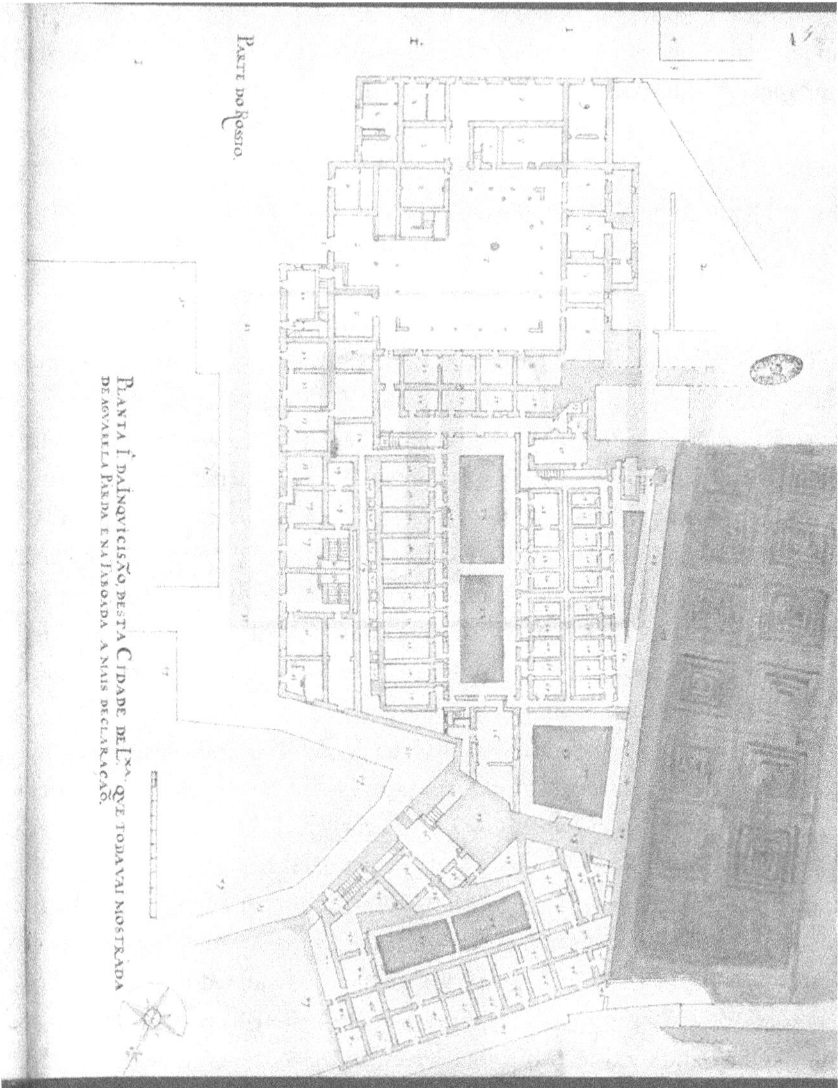

Figure 5 The 1634 plan of the ground floor of the Inquisition's *Estaus* Palace in Lisbon. ANTT., *Tribunal do Santo Ofício, Conselho Geral, livro* 470, fol. 4r. CC BY-SA 4.0.

Protestant and freemason arrested by the Lisbon Inquisition in 1743, penned an eyewitness account after his release upon the intervention of the British government. Coustos and Maria were both prisoners in 1743, possibly in cells located along the same corridor or perhaps even sharing a wall. Coustos's account vividly describes the conditions in the cells and the psychological trauma suffered by prisoners:

> They then led me to a lonely dungeon, expressly forbidding me to speak loud, or knock at the walls; but that, in case I wanted anything, to beat against the door, with a padlock, that hung on the outward door; and which I could reach, by thrusting my arm through the iron grates. 'Twas then that, struck with all the horrors of a place, of which I had heard and read such baleful descriptions, I plunged at once into the blackest melancholy; especially when I reflected on the dire consequences with which my confinement might very possibly be attended.
>
> I passed a whole day and two nights in these terrors, which are the more difficult to describe, as they were heightened at the every little interval, by the complaints, the dismal cries, and hollow groans (echoing through the dreadful mansion) of several other prisoners, my neighbours; and which the solemn silence of the night made infinitely more shocking. 'Twas now that time seemed to have lost all motion, and these threescore hours appeared to me like so many years.[13]

While Coustos was an embittered ex-prisoner and Protestant who wrote an avowedly anti-Catholic pamphlet, there is no cause to doubt the general accuracy of this description. Neither does it clash with the available evidence on conditions in the cells of Lisbon's Inquisition.[14]

Even though Maria was now cut off from the outside world, word of her story was circulating in Lisbon. As a manuscript newsletter dated Saturday 4 March 1741 records, rumours and gossip about the 'Catalan hermaphrodite' were rife:

> A case similar to those recorded many times in histories, and which goes against the perfection of Nature, is now the subject of conversations in Lisbon. A woman was born in the principality of Catalonia and, because she was of noble status, she wanted to conceal the flaws made by Nature [in her genitalia]. She was due to marry and, since the marriage would expose something for which she could not be blamed, she preferred to ignore social propriety and fled from her parents' house. Given that neither the [female] attire she wore until that point, nor the male clothing she acquired contradicted her choice of sex outside of those places where she was known, she secured a position as a soldier, serving with distinction and resolution and was promoted to the rank of Ensign, or *alferes*. Later, after wandering during various years from one kingdom to another in Spain, she came to this Kingdom of Portugal and resided in Lisbon. Father José Jofreu, a cleric of well-known virtue in the Order of Saint Vincent de Paul who was born in Catalonia, also lives here in Lisbon. She was tired of being a man and when she learned of his exemplary life, and the many conversions [of sinners] that Jofreu had achieved, she went to him and revealed her story as well as the natural problem that had led her to reject marriage. With indefatigable zeal, Father Jofreu steered that wayward soul towards a spiritual life and got her to dress as a woman. Since these clothes could not hide the fact

> she was a hermaphrodite, he sent her to the house of Luisa das Chagas, a lady of impeccable lifestyle who resides close by the church of the *Menino Deus*, so that she could receive some instruction in virtue. After a few months, she entered into the illustrious *Recolhimento do Menino Deus*. The illustrious and excellent Vicountess of Barbacena, a lady of great piety who lives in Évora, wishing to demonstrate her unusual charity, took her to that city and placed her in the convent of Our Lady of Paradise. She stayed there eleven months. The Devil was able to enter that convent and he persuaded her to become a man again. This new choice [of sex] proved that her status as a nun could not stop the damage caused by her previous life as a soldier. She irreverently offended and affronted her [religious] vows, the cloistered life [of the convent] and went back on her previous choice to live as a woman. She was arrested on the orders of the Holy Office [of the Inquisition] by the Count of Soure on Tuesday 14 February and they brought her to the Inquisition of Lisbon, where she currently is [jailed].[15]

The following week, the newsletter added the following note:

> The Catalan hermaphrodite, of whom the previous newsletter gave news, continues to be the subject of most conversations. It is also known that she was a *Donata* in a convent of nuns. While she was a novice in that of Saint Catherine, which is Dominican, she was able to become a man some times and a woman at other times in accordance with her accursed [sexual] appetites because of a pact made with the Devil. By order of the King, she was brought to Lisbon where she will be punished by the Holy Office [of the Inquisition], where she is currently under arrest.[16]

The newsletter offers interesting evidence of the interest that Maria's story generated in Portugal. The sensationalized outline of Maria's early life seems to be mostly based on rumour, and the claim that she was taken to Évora by a charitable aristocrat does not match with the evidence collected from Maria Duran and contained in the inquisitorial trial dossier. The newsletter presents Maria here somewhat sympathetically as a victim of an 'error of Nature', a hermaphrodite who fell prey to the Devil.

Oblivious to the public sensation her arrest was causing in Lisbon, Maria Duran waited for over two weeks in her cell before her first interrogation, which occurred on 13 March 1741. A single inquisitor, Francisco Mendo Trigoso, was present and took charge of the proceedings, assisted by a notary who carefully recorded both the questions put to Maria and her answers. The Inquisition followed a set procedure. Before Maria could be officially indicted and the trial could commence in earnest, she would be subjected to three interrogations. At the start of each one, the inquisitor ordered Maria to place one of her hands on a copy of the Gospels and swear an oath to tell the truth. Following this, the inquisitor asked Maria whether she had examined her conscience and wished to confess any crimes, thereby saving her soul. The first interrogation focused on helping the Inquisition gather essential information about Maria's background and confirm her identity. The inquisitor questioned Maria about her family, place of birth and baptism, and her youth. Moreover, she was asked about the reasons that had motivated her to leave her husband and village as well as 'which lands she travelled through'.

During the second interrogation, nearly four months later, on 8 July 1741, the inquisitor approached the subject of Maria's cross-dressing in Spain. The inquisitor seemingly dismissed Maria's explanation that it was safer for a lone woman to travel dressed as a man and hinted at sinister motives. He was also highly sceptical about Maria's ability to conceal her lack of male genitals in normal everyday interactions with men and women. As was the standard procedure in inquisitorial trials, the inquisitorial notary recorded this fascinating exchange in the third person:

> She was asked how she can expect her claims [to have worn male clothing out of fear of her husband's relatives] to be believable when she did not wear male clothing whilst she was [in Catalonia and Andorra] and therefore in greater danger [from her husband's relatives].
>
> She says that she has spoken the truth.
>
> She was asked whether she knows that many women from more distant lands than her native village have completed far more perilous travels than her own journey, and have worn their own [female] clothing without these female clothes endangering their travels or honour.
>
> She says that she is well aware that many women travel wearing their own clothing. Nonetheless they do so in clear danger of losing their honour.
>
> She was asked whether, when she travelled within Catalonia dressed as a woman as she has declared in her [prior] testimony, she was able to preserve her matrimonial chastity and experienced any of the dangers that she has claimed women face whilst travelling.
>
> She says that she always lived chastely during her travels, despite the dangers.
>
> She was asked why, if she was in fact able to preserve her honour during her travels through Catalonia as she claims, she then chose to change [into male clothing]. For it follows that such a change did not originate for the reasons that she claims but rather for other reasons that she is obviously hiding.

> She says that she did not have any other motives [to wear male clothing] than those she has described.
>
> She was asked whether, during her travels in different lands and places, she became friends with her bedfellows and with those with whom she shared meals, both male and female.
>
> She says that, after leaving her homeland, she made many male and female friends, singing songs and exchanging jokes with them. She shared a bed with many men.
>
> She was asked whether she revealed that she was a woman and not a man, as she was pretending to be, to any of her friends. Also if, during the confidences that occur during the jokes and games that men play with women or with each other, one of them managed to touch her and discover her sex.
>
> She says that prior to entering this kingdom [of Portugal] she did not reveal [her sex] to any of her male or female friends and neither did she allow them to touch her [crotch]. She is not aware that any of them discovered [her sex]. All she can say is that many of them used to say that she had a feminine face and must be a eunuch. She herself used to make jokes about being a woman.[17]

The questions of inquisitor Francisco Mendo Trigoso reveal that he held conventional ideas about gender and sexuality. For the inquisitor, a daughter of Eve could never hope to conceal her sex or resist sexual temptation for long when freed from the restraining shackles of male oversight. The inquisitor simply refused to accept that Maria could have successfully concealed her sex whilst living in such close proximity to men and women. When Maria stated that she had never had sexual relations with the men who were her bedfellows in Spain, the inquisitor simply refused to believe her. The inquisitor scoffed and retorted:

> If she says this, then it is clear that she is not a woman but a man since, by placing herself in positions so propitious for sin such as sleeping in the same bed as men with whom she had a close friendship, it would be morally impossible for her not to fornicate with them if she was a woman and not a virgin but rather a married woman or widow.

The reference to Maria's marital status implied that Maria, having previously experienced heterosexual intercourse during her unhappy marriage in Catalonia, must have developed a taste for sex. It is important to note that men sharing beds was a common cultural practice in early modern Europe and did not carry the same sexual connotations that it presently does. After noting that it would be impossible for Maria to maintain her pretence and avoid arousing suspicions even if she exercised the greatest care, the inquisitor asked her insistently, 'Why are you not telling the truth?' To this, Maria could only respond by insisting that she had indeed spoken the truth.

The notion that women behaved in stereotypical ways and that, consequently, Maria would never have been able to successfully usurp a male identity is articulated in a number of aggressively phrased questions that the inquisitor fired at Maria. How could it be believed, he asked, that Maria did not betray her identity as a woman through her appearance and gestures, 'which it is impossible to hide for long, as she dares to claim'? How could Maria, who admitted having voluntarily revealed her sex and submitted to a physical examination in order to avoid being sent with the Spanish army to Italy, seriously claim that no one knew of her sex for so many years? Did Maria not know that 'the forces of profane love and lust' would obviously be stronger than her need to conceal her sex? If Maria had so easily revealed her sex to Father Jofreu upon her arrival in Lisbon 'without having any urgent need to do so', how could it be believed that she would have refrained from doing so when she felt 'a profane and impure love for one of the many men with whom she had dealings'? How could Maria, who was 'not a saint but a perverse individual', expect anyone to believe her claims to have preserved her chastity and honour whilst living among 'men who led a depraved life and with the full freedom to do whatever she wanted as well as being of a hot-blooded and vigorous age'? The terse responses of Maria rejected any suggestion of having had casual sexual relations with men or that she was a man. Instead, Maria consistently insisted that she was 'a true woman' (*uma verdadeira mulher*) who had only pretended to be male. When the inquisitor asked Maria if she had a penis concealed inside her body that only emerged occasionally and, if so, whether she had been born with this condition? Maria resolutely responded that 'she is a true woman and only has the [physical] parts that other women have'.

The inquisitor next turned to the subject of Maria's sexual behaviour and genitals when the interrogation resumed on 15 July. What 'obscene touchings' (*tocamentos obcenos*) had she engaged in? Who had her partners been, and had these sexual relations resulted in 'full penetrations'? Why had Maria told other people that she was a man? If she was 'so lascivious, and had masturbated herself with her hand, then why had she not allowed others to pleasure her'? If Maria had nothing to hide, what was the 'true reason' she had not consented to allow the surgeon Antonio Soares Brandão to conduct an internal examination of her vagina following her expulsion from the *recolhimento* of Our Lady of the

Incarnation in Lisbon? Why was she, during her sexual relations with women, always the 'active partner' (*agente*) and always refused to allow her partners to touch her genitals?

Maria never denied that she had sexual relations with the women in Lisbon and Évora. Maria's description of the sexual acts was also very frank:

> She would penetrate them with the thumb of her right hand, sometimes wrapping it in her shirt, and sometimes without wrapping it up. At the same time, a few times, she would masturbate herself with the other fingers of that hand. She never allowed any of her friends to touch [her genitals] or do the same thing to her.

Maria also admitted to using a pincushion (*agulheiro*) about 'half a palm' (*c.* 10 centimetres) long that she had manufactured from cloth as a dildo. The accusation that she was a man stemmed, Maria claimed, from the deep hatred that one of the *recolhidas* in Lisbon, Maria de Jesus, harboured against her. In answer to the question about always being the active partner, Maria candidly stated that 'she never wanted to be the passive [partner] because she never wanted one of [her sexual partners] to touch her'. Maria asserted that her main motive for not allowing her partners to touch her groin was the need to persuade them that she was a man. Furthermore, she claimed that her refusal to allow Antonio Soares Brandão to examine the inside of her vagina was because 'she was angry about all the examinations [she was forced to undergo]'.

Finally, on 29 August, the inquisitor summoned Maria to answer questions linked to the claims that she had made a demonic pact. Once again, Maria faced a veritable avalanche of questions. Had she ever believed that the Devil was God and could save her soul? Did she think that the Devil was not the enemy of the human soul and of all humankind? Had she seen the Devil, either when she was awake or in her dreams, and, if so, where, in what form and had she invoked him? Had she made a pact with the Devil who 'as a vile and foul soul promptly helps in all things that are obscene'? Had she had sexual relations with him? Was she ever pursued by, or obsessed with, the Devil? Did she practice any 'vain and superstitious arts' to achieve what she wanted? Did she practice witchcraft? Did she understand that anyone who exceeds the forces of Nature does so either through the intervention of God or the Devil? Finally, did she know that it was 'an extraordinary and naturally impossible thing' for a 'pure woman who does not have a penis to have one or more acts of fornication with persons of the female sex resulting in complete vaginal penetration'? Did she understand that God, in His infinite mercy, would never cause sin to occur and that, consequently, any aid she might have received 'to commit so many offences against God and Nature' must have come from the Devil?

Obviously, these leading questions sought to direct Maria towards making a confession. Her responses were nearly always terse and either agreed with the premise laid out by the inquisitor or denied any pact or contact with the Devil (such as 'she says she agrees with this' or 'she says that she never used magic'). Maria insisted that she achieved her sexual relations with women in the *recolhimentos* in Lisbon and the convent in Évora 'naturally and without any assistance from the Devil'. The longest response was a lengthy rebuttal of the notion that she might have been pursued by, or obsessed with, the Devil. Maria claimed that a mysterious 'shape' (*vulto*) caused the scratches on her body and that she took it to be a cat that had jumped onto her bed at night. At the time, Maria had assumed that 'the shape must be the Devil' but she rapidly came to disbelieve this. Maria blamed Father Jofreu for credulously believing that the Devil had possessed her and for subjecting her to exorcisms.

On 30 August, the inquisitors gathered to review the transcripts of these interrogations as well as the interrogations of the *recolhidas* in Lisbon and the nuns in Évora. They unanimously agree that the evidence of nearly all witnesses claiming that they had sensed a penis during 'carnal copulation' (*copula carnal*) with Maria Duran was compelling. It seemed 'morally impossible' to the inquisitors that the women should all be mistaken. Moreover, it is at this point in the trial dossier that the inquisitors make a startling revelation. They noted that the *recolhida* Maria de Jesus in Lisbon had been married. They used the past tense, indicating that Maria de Jesus must have been a widow. Maria de Jesus did not refer to this crucial 'detail' in her testimony and the inquisitors did not reveal how they knew this. The implication was clear, however. Since they thus presumed that Maria de Jesus knew what heterosexual sexual intercourse was like, it seemed impossible to the inquisitors that Maria de Jesus could have been mistaken.

The case was considered sufficiently troubling to warrant a further measure. Since it was obvious that Maria Duran had made a habit of lying about, or exaggerating, her identity, the inquisitors wanted more evidence to confirm her claims about her past. They decided to write to their colleagues in Barcelona, on the other side of the Iberian Peninsula, to request a 'verification of her claims about her name, identity, marital and social status, the circumstances of the claims about her life and travels'. To achieve this, they sent their colleagues in Barcelona the names and details of the people in Catalonia whom Maria had mentioned during her interrogation. The Lisboan inquisitors were taking no chances and noted that they particularly wanted these witnesses in Catalonia to confirm Maria's age and to provide physical descriptions of her 'to know whether Maria [in Lisbon] is the same person that [the witnesses in Catalonia] are talking about'. Such collaboration between the Portuguese and Spanish Inquisitions was relatively frequent. Given the long land border that linked Spain and Portugal in Europe and the links between their colonies, the movement of people and flight of fugitives across political borders was a problem for both Inquisitions. From the sixteenth century onwards, both Inquisitions regularly exchanged information, responded to each other's queries and sometimes even extradited wanted men and women. Of course, onerous bureaucratic procedures governed such exchanges. The governing councils of both Inquisitions – the Supreme Council of the [Spanish] Inquisition in Madrid and the General Council of the [Portuguese] Inquisition in Lisbon – had to approve such requests, and the time that it took for mail to travel between tribunals caused significant delays in trials.[18]

In the meantime, while they awaited news from Barcelona, the inquisitors in Lisbon decided to proceed with the trial. Inquisitorial regulations mandated that Maria Duran must be subjected to a series of three interrogations named *Genealogia*, *In Genere* ('In Kind') and *In Specie*. The first, as its name indicates, involved a comprehensive examination of the defendant's family, life and religious beliefs. The second would, without revealing the specific details of the accusations against her, seek to tease out from Maria Duran information that might be relevant to the case, especially regarding the doubts about her biological sex. Finally, the third interrogation would focus on the specific accusations of witchcraft and dealings with the Devil made against Maria Duran. Each interrogation ended with a legal ritual. Maria was officially warned that 'the Holy Office [of the Inquisition] does not arrest people without possessing considerable evidence'. Maria was therefore 'admonished with great charity on behalf of Our Lord Jesus Christ to open the eyes of her soul and truly confess all her sins in order to unburden her conscience and save her soul'. Should Maria choose to do this, the inquisitor promised, 'she would receive the mercy that the Holy Office [of the Inquisition] offers to good and truthful prisoners'.

The *Genealogia* interrogation took place on 2 September 1741. Inquisitor Francisco Mendo Trigoso questioned Maria about her racial ancestry (to ensure she was not descended from Jews or Muslims), the identity of her parents and her grandparents before moving on to her place of baptism, confirmation and the identity of her godparents. As the inquisitorial regulations demanded, Maria underwent an examination of her religious beliefs. The inquisitor ordered Maria to kneel, make the sign of the cross, as well as to recite the Lord's Prayer, the *Ave Maria*, the *Salve Regina*, the Ten Commandments and the Commandments of the Catholic Church (also known as the Precepts of the Church). The inquisitorial notary present noted that Maria knew all of them without error.

The *In Genere* interrogation took place on 11 September 1741. Maria insisted that she had no crimes to confess that could be 'relevant to this tribunal'. The questions put to Maria were quite general to begin with. By way of illustration, they included, 'Has she ever abandoned the faith of our holy Catholic Church and adopted another religion or sect, believing that she would save her soul through it'? or 'Has she ever doubted the tenets of the Catholic Faith'? Only later in the interrogation did the questions become more relevant to Maria's case. Maria was asked whether she had ever invoked and venerated the Devil or used powers received from Satan to be able to have sexual relations with women. The final question was 'whether she has used some superstitious remedy or diabolic art to conceal her true sex and confuse those [doctors and midwifes] who have examined her body'. Maria responded in the negative to all the questions put to her. The inquisitorial notary's record indicates Maria's frustration with the process, as he recorded that 'she said that she has already said many times that she has never interacted with the Devil, nor has she sought to acquire powers from him for any reason'.

It was only, as planned, during the *In Specie* interrogation on 23 October 1741 that the inquisitor questioned Maria about specific aspects of the case and the accusations against her. Once more, Maria admitted having sexual relations with women in Lisbon and Évora but only with the aid of her fingers or a dildo, and never with a penis. Moreover, Maria also confessed to having 'lied a lot', telling many of these women that she was a man in order to deceive them and that her other statements about possessing supernatural powers of seduction and having impregnated women were 'jokes'. The women accusing her must have mistaken her dildo for a penis and Maria denied that she had ever claimed to be a hermaphrodite. Likewise, Maria confessed that claims made to her lovers that she would not climax in order to avoid ejaculating and a possible pregnancy was made 'in order to deceive them and make them believe that she was a man'. At the end of the interrogation, Maria repeated that 'she has never seen the Devil or spoken to him, if she ever told this to someone then it was false'. With the last of the preliminary interrogations of Maria concluded, the trial of Maria Duran could begin in earnest.

7

Maria on trial

With the initial interrogations of Maria Duran and the witnesses in Lisbon and Évora concluded, the inquisitors turned their attention to the start of the trial without waiting to hear back from their colleagues in Barcelona. The next step in the Inquisition's trial procedure was the reading of the *libelo*, the official indictment against Maria Duran. The *libelo* marked the official start of the trial. Since Maria had not confessed to having made a pact with the Devil, the inquisitorial prosecutor could now lay charges against her, and Maria would have access to these charges. After this, Maria would have the opportunity to put together a defence, although the charges against her were pruned of any details that could compromise the anonymity of witnesses, making it difficult for Maria to precisely identify her accusers.[1]

To properly understand the trial of Maria Duran, it is important to never lose sight of the fact that the Inquisition prosecuted Maria Duran because she was accused of having made a pact with the Devil and not because of any homosexual relations with women. Whilst the Portuguese Inquisition prosecuted male homosexuals, same-sex acts between women, or 'female sodomy' to use the early modern legal terminology, had long been a problematic issue. The New Testament did offer Catholic theologians and jurists an isolated yet clear condemnation of female homosexuality in Rom. 1.24–26. In the thirteenth century, Saint Thomas Aquinas listed same-sex sexual relations between women alongside same-sex male anal intercourse as pertaining to the 'vice of sodomy' in his hugely influential work *Summa Theologiae*.[2] Portuguese law mentioned same-sex relations between women for the first time in an edict promulgated by King Manuel I of Portugal (1495–1521) on 20 December 1499. The Crown's condemnation of such acts was unambiguous:

> Sitting in judgment, the King Our Lord, was informed that there existed some doubts amongst lawyers whether, when a woman slept with another woman as if [one of them] were a man, she should be sentenced like a man who has

> committed the sin of sodomy in accordance with the Law. A gathering of lawyers who were present determined that the sentence should be the same as that of a man who commits such a sin with another man ... This applies just as much to the active as to the passive woman.[3]

This decree was incorporated into Portuguese law via the published legal ordinances (*ordenações*) of King Manuel, and the sentence imposed on female homosexuals was death by burning at the stake and the scattering of their ashes. Any woman convicted of this crime would also face the confiscation of her property, which would be split between the Crown and those who had denounced them as a reward.

For all the severity of King Manuel's edict, there is little evidence that the state and church proactively hunted 'female sodomites' or perceived them to be as much of a threat to society as male homosexuals. The prevailing attitude in Portugal seems to have mirrored that of the sixteenth-century Spanish jurist Gregorio López, who argued in a legal commentary that women who had sexual relations with other women 'cannot compare to the abominable vice of sodomy committed between men. Sodomy between men perturbs the order of Nature far more than sodomy between women'.[4] 'Female sodomy' was difficult to define in a strictly legal sense. If the law defined 'male sodomy' as anal penetration with a penis, how could women commit the crime of 'sodomy', since they did not possess a penis? The inquisitors in neighbouring Spain debated this issue during the sixteenth century and eventually decided not to prosecute cases of female homosexual intercourse unless they involved the use of dildos, or other instruments serving as penis substitutes. Prosecutions, however, appear to have been extremely rare.[5]

In Portugal, the regulations of the Portuguese Inquisition published in 1640 stipulated that the inquisitors must sentence any 'woman accused of sodomy' to serve a sentence of exile either on the islands of São Tomé and Príncipe (situated off the coast of western Africa) or in Angola (southern Africa). It was noted that 'because of the great scandal and injury that can result from the publication of such crimes in public *autos*', women were preferably to be sentenced in secret, within the walls of the inquisitorial palace and not during a public *auto-da-fé*. If a woman did receive her sentence in public, then the regulations instructed the inquisitors to ensure that she also received a public flogging.[6] Recorded cases of 'female sodomy' prosecuted by the Portuguese Inquisition are extremely rare.[7] The reason for this may well be due to a mixture of the lack of anxiety that it provoked in a male-dominated society and the fact that female homosexuality, by its very nature, rarely came to the attention of male observers. The inquisitorial tribunal of Lisbon judged a number of cases of 'female sodomy' during the 1630s, but these involved heterosexual anal intercourse with men and not sex between women.[8]

The prosecution of female homosexuals caused considerable uneasiness among Portuguese inquisitors. In the middle of the seventeenth century, almost a century before the arrest of Maria Duran, the General Council of the Portuguese Inquisition received a letter from the inquisitors of the tribunal of Goa in India asking for direction concerning the prosecution of same-sex acts between women. The question, simply put, was the following one: should the inquisitors prosecute a woman who had intercourse with another woman either passively or actively when such acts occurred without vaginal or anal penetration or through one woman's use of a dildo to penetrate her partner vaginally or anally? The General Council was equally perplexed and created a panel of legal and theological experts composed of three inquisitors and four theologians to consider the question. The panel poured over the available literature. Their recommendation to the General Council was that, barring any new edict or decision issued by the Holy See in Rome, the Portuguese Inquisition should neither investigate nor prosecute cases of female homosexuality in Portugal or its colonies. Citing no less than fifteen learned works in their final report, including the 1643 *De jurisdictione tractatus* of Francisco Ansaldi and the 1639 *De defensione inquisitorum, carceratorum, reorum et condemnatorum super quocunque crimine* of Sebastiano Guazzini, the experts concluded that 'such business is highly dubious' (*sendo a material duvidosa*).

On 7 November 1741, an inquisitorial official took Maria out of her cell and brought her into the presence of all three of the inquisitors of the Lisbon tribunal: Francisco Mendo Trigoso, Simão José da Silveira Lobo and Manuel Varejão de Távora. After asking Maria one last time if she had anything to confess and receiving a negative response, the inquisitors summoned the prosecutor (or *promotor fiscal*) to come forth and read out the charges against her. The prosecutor duly read out a list of thirteen charges. He started by stating that Maria, despite being a baptized Christian and 'as such obliged to believe and hold as true all that the Holy Mother Church of Rome believes and teaches' had communicated with the Devil 'without fear of God or the law'. The proof of this lay, first of all, in the accounts of the suspicious cuts and bruises Maria had received and which were healed when holy water was applied to them, and then, secondly, 'that being a perfect woman without any distinctive part of a man, she used a penis as if she were one'.

The reading of the *libelo* must have been an intensely frustrating experience for Maria Duran. After the first charge, the prosecutor read out the remaining twelve charges, which all referenced instances in which a witness had claimed that Maria had a penis during intercourse or had exhibited other signs of being male. To protect witnesses against possible reprisals, inquisitorial rules mandated that these charges must be pruned of any details (precise places and times as well as names) that could help the defendant identify them. As a result, every single one of the charges was phrased in a generic manner. Charge number 10, for example, reads as follows:

> It will be proved that being present in another certain place, at some point before now, the defendant had carnal intercourse with a person of the female sex on a couple of occasions. She placed herself on top of that person and always touched [that person's] genitals with an organ that seemed to be a penis. On those same occasions, she ejaculated semen where [the penis] touched that person and told [that person] that all the women upon whom she cast her eyes would be seduced into committing the disgusting acts that she desired and which she had already committed with others. [She also claimed that] one woman had borne her a son and that she could conceal the signs of her manhood when she wanted to, so that people would only see her female organs.[9]

Having finished reading the *libelo*, the prosecutor asked the inquisitors to ensure that Maria Duran 'be punished with the greatest and most severe legal penalties that she deserves for her crimes'. The inquisitors then asked Maria whether she wished to confess to any of the charges laid against her, but she stated that, beyond the fact that she was indeed a baptized Christian, none of those were true.

The Inquisition's system functioned on the assumed guilt of the defendant and today it has become synonymous with arbitrary justice. This does not mean, however, that it did not care about ensuring due process, at least officially. The 1640 regulations of the Portuguese Inquisition stipulated that defendants must have access to a qualified defence attorney to assist them. Defence attorneys were considered particularly important 'if the defendant is a rustic person, or one with little understanding or is illiterate … In such a case, [the attorney will explain with the greatest detail the substance of the charges against them'.[10] Accordingly, Maria was offered an attorney, but she could only choose from a roster of attorneys employed by the Inquisition. Three such individuals, all of them graduates in law (*licenciados*), were duly presented to Maria, who chose João Nunes de Silveira as her attorney. Maria's choice must have been largely arbitrary since there was no time for her to question or compare the attorneys.

João Nunes de Silveira took up his duties as Maria's attorney on 8 November during a ceremony in which the attorney swore an oath and committed himself to 'defend [Maria] and advise her during her trial on all things that serve the interests of justice'. In line with the regulations of the Inquisition, an inquisitorial official was present at all meetings between Maria and her attorney.[11]

On 15 November 1741, Maria and her attorney met to discuss her defence, armed with a copy of the indictment. Maria's defence options rested on three lines of attack. Firstly, she could question the jurisdiction of the Inquisition over her case. Secondly, she could question the logic of the accusations against her. Thirdly, and finally, she could try to identify the prosecution's witnesses and discredit their evidence by demonstrating that they had committed perjury. Merely claiming this was not enough, however. It was up to Maria to prove that the prosecution's witnesses were her 'mortal enemies' and therefore had a good reason to commit perjury against her. Maria's defence articles, presented on the same day, fielded all three arguments.

To begin with, Maria and her attorney reminded the inquisitors that the Inquisition did not have jurisdiction over crimes of 'mere sensuality' and that they could only prosecute her for the suspicion of having made a pact with the Devil. Secondly, Maria argued that she had led an exemplary Christian life, 'always attending mass on nearly all the days of the week, confessing her sins frequently' and receiving communion whenever her fellow *recolhidas* or novices and nuns did. She had willingly sought to lead a religious life, joining *recolhimentos* and finally a convent, taking part in communal acts of worship. This exemplary religious life was evidence that she had not made a pact with the Devil. Thirdly, if the Devil had granted her the ability to have a penis, it would have made greater sense for Maria 'to continue living freely in the secular world where there are more opportunities to live lasciviously than in a cloistered religious community where fewer people are available with whom sexual lust can be indulged'. To the potential rebuttal that the Devil would especially enjoy corrupting the lives of women dedicated to God, Maria answered by repeating that her motivation to seek a religious life had been solely inspired by the realization that she was naturally 'inclined to the sin of lust' and needed to protect her soul. Unfortunately, this 'weakness in her nature', without any help from the Devil, had caused her to continue to commit 'many depraved acts' (*muitas torpezas*) in religious institutions. Finally, Maria affirmed that she had sought to control her sexual urges through acts of bodily self-mortification: fasting, wearing hairshirts and disciplining herself with a scourge. Again, Maria presented such actions as evidence that she could not have made a pact with the Devil.

In the following weeks, on 22 and 26 November 1741, Maria and her attorney used the list of charges in the indictment to formulate more questions for the prosecution witnesses. These questions all focused on the claims that Maria had made a pact with the Devil and the nature of the sexual relations these witnesses had with Maria. The defence asked the witnesses to reveal whether they were 'enemies' of Maria because of any personal conflicts or jealousy due to Maria's sexual relations with other women or for any other reason. If Maria had indeed claimed that the Devil caused her wounds, why did the witnesses think she was talking seriously and not speaking out of 'mockery and trickery, as she often did during these games'? The witnesses were indeed asked to confirm whether Maria was generally 'inclined to play tricks or similar jokes in games' or whether she often 'told fabulous tales' to pass the time, so that it could be assumed that any claims she had made about the Devil were spurious, harmless jokes.

Regarding the testimony accusing her of having a penis, Maria and her attorney's questions aimed to bolster her claims to have used a dildo during intercourse and that the witnesses were either confused, mistaken or lying. Why did the witnesses not think that Maria had employed a dildo that simulated a human penis? What 'new actions' had Maria performed during intercourse that differed from those that usually occurred between women during sex? Why had these 'actions' led them to believe that Maria had a penis? Had Maria's right hand been visible during intercourse or had she used it between her legs? How could the witnesses be sure that the 'fluid' (*humor*) that they found on their body was human semen and not 'some other fluid that she produced as a result of her pleasure', apparently a reference to vaginal discharge caused by orgasm, or even 'a small amount of urine'? Maria appears to have rapidly guessed that one of the prosecution witnesses must be Agostinha, her lover in the *Recolhimento do Menino Deus* in Lisbon. She specifically requested that Agostinha be asked how she could be certain that the 'penis' was not actually the 'instrument that she, Agostinha, once found in Maria's sleeve, made from cotton or baize and covered with silk' and that Maria used for her 'depraved ends'.

One particularly interesting question formulated for Maria's defence concerned how the witnesses could be certain that the 'penis' they had felt was not 'some nerve that naturally comes forth from the vagina, which some women possess without having changed sex or having both sexes'. It would appear that this is a reference to the clitoris but whether this was a question originating from Maria or her attorney is not clear. This female sex organ had been discussed in Italy by the theologian and inquisitorial advisor Ludovico Maria Sinistrari d'Ameno (1622–1701) in a discussion of 'female sodomy'. In his 1700 published work *De Delectis e Poenis*, Sinistrari stated that he had consulted numerous 'learned men' who had all candidly confessed to him that they were 'completely ignorant as to how [female homosexuality] can be different from the pollution produced by [women] rubbing their private parts together'. In Sinistrari's opinion, the use of dildos or other inanimate objects such as fingers in same-sex female sexual relations did not constitute an act of 'female sodomy'. 'Sodomy' between women could only take place in instances where one woman possessed an abnormally developed and long clitoris that, when erect, could penetrate the vagina of another woman.[12] Although they predated Maria's trial by decades, Sinistrari's writings do not appear to have circulated in Portugal. The inquisitors in Lisbon never mentioned them. Given that it could have led to an accusation of 'female sodomy', it was probably a stroke of good luck for Maria that this striking defence question did not attract the attention of the inquisitors.

The inquisitors put the questions about Maria's religious life to five of the more senior (and older) nuns in the convent of Our Lady of Paradise in Évora rather than to the women who claimed to have had sexual relations with Maria. The inquisitors doubtless hoped to obtain a more objective evaluation of Maria's professed Christian zeal. These witnesses all insisted that they were not 'enemies' of Maria. Contrary to Maria's claims to have led an exemplary religious life, most witnesses expressed negative assessments of it. In particular, they deemed that Maria had demonstrated 'little devotion' in her attendance at communal acts of worship, sometimes acting in a disruptive manner that upset the conventual community.

The questions that Maria and her attorney formulated for the witnesses accusing her of having a penis and making a pact with the Devil were then put to the prosecution witnesses. This began a long drawn-out process in which the inquisitors contacted these witnesses to have them answer the defence questions. In January 1742, they sent copies of these questions to the inquisitors in Évora so that one of their agents could question the nuns of the convent of Our Lady of Paradise, another agent was tasked with questioning the *recolhidas* in Lisbon. Tracking down all the original witnesses was not always an easy task, as some no longer lived in Lisbon. One *recolhida*, Veronica Maria, had moved to the town of Leiria, over 100 kilometres north of Lisbon, to become the servant of the cantor of Leiria's cathedral. Likewise, Agostinha, Maria's lover in the *Recolhimento do Menino Deus*, had left that establishment by the time the inquisitors sought to put Maria's questions to her. The inquisitors eventually tracked Agostinha to the convent of Our Lady of the Conception (*Nossa Senhora da Conceição*) in the town of Beja, *c.* 150 kilometres south of Lisbon, where she had become a novice. This same convent had received unwelcome fame across Europe when the sensational fictional correspondence of one of its nuns and a French officer who was her lover was published in 1669 and became a bestseller translated into various languages as the *Letters of a Portuguese Nun*.

The responses to Maria's questions did little to undermine the prosecution's case against her. When questioned in her convent, Agostinha stood by her claims that 'she always believed that [Maria] was a man and used a penis' during intercourse. Moreover, Agostinha added that Maria 'sometimes held her penis with her right hand to penetrate [Agostinha's] vagina and withdrew her hand before ejaculating. Sometimes copulation occurred without [Maria] having to hold her penis'. Agostinha was also clear that the fluid she found on her clothes was 'human semen by its colour and consistence', although she did not explain why she was so seemingly familiar with the nature of semen. Regarding the dildo, Agostinha was adamant that it had belonged to another *recolhida* and not Maria, who had 'never used it in the [sexual] acts between them'. Finally, Agostinha noted that her former lover 'always spoke seriously' and that she had not seen any evidence that 'Maria was accustomed to playing tricks'.

The other witnesses against Maria Duran similarly confirmed their original testimony or only made small alterations. The nun Teresa Maria Evangelista retracted her original claim that Maria had ejaculated semen asserting that it was 'an error on her part and made inadvertently'. While Sister Teresa claimed not to be able to remember what Maria had done with her hands during sex, she nonetheless stood by her original declaration to have felt a penis touching her because it was 'something warm and erect and not cold'. Some witnesses even added further incriminating details that they claimed to now remember. The *recolhida* Vitoria Rosa insisted that she had seen 'some old odds and ends as well as unguents [belonging to Maria] that frightened her and which she took to be related to witchcraft'. Alarmingly, Maria would shut herself in her cell and 'seal all the holes in the ceiling and door so that they could not observe what she was doing'. Furthermore, Vitoria Rosa remained adamant that Maria Duran had not used a dildo and was a man. Vitoria Rosa told the inquisitors that Maria had ejaculated in her vagina during sex 'like any man' and that she was certain of this because she had 'felt it happen inside her'. On the basis of 'wet dreams' experienced earlier in her life, Vitoria Rosa maintained that she could distinguish her own 'ejaculation' (i.e. vaginal secretions) from Maria Duran's ejaculation. None of the witnesses would pronounce themselves on the suggestion that what they had felt could have been Maria's clitoris, but they discounted the possibility that Maria's wounds were fake or that her claims about the Devil were idle jokes.

At some point in late 1741 or early 1742, whilst the questions of the defence were put to witnesses across central and southern Portugal, the inquisitors in Lisbon finally received news from Barcelona. The inquisitors in Barcelona had received the request for assistance. Between 28 October and 3 November 1741, they proceeded to order the interrogation of the various witnesses Maria named in her testimony, who could confirm her claims as well as her identity. For reasons that are left unexplained, the inquisitors of Barcelona contented themselves with questioning four witnesses who were close at hand and had known Maria in the mid-1730s. These witnesses were Doctor Guillermo Colomer, a churchman from the town of La Seu d'Urgell; Maria Soldevila, a midwife who had examined Maria Duran after her expulsion from the Spanish army; Miguel Senant, a Dominican friar in Barcelona and, finally, Don Antonio de Camprodor, the Baron of Prullans, Maria's place of birth and initial home. The inquisitors of Barcelona made no effort to send an agent to the village of Prullans to interrogate Maria's husband, Ignacio de Sulsona, or any other relatives. This was despite the fact that Don Antonio de Camprodor told the inquisitors that Ignacio de Sulsona was still alive and that he had seen him in Prullans only six weeks before. The baron of Prullans did confirm the reality of Maria's marriage in Prullans as well as the birth and death of an infant child. It is possible that the inquisitors did not want to delay the despatch of their response to Lisbon and, just as likely, that they did not want to incur unnecessary costs gathering evidence for a trial run by another tribunal.

As requested by the inquisitors in Lisbon, all four witnesses in Catalonia provided separate physical descriptions of Maria Duran. These all broadly agreed that Maria was of 'good stature', tall, long-faced, 'brown skinned' with long black hair and a thin face. One witness noted that Maria was flat chested and another remembered that he had noticed that Maria had once worn earrings. One witness recalled that, when they met, Maria's hair was worn 'in the fashion of a dragoon', a reference to the common practice of men serving in cavalry regiments growing their hair long and in a single braid or pigtail gathered at the back of the head to avoid it becoming a nuisance when riding on horseback. Regarding any particular physical marks, two of the witnesses remembered that Maria bore a mark on one of her cheeks. For one, it was 'like a dimple' while another recollected that it was a scar 'like that made by a bullet'. A third witness maintained that Maria had 'scar like that made by a bullet wound on one of her legs'. What is striking in these physical descriptions is that none of the four witnesses insisted that Maria was particularly 'manly' or 'masculine'. Two witnesses claimed that Maria had a *voz abultada*, which translates roughly as a 'big voice' or perhaps a 'low-pitched voice' more commonly associated with men than women. Nevertheless, the fact that only two out of four witnesses remembered this detail suggests that this aspect of Maria's speech must not have been particularly pronounced.

By 30 April 1742, the inquisitors were ready to proceed on to the next stage of the trial of Maria Duran: the 'publication'. Since Maria still refused to confess, the prosecutor presented ('published') a list of the seven key witnesses against Maria: the *recolhidas* Josefa Maria Xavier, Maria de Jesus, Vitoria Rosa, Veronica Maria, Agostinha and the nuns Teresa Maria Evagelista and Isabel Elena. The document listed redact summaries of their accusations and withheld the names of the witnesses. It was Maria's responsibility to try to identify them and then offer credible *contraditas*: evidence that they were her enemies and thus discrediting them. It was a high-stakes game and, on 18 May, Maria named the *recolhidas* Agostinha, Maria de Jesus, Vitoria Rosa, Veronica and the nuns Ignacia Candida, Teresa Maria Evangelista and Iria Joachina. All of these women, Maria claimed, were her 'enemies' because of various jealousies and disagreements. Maria added that most of them were motivated by sexual jealousy and 'vengeful passions' and, deciding to throw as much mud as possible at the reputations of her potential accusers, Maria claimed that 'despite being nuns and religious persons, they have all taken lovers and led a life that was far from exemplary'. For good measure, and to be on the safe side, Maria added a servant boy whom she had once dismissed for stealing some of her shirts to the list of her enemies. Crucially, the list of these 'enemies' did not include two of the witnesses against Maria: the *recolhida* Josefa Maria in Lisbon and the nun Isabel Elena in Évora.

It was not enough for Maria to name her 'enemies' in order to discredit them. Maria had to confirm her claims by providing witnesses whom she listed under the name of each 'enemy'. This led the inquisitors to order yet another round of interrogations of witnesses during the month of June 1742. When it came to confirming the claims Maria made about her 'enemies', many of the witnesses proved reticent. In the convent of Our Lady of Paradise, Sister Josefa Teresa da Assumpção confirmed the fracas that had led Maria Duran to seek to beat Teresa Evangelista with a stick but stated, somewhat ridiculously, that she did 'not know whether it is certain that hatred and enmity resulted between Maria Duran and Teresa Evangelista from this [incident]. She only knows that they stopped speaking to each other'. Likewise, the regent of the *recolhimento* of Our Lady of the Incarnation in Lisbon recalled that 'on one occasion [Maria Duran] fell out with Maria de Jesus and with considerable anger threatened to kill her. The reason, she suspects, was [because Maria de Jesus wanted] to know if Maria Duran was a man or a woman'. The incident, however, was presented as an isolated one and the regent concluded that 'during the time Maria [Duran] spent in the *recolhimento* there were no differences or arguments that could have caused hatred or enmity, even though all the *recolhidas* wanted her expelled because of her poor behaviour and low [social] status'.

Even while they were going through the process of gathering the testimony required to confirm the claims of the defence, the inquisitors decided to take decisive action to tackle the issue of Maria Duran's sex. It was clear to the inquisitors that the witness testimony accusing Maria Duran of being male or even a 'hermaphrodite' stood at odds with medical evidence that Maria only had female sex organs. This medical evidence included not just the reports of physical examinations conducted in Spain when Maria was expelled from the Spanish army but also that of the reputable surgeon Antonio Soares Brandão, who had conducted a careful examination of her genitals following her expulsion from the *recolhimento* of Our Lady of the Incarnation in Lisbon. The surgeon had declared that Maria Duran was female but, in retrospect, confided some doubts to the inquisitors. On 23 May 1742, the inquisitors of Lisbon wrote to their superiors in the General Council of the Portuguese Inquisition to inform them that they intended to undertake an unusual step in an inquisitorial trial: a full anatomical examination of Maria Duran's body in general and genitalia in particular. The inquisitors hoped that such an examination, conducted by the Inquisition's own experts, would settle the matter of Maria's biological sex once and for all.

8

'A real woman and not a hermaphrodite': The anatomical examination of Maria Duran

Taking into consideration the witness testimony they had collected in Portugal and those collected on their behalf by their colleagues in Barcelona, the inquisitors of Lisbon faced a quandary. There existed a fundamental contradiction between the testimony of multiple, seemingly credible witnesses in Portugal alleging that Maria possessed a penis and the reports of the Portuguese and Spanish surgeons and midwives who had previously examined Maria and found no evidence to support these claims. This discrepancy opened room for doubt: could it be that Maria had experienced a natural sex change? Alternatively, might Maria be a 'hermaphrodite'?[1]

Maria Duran's trial coincides with a particularly significant point in the development of European attitudes towards the anatomy of the sexes. According to Thomas Laqueur, the eighteenth century marked a turning point in European attitudes to, and discourses about, the division between the sexes.[2] The Galenic 'one-sex model' inherited from Greco-Roman Antiquity argued that male and female genitalia were essentially the same and continued to be influential in early modern Europe. The female sex organs (vagina, womb and ovaries) were perceived as an inverted form of the male genitalia (penis and testes) and the body's thermodynamic forces influenced their development in human foetuses. Since male bodies were thought to be warmer than those of females, genitals in male foetuses were expelled from within the body to hang outside of it, whilst those of the cooler female foetuses were retained within the body. Both males and females thus produced semen or 'seed' – believed to be a distilled form of blood – that combined to create a foetus at the point of conception. Consequently, some medical authorities admitted the possibility of, admittedly rare, natural sex changes after birth due to changes in the body temperature of an individual. One such authority was the celebrated French surgeon Ambroise Paré (*c.*1510–90), who pointed to bodily thermodynamics as a cause of the possible 'degeneration' of women into men in his 1573 work *Monstres et Prodiges*:

> The reason why women can degenerate into men is because women have as much hidden within the body as men have exposed outside; leaving aside, only, that women don't have so much heat, nor the ability to push out what by the coldness of their temperament is held as if bound to the interior. Wherefore if with time, the humidity of childhood which prevented the warmth from doing its full duty being exhaled for the most part, the warmth is rendered more robust, vehement, and active, then it is not an unbelievable thing if the latter chiefly aided by some violent movement, should be able to push out what was hidden within. Now since such a metamorphosis takes place in Nature for the alleged reasons and examples, we therefore never find in any true story that any man ever became a woman, because Nature tends always toward what is most perfect and not, on the contrary, to perform in such a way that what is perfect should become imperfect.[3]

To be sure, Thomas Laqueur's iconic 'one-sex' paradigm has been critiqued by modern scholars who argue that the model glosses over a lack of homogeneity in ancient and early modern medical attitudes to sex and the human body.[4] In the sixteenth century, the University of Montpellier professor and royal physician to the French king André du Laurens rejected the idea of natural sex changes from female to male as impossible. André du Laurens argued that the impossibility was clear since 'no similarity comes in between the vagina and the male penis; none between the uterus and the scrotum; neither is the structure, form and size of the testicles the same, nor in the distribution and insertion of the spermatic vessels'.[5] Nevertheless, numerous Iberian medical authorities in the sixteenth and seventeenth centuries were influenced by the Galenic and Hippocratic theories of the mixing of male and female semen and accepted that the imperfect mixing of the two could result in a range of intermediates between the categories of 'perfect' virile men and 'perfect' feminine women.[6] It is noteworthy that the witnesses in the trial of Maria Duran, or at least the notaries who wrote down their testimony, used those same expressions: *homem perfeito* and *mulher perfeita*.

Authors and medical authorities in both Spain and Portugal also considered the problem of seemingly natural sex changes from the sixteenth century onward. Regarding natural sex changes, the sixteenth-century Portuguese physician João Rodrigues de Castelo Branco (better known under his penname of Amatus Lusitanus) noted the case of Maria Pacheca, 'who at the time that girls usually start to menstruate' experienced the emergence of a penis (*priapum*) 'which had until then remained concealed within her'. In this manner, Maria Pacheca had 'transformed from a woman into a man' and taken the name Manuel. Amatus Lusitanus offered the case to his readers as a medical curiosity without seeking to discuss it in any detail although in the rest of his work he follows conventional Galenic and Hippocratic theories.[7] In neighbouring Spain, Juan Huarte de San Juan (1529–1588), a renowned Spanish physician and physiognomist, claimed that 'if Nature, having made a perfect male, wants to change him into a female, it merely has to turn his reproductive organs back inside the body'. Juan Huarte de San Juan argued that such a transformation was likely to happen to a foetus during gestation (e.g. if the body temperature of a pregnant woman changed for any given reason) rather than after birth.[8] Just as in the rest of Europe, the Galenic 'one sex model', and the possibility of natural changes of sex, provoked debates among Iberian medical authorities. Some Iberian authors assigned the possibility of a natural sex change to an excess of matter provided by the parents during conception, others to the delayed mixing of the 'seed' produced by the parents. Finally, there existed authorities like the Spaniard Gaspar Bravo de Sobremonte (1603–1683) who rejected the existence of natural sex changes entirely, dismissing them as 'figments'. Bravo de Sobremonte links such tales to errors in the identification of an individual's sex, such as cases of cryptorchidism (boys whose testicles remain within their bodies and descend into the scrotum later in life) or women with an abnormally large clitoris.[9]

Beyond the possibility that Maria Duran might be, to use Ambroise Paré's expression, a woman 'degenerating' into a man, the inquisitors also had to consider the chance that Maria Duran might be a 'hermaphrodite'. The existence of hermaphrodites – individual humans or animals who were born possessing both male and female sexual organs – was discussed in Antiquity by the Greek philosopher Aristotle in book IV of his work *On the Generation of Animals* and by the Roman Pliny in book XI of his *Natural History*. The influential theologian and philosopher Saint Augustine listed *androgynes* or 'hermaphrodites' among 'monsters' such as cyclopes or pygmies in his work *City of God*, but he asserted that they were not unnatural. On the contrary, for Augustine, they were natural in origin and evidence of God's power over the natural realm. For, Augustine noted, 'no faithful Christian should doubt that anyone who is born anywhere as a man – that is, a rational and mortal being – derives from that one first-created human being. And this is true, however extraordinary such a creature may appear to our senses'.[10]

Later, in the sixteenth and seventeenth centuries, numerous authors considered hermaphrodites to exist as a discrete category of 'monsters' or 'marvels' of nature and sought to offer medical explanations for their existence. The Frenchman Ambroise Paré discussed 'hermaphrodites or androgynes, that is to say which have two sets of sex organs in one body' in a chapter of his *Monstres et Prodiges*. Paré reasoned that the existence of 'those born with double genitalia' was brought about when 'the woman furnishes as much seed as the man proportionately, and for this [reason] the formative virtue [property], which always tries to make its likeness – to wit, a male from the masculine matter and a female from the feminine – operates so that sometimes two sexes, called hermaphrodites, are found in the same body'. Such hermaphrodites could, Paré argued, be distinguished into four different categories depending on the varying degree of development of the male and female genitalia.[11]

Prior to the eighteenth century, the existence of 'hermaphrodites' was seemingly a far less controversial topic than the subject of natural sex changes. In line with the writings of Aristotle, Pliny and Saint Augustine, many early modern Iberian writers considered hermaphrodites to be grotesque 'monsters', or errors of nature. Even a harsh critic of the notion of natural sex changes like Gaspar Bravo de Sobremonte considered hermaphroditism a possibility in cases linked to the imperfect mixing of the male and female semen at the time of conception and the development of both sexes in a foetus. Theologians and jurists who considered the problem of hermaphroditism, emphasized the need to assign a sex to such rare individuals in order to ensure their proper assimilation into society. When an inquisitorial tribunal in seventeenth-century Spain prosecuted a priest described as a 'hermaphrodite' – and colloquially known by some of his parishioners as 'the priestess' – its primary concern was not the priest's sexual organs. Instead, its primary focus was on claims by witnesses that the priest claimed to be a woman and the risk of causing a scandal within the community by leading his parishioners to believe that women could be ordained into the priesthood.[12]

In the eighteenth century, anatomists and surgeons increasingly advocated for a new model of the human body with a clear distinction between the sexes. For such authors, females were a different biological sex entirely rather than an 'imperfect' version of the male. The Galenic notion of a human body whose sexual organs could be altered by humours or thermodynamics was rejected. In 1741, the very year of Maria Duran's arrest, the English physician James Parsons published a work entitled *A Mechanical and Critical Enquiry into the Nature of Hermaphrodites*. James Parsons condemned those who saw 'hermaphrodites' as a separate monstrous category:

> What, but ignorance or superstition, could persuade Men to imagine, that poor human creatures (which were only distorted in some particular part, or had anything unusual appearing about them, from some morbid cause affecting them, either in the Uterus, or after their births) were prodigies or monsters in Nature?[13]

For Parsons, hermaphrodites and hermaphroditism simply did not exist, and to argue otherwise was just 'ignorance of the fabric of the body'. Those individuals misidentified as hermaphrodites were only women with enlarged clitorises, or *Macroclitorideae* to use a term Parsons coined. Similarly, Parsons's compatriot Robert James was uncompromising in his three-volume *Medicinal Dictionary* (1743–5), when it came to defining hermaphrodites:

> As I look upon all the histories related of hermaphrodites to be merely imaginary, I shall only observe, that of many I have seen who have been reported to be so, I have met with none who were any more than mere women, whose clitoris was grown to an exorbitant size, and whose *Labia Pudendorum* were preternaturally tumid.[14]

Similarly, the French scholar Chevalier Louis de Jaucourt examined hermaphrodites in a contribution to Diderot's famous *Encyclopaedia* and repeated this firm stance a few years later. Using Parsons and Roberts as two of his sources, Jaucourt asked the rhetorical question, 'But are there true *hermaphrodites*'? to which his answer was uncompromisingly biting:

> One could raise this question in the times of ignorance; one should no longer propose it during these enlightened centuries. If nature wanders sometimes in the production of man, it does not go as far as metamorphoses, confusions of substances, and perfect assemblages of two sexes. … We conclude, therefore, that *hermaphrodism* is nothing more than a chimera, and that the examples that one hears of married *hermaphrodites*, who have both had children, each as man and woman, are childish fables, drawn from the heart of ignorance in the love of marvels, which are so difficult to dismantle.[15]

Jaucourt discussed some case studies of seventeenth- and eighteenth-century individuals held to be hermaphrodites and dismissed these as the result of the understandable confusion that is caused by 'the very strange tricks that Nature plays on natural parts'. The eighteenth century, thus, contributed to the acceleration of what Julia Epstein has described as the 'medicalization' of sex and sexual ambiguity. The adoption of a clear-cut distinction or binary between two sexes by anatomists and medical jurisprudence, which left no space for the existence of 'hermaphrodites' or a range of 'intersex' individuals.[16]

Such ideas also gained currency in the Iberian Peninsula. In Spain, the anatomist Martín Martínez published his *Noches anatómicas, o Anatomía compendiosa* (Anatomical Evenings or Compendium of Anatomy) in 1717 and the *Anatomía completa del hombre* (Complete Anatomy of Man) in 1728. Influenced by the writings of European anatomists like the Austrian Paul de Sorbait (1624–1691) as well as his own observations, Martínez not only criticized the notion of spontaneous, natural sex changes but also the existence of 'hermaphrodites' as 'popular fables' that only the ignorant populace could believe. In his work, Martínez carefully described the female genitalia, including the clitoris, 'a sort of glandular body, round and large, very similar to the virile member'. Whilst it is similar to a penis and is described as a woman's principal organ of 'sensual pleasure' (*deleite sensual*), Martínez is clear that it is not a penis. Martínez notes that the clitoris could sometimes grow and become hard like a penis 'to the point that [some women] have been able to abuse Venus with other women, and give occasion to the populace to believe fables of women turned into men'.[17]

Of course, irrespective of the changing discourse about the sexes in the writings of anatomists, the figure of the hermaphrodite continued to elicit fascination and curiosity across Europe. Works written for a popular readership that proclaimed the existence of hermaphrodites continued to appear in print in the Iberian Peninsula during the late seventeenth and eighteenth centuries. This was the case of the seventeenth-century author Andrés Ferrer de Valdecebro's popular *El Por qué de todas las cosas* ('The Why of All Things'), which appeared in a 1727 edition and briefly sought to explain why hermaphrodites were born.[18] Moreover, as we have seen in Chapter 6, the manuscript newsletters written in March 1741 described Maria Duran as the 'Catalan hermaphrodite' or, alternatively, 'a case similar to those many times recorded in stories, and which goes against the perfection of Nature'. These sensationalized newsletters were destined for a literate readership and reveal how the topic of hermaphroditism continued to fascinate the educated, literate classes in Portugal. Even among Iberian medical practitioners, the rejection of hermaphroditism was far from the norm, and we must certainly not assume that the new theories on 'hermaphrodites' achieved a consensus. Moreover, the existence of 'hermaphrodites' continued to be assumed in a variety of contexts. It is possible, for instance, to find 'hermaphrodites' mentioned as a special category in a 1771 discussion of the separate legal rights of men and women in Castile.[19] As late as 1796, a Spanish translation of the Austrian physician Joseph Jakob von Plenk's work on forensic medicine still included an earnest discussion of the different types of hermaphrodites, including 'the true hermaphrodite, who truly possesses the corresponding parts of both sexes'.[20]

In the request that they submitted to the General Council of the Portuguese Inquisition on 23 May 1742, the inquisitors of Lisbon outlined the problem they faced regarding Maria Duran's sex:

> Maria Christina Duran, a Spaniard and novice in the Convent of Our Lady of Paradise in Évora, is a prisoner in this Inquisition because of a suspected pact with the Devil. This suspicion was born from having had carnal copulation with various women as a true man. Her trial has gone ahead and she continues to deny the accusation, always protesting that she is a true woman, who has already given birth to a child, a claim confirmed by the investigations carried out in Catalonia, where she lived and resided before coming to Lisbon. This tribunal has received information from Antonio Soares, the surgeon of the jails of the Inquisition, who was ordered by Father José Jofreu to conduct an examination. In this examination, he was not able to certify [categorically] that the accused did not possess a penis. Moreover, the witness Veronica Maria stated during one of her interrogations that the midwife ordered by Father José Jofreu to examine the accused had misgivings about her sex and told her that she should not be permitted to live among [religious] women.[21]

The contradictory evidence baffled the inquisitors. On the one hand were multiple witnesses who resolutely stood by claims that Maria Duran was a man and, on the other hand, was reliable information from witnesses in Catalonia that asserted the contrary, namely that Maria had married and given birth to a child. Furthermore, while the previous physical examinations of Maria's genitals had not found any evidence of a penis or abnormally large clitoris, there were doubts about the reliability of the findings of these examinations. The inquisitors concluded that 'to shed light on this case, it seems expedient to us to order a new examination and precise anatomical inspection to determine if she possesses a penis or another genital organ or some other thing that is similar'.[22]

The anatomical examination of Maria Duran took place on 18 June 1742. The medical authorities selected by the inquisitors consisted of three men and one woman. The men were Bernardo Santucci, José Ricord and Antonio Soares Brandão, the latter of whom had already examined Maria before. The woman was Mariana Lopes, a midwife employed by the Inquisition to look after the medical needs of pregnant prisoners. To follow the rules of the Inquisition, the examination took place in one of the cells and in the presence of an inquisitorial notary. The 'expert witness' was without doubt Doctor Bernardo Santucci

(1701–1764). As his name indicates, Santucci was of Italian origin. Born in the town of Cortona in Tuscany, Santucci studied at the University of Bologna and was invited to come to Portugal in 1729 by the Italophile King João V. Santucci was the resident expert and professor in human anatomy at the Royal Hospital of All Saints (*Todos-os-Santos*) in central Lisbon. Only a few years before, Santucci had authored the first comprehensive work of anatomy printed in Portuguese. The work featured two chapters with detailed anatomical descriptions of male and female genitalia, including the clitoris.[23] With an expert in the anatomy of human genitals so close at hand, it is hardly surprising that the inquisitors sought Santucci's help even though he was not a 'familiar' or sworn agent of the Inquisition, unlike José Ricord and Antonio Soares Brandão.

Even though they all examined Maria Duran together, inquisitor Francisco Mendo Trigoso interrogated the four witnesses individually during the following week. The first one questioned under oath – another clear indication of his significance as an expert in human anatomy in the eyes of the inquisitors – was Bernardo Santucci. Asked to describe the examination, the Italian anatomist recalled that Maria Duran undressed 'with no small disgust … and exposed her private parts'. Santucci conducted a visual examination not just of their exterior but 'also of those parts inside that could be seen with the eyes'. He could not see anything that differed from the usual anatomy of a human female and the only 'novelty' (*novidade*) he did note was that space separating Maria's pubic bone (*pubis*) and coccyx was extremely short. In his opinion, this constricted the birth canal to such an extent that, in the event of a pregnancy, it would be impossible for Maria to deliver a child via a vaginal birth. Moreover, Santucci pointed to other signs that suggested Maria had never been pregnant. He noted the absence of stretch marks on her stomach and the presence of *carunculae myrtiformes* – the remnants of the hymen in a post-pubertal individual – that suggested Maria Duran had 'never copulated with a man' and was still a virgin.

Santucci was adamant that 'he clearly observed that [Maria] is not a hermaphrodite because she does have a penis, not anything resembling part of one, nor does she have testicles'. Santucci told the inquisitors that he remembered reading 'in some of his books' that the clitoris could swell up and increase its length during 'lascivious acts, so that it imitates a penis'. The only source he named was Philip Verheyen (1648–1710), a Flemish anatomist whose 1693 work *Corporis Humani Anatomia* had indeed discussed the clitoris. Santucci cited the Latin passage in Verheyen's work where the Flemish anatomist noted that the clitoris was frequently mistaken for a penis, giving cause to the mistaken belief that some women were hermaphrodites.[24] Despite the claims of authorities like Verheyen, Santucci remained sceptical that a clitoris could act like a penis. He told inquisitor Francisco Mendo Trigoso that 'in reality, it is not the case'. Santucci examined Maria's clitoris 'with the greatest of attention and found it to be very small and almost absent'. As such, he deemed Maria's clitoris incapable of 'imitating a penis'.[25]

In their own, separate individual interrogations, José Ricord and Antonio Soares Brandão broadly agreed with the findings of Bernardo Santucci. José Ricord examined Maria's genitals and even went so far as to use one of his fingers 'to probe' Maria's vagina for any evidence of male genitals but could only conclude that 'her external and interior genital parts are the same, and have the same form, as those of any woman'. Ricord noted that Maria's *labia* were flatter and harder 'than those of other women', which he attributed to friction caused by horse riding when Maria had been a dragoon, and that 'she is flat chested', which he attributed to the tight fit of the male clothing Maria had worn for many years. Antonio Soares Brandão examined Maria Duran with his eyes and fingers before likewise concluding that Maria 'is a true woman like any other and not a hermaphrodite and does not have male parts that are fully or imperfectly formed'. Seemingly referring to the clitoris, Brandão stated that he had not found 'any instrument inside or outside her that could be apt to have coitus with a woman'. Remaining cautious, however, Brandão stated that it would only be possible for Maria to have penetrative sexual intercourse with a woman due to 'some monstrosity of Nature until now never observed in a woman'. Finally, both Ricord and Brandão excluded the possibility of Maria having given birth for the same reasons outlined by Santucci.[26]

Marianna Lopes, the midwife, was the last to be interrogated. It was a telling sign that the inquisitors, reflecting cultural and social prejudices, assigned less importance to her medical expertise than to those of the three male medical practitioners. Like them, Marianna affirmed under oath that Maria Duran was not a man or a hermaphrodite but 'a true woman like any other' with no evidence of any male genitals being detected either outside or inside her body. She also categorically rejected any possibility that Maria might once have been pregnant and given birth 'because examining and observing very closely Maria's stomach and breasts, she did not see the signs that are to be found in all women who have given birth'. Moreover, Marianna was also certain that Maria was still a 'maiden' (*donzella*), thereby indicating that Maria was a virgin.[27]

The medical examination of Maria Duran's body thus seemed to offer some clarity to the inquisitors on the issue of Maria's sex. Bernardo Santucci, José Ricord and Antonio Soares Brandão all found no evidence of male sex organs, although the opinion of Antonio Soares Brandão was not as definite as that of the first two. The midwife Marianna Lopes also backed this opinion. Moreover, Antonio Soares Brandão and Bernardo Santucci, the real experts in human anatomy among these four, were both categorical that Maria's clitoris could not have been mistaken for a penis. Yet, just as the medical examination seemed to solve one question, it also raised another problem: all four witnesses were adamant that Maria Duran could not have given birth, and both Santucci and the midwife opined that Maria was a virgin. This was in complete contradiction with the claim that Maria Duran made about having given birth to a son, a claim confirmed by the evidence from Catalonia provided by the inquisitors in Barcelona.

9

Torture, verdict and punishment

On 12 September 1742, a conference took place in the *Estaus* Palace to consider the status of Maria Duran's trial. Those gathered included not just the inquisitors Francisco Mendo Trigoso, Simão José da Silveira Lobo and Manuel Varejão e Tavora. The inquisitors were joined by five *deputados* ('deputies'): ordained members of the church who were called in by the inquisitors when it was necessary to discuss how a trial should progress, or to determine a verdict. An inquisitorial notary recorded the resulting discussion in eight pages of small and densely written script. The inquisitors and *deputados* reviewed all the witness testimony and the results of the anatomical examination. The transcription of the meeting provides a fascinating insight into the robust discussions that followed. Given the complexities of Maria's case, it is hardly surprising that there was no consensus, even among the inquisitors. The men were divided into two groups with very different opinions. One group, which for the purposes of convenience will be described as the 'first group', considered that sufficient evidence existed to convict Maria Duran of having made a demonic pact. The remainder, the 'second group', disagreed entirely and wanted to absolve Maria.

The first group was comprised of inquisitors Francisco Mendo Trigoso and Manuel Varejão e Tavora and two of the *deputados*. Pointing to the witness testimony, these men concluded that it was 'legitimately proven that the defendant engaged in repeated acts of carnal copulation as if she were a man, with vaginal penetration and ejaculation of semen both inside and outside of the women with whom she had [carnal relations]'. It was not credible, they pointed out, that the claims of so many women could be wrong or simply dismissed as those of 'simple, ignorant or stupid [women]' when it came to the alleged sexual relations. Indeed, they noted that the witness Maria de Jesus was previously married and thus presumably familiar with heterosexual intercourse. They also highlighted the findings of the anatomical examinations performed by 'three of the most expert surgeons in Lisbon, one of whom is a professor in anatomy, as well as a midwife' that Maria 'is truly a woman and does not possess a penis either outside or inside her body'. One of the surgeons, Antonio Soares Brandão had even examined Maria twice and on the first occasion had placed her in a tub of hot water to see if her muscles would relax and reveal a penis hidden within her body, but this had not been the case. Moreover, Maria herself had never ceased to assert that she was a woman during her various interrogations. Since Maria was therefore a woman, it was 'not possible' for her to 'accomplish what she is accused of naturally, since [heterosexual] carnal copulation requires the instruments of a man'.[1]

The first group concluded that the only logical conclusion must be that Maria had received aid 'from some higher force' and made a pact with the Devil, 'who hides her penis if she has one or, if she does not have one, makes one for her, though not a real one, that appears and seems real'. This presumption of a pact with the Devil was supported by the testimony of various witnesses, including the eminently respectable Father José Jofreu, that Maria had claimed that the Devil visited her and the fact that Maria had been successfully treated with holy water for strange scratches and bruises. In addition to this, there was the disturbing discrepancy between the claims of the three surgeons and midwife who had examined Maria that she had never given birth and was, in fact, a virgin and the evidence received from Barcelona stating the exact contrary. This 'novelty"' they argued, must also be attributed to the Devil's dark arts. With the exception of one dissenting *deputado*, the recommendation of the first group was that Maria be tortured 'in order to clarify the evidence'.[2]

The second group, composed of the inquisitor Simão José da Silveira Lobo and three *deputados*, took a radically different approach to the case. They began by immediately advocating that Maria must be absolved of the charges against her. The variety of reasons they presented for reaching such a conclusion are detailed in the transcript of the meeting. To start with, they underlined the fact that the Inquisition did not have jurisdiction over cases of 'execrable obscenities' (female homosexual acts) such as the ones Maria had committed with 'other women' and the Inquisition could only prosecute Maria for the crime of having concluded a pact with the Devil.

Insofar as the possibility of a pact with the devil was concerned, the second group did not believe that the evidence was sufficient to convict Maria. The anatomical examination ordered by the Inquisition had shown Maria to be 'only a woman', as she had claimed all along. Beyond the possibility of a demonic pact, there existed perfectly credible explanations that could account for the discrepancy with the testimony of the prosecution's witnesses. To support his claim, they referred to a number of medical sources referring to clitorises. These included the work of the Frenchman Jean Riolan (1577–1657), an anatomist and a member of the medical faculty of the University of Paris and the Italian Matteo Realdo Colombo (1516–1559), a surgeon and professor of anatomy at the famous university of Padua, whose manual of anatomy (*De Re Anatomica*) was published in 1559. They set particular store by the work of 'the eminent medic' Paolo Zacchia (1584–1659), an Italian whose influential work on forensic medicine, *Questionum medico-legalium* (Medicolegal Problems), appeared in print in Rome in 1621. Zacchia discussed in detail the cases of two women with an enlarged clitoris that allegedly enabled them to penetrate women as if they were men.[3] They noted that there existed considerable similarities between the cases described by Zacchia and that of Maria Duran:

> Although their bodies were visibly those of women, a swollen excrescence or penis [emerged from their bodies] on those occasions when they were seized by a lascivious fury, with which they penetrated and deflowered those maidens whom they were very fond of and, once their passions abated, these retracted [into their bodies] and were concealed so that they could neither be seen nor felt when they were examined and they were consequently thought to be women.[4]

The members of the second group argued that such cases, although very unusual, could be attributed to 'nature itself', which sometimes causes aberrations in human bodies. Maria's case was 'in everything similar' and they noted that one witness, the nun Sister Elena in Évora, has described the 'penis' as 'short and hard'. If Maria did not confess to it then this could only be because of her 'ignorance'.

The second group admitted that even though it was not possible to be certain that Maria Duran might have a condition similar to that described by Zacchia, 'this was no reason to assume that she had made a pact with the Devil because there are other explanations that could be natural in origin'. Indeed, they identified other 'natural' explanations for Maria Duran's case. Another possible explanation was that Maria had used the fingers of one of her hands to fool the witnesses into believing that she had a penis. The 'perturbation of the mental faculties and senses' that occurred during sex could 'easily' explain why the witnesses might have been convinced that they were being penetrated by a penis. They further noted that experience had shown that it was particularly difficult to establish the existence of a demonic pact. A defendant might be accused of witchcraft and committing murder 'through the arts and power of the Devil' but it was extremely difficult to prove that the death was not natural or 'bought about by natural means' (such as through poison). They concluded that, likewise, it would not be possible to prove beyond a shadow of a doubt that Maria Duran's actions were the result of a pact made with the Devil. Instead, they quoted 'the axiom of law that in doubtful circumstances, defendants should receive the benefit of the doubt'.[5]

Regarding the witness testimony, the second group emphasized that the witnesses had never actually seen Maria's alleged penis. Whilst they claimed to have felt it brush against them, such a claim was hardly convincing. As churchmen, inquisitor Simão José da Silveira Lobo and the three *deputados* who sided with him naturally looked to the Scriptures for guidance and authoritative arguments. They pointed to a biblical precedent in the Old Testament that illustrated how easy it was to deceive the sense of touch. According to the book of Genesis (chapter 27), had not Jacob laid goatskins on his arms to pass himself off as his brother Esau in order to deceive their blind father Isaac and receive his blessing?[6]

Returning to the issue of Demonic possession, the second group noted that it was impossible for the Devil to alter the physical body of any creature 'since this is not something that falls within his power'. Although they did not cite any sources, the question of whether the Devil could alter the human body had been extensively discussed in previous centuries within the context of witchcraft accusations and trials. The popular witch-hunter's manual *Malleus Maleficarum* (Hammer of the Witches), written by the fifteenth-century German Dominican Heinrich Kramer and widely read by Iberian theologians, examined the question of whether witches could, with the aid of the Devil, cause a man's penis to disappear. Citing Saint Augustine and Saint Thomas Aquinas, Kramer concluded that the devil had the power, by means of a spell, to deceive the 'external' senses of individuals – namely their sight and touch – and cause them to believe that their genitals, or those of others, had disappeared or been altered when in reality they had not. Thus, Kramer argued that the victim of such a spell, deceived by their senses, perceived the transformation as a real one.[7] Likewise, the Italian priest Francesco Maria Guazzo, the author of another widely read and consulted treatise on witchcraft, shared this view. In his 1608 work *Compendium Maleficarum* (Compendium of Witchcraft), Guazzo discussed whether the Devil and witches could interchange sexes. Guazzo argued that changes of sex could only take place naturally rather than through witchcraft. Guazzo, however, added an important caveat. Since only God had to power to cause physical alterations to the human body, then 'with God's permission it is possible for the Devil [to cause such transformations of an individual's sexual organs], relying upon natural causes'.[8]

The fact that witnesses had seen scratches and bruises on Maria's body, and that Maria had allegedly claimed that 'the Devil and witches' had inflicted them was hardly convincing proof of a pact with the Devil. The second group pointed out that these claims were not satisfactory because Maria's confession had been 'extrajudicial', the witnesses were too vague regarding the place and time in which these alleged assaults took place and Maria denied it when questioned by the Inquisition. Moreover, 'the Devil could just as well have mistreated her that way if she were a saint, just as he had physically abused many virtuous people'. Although the notary did not record that any examples were provided, the second group probably did not feel the need to elaborate on this point. Hagiographies recorded numerous cases of saints assaulted by the Devil and his minions. One of the most famous was Saint Anthony the Abbot in the third and fourth centuries CE, whom demons had grievously beaten during his time in the wilderness. As churchmen, all the men who had gathered to consider the case of Maria Duran would have been familiar with this and other examples.[9]

The final observations of the second group related to the anatomical examinations that Maria Duran underwent. They noted that Maria had refused to allow the surgeon Antonio Soares Brandão to examine the inside of her vagina during the first examination, when he placed her in a tub of hot water. The second group pointed out that Maria was not placed in a tub of hot water during the second examination and that the experts did not examine her internally once her body temperature had increased. How then could the experts who examined Maria be so categorical in their assessment that she was a 'perfect woman'? Without having examined the inside of her vagina after her body temperature was raised, it was simply not possible to discount the possibility that Maria was an individual similar to those two women whose cases were described by Paolo Zacchia. After all, they noted, the same experts had apparently also been completely wrong in their assessment that Maria was a virgin and had never given birth.[10]

The inquisitors always sought to find precedents when judging an unusual and difficult case. Of course, the Portuguese inquisitors only had access to the archives of the Portuguese Inquisition and this means that they were not aware of a handful of previous inquisitorial cases involving alleged 'hermaphrodites' in neighbouring Spain during the sixteenth and seventeenth centuries. This included the trial of the cross-dressing 'hermaphrodite' Eleno(a) de Céspedes, which has been the subject of many modern studies.[11] Although Maria's case was extremely unusual, the inquisitors in Lisbon did find one previous trial with interesting similarities: the trial of Father Pedro Furtado in 1699–1701. A priest in the remote village of Sambade in northern Portugal, Pedro Furtado was arrested and put on trial by the inquisitorial tribunal of Coimbra further north in Portugal. His arrest came after multiple men in different locations, who could not have known each other, claimed to have had sexual relations with him and that the priest possessed a vagina. The inquisitors in Coimbra had considered the possibility of a demonic pact but discarded it because of insufficient evidence. Father Furtado was known in his parish as 'Father Paula' and was ultimately found guilty of misleading his parishioners regarding his gender and of the serious charge of leading them into theological error by implying that women could become ordained priests. His sentence had been relatively light. Pedro Furtado was condemned to pay the costs of the trial, and three years of exile served in the town of Almeida on the border with Spain, the same town through which Maria Duran had entered Portugal decades later.[12]

When discussing the precedent of Father Furtado's trial in relation to that of Maria Duran, the first group deemed that the two cases were too different in terms of the level of evidence of a demonic pact. Thus, they argued, there existed sufficient evidence to convict Maria. The second group, however, noted the strange parallel that existed between the cases in terms of the contradiction between the witness testimony and the results of multiple anatomical examinations. Accused by credible witnesses of possessing a vagina, Father Furtado was examined twice by medical practitioners who could find 'not even the slightest trace' of female genitalia. Consequently, the inquisitors in Coimbra, they noted, had set aside these allegations against the priest and just condemned him for causing a public scandal that risked leading his parishioners into heretical beliefs.[13]

Deadlocked and unable to reach a verdict, the inquisitors followed the procedure established in the regulations of the Inquisition and wrote to the General Council of the Portuguese Inquisition to request further guidance. It was to be over thirteen months, during which Maria languished in her jail cell, before the inquisitors received a response in October 1743. There is no explanation for this extended delay in the inquisitorial file. While it may be tempting to see a sinister motive, the cause was almost certainly quite prosaic. The inquisitors in Lisbon were particularly busy in the early 1740s, juggling a large number of trials. The Papal Bull *In eminenti apostolatus specula*, issued by Pope Clement XII on 28 April 1738, had banned Catholics from becoming freemasons. In response, the Portuguese Inquisition arrested a number of suspected foreign freemasons in Lisbon, including John Coustos, who later published a vivid description of the jails of the Inquisition. Other trials involved allegations of crypto-Judaism, witchcraft, Protestantism, bigamy and various heretical propositions. One of the most important trials taking place at the same time as Maria Duran's was that of Pedro de Rates Henequim, a man whose unorthodox millenarian ideas had led him to expound the belief that a brother of the aging King João V should become king of an independent Brazil. Given the threat that such an idea presented to the Portuguese Crown, it ordered Henequim's arrest for treason and handed him over to the Inquisition in 1741. The Lisboan inquisitors were under considerable political pressure to conclude Henequim's trial and convict him. Indeed, by the month of April 1744 the inquisitors held no less than forty-one prisoners in the cells of the *Estaus* palace in Lisbon. The trials of these prisoners were either concluded or nearing their conclusion.[14]

In its response, the General Council authorized the use of torture to extract a confession from Maria Duran. While Protestant propaganda insisted that the Spanish and Portuguese inquisitors freely used torture with sadistic relish, in reality the use of torture was limited and carefully regulated. The regulations of the Portuguese Inquisition devoted an entire section to defining when and how torture was administered. Torture was a last resort, to be used only when a trial had reached an impasse and the inquisitors had valid reasons to believe that a suspect was withholding evidence.

Since the Fourth Lateran Council in the thirteenth century, Canon Law explicitly forbade churchmen from shedding blood. Accordingly, the methods of torture employed by the Inquisition had to be 'bloodless' ones. Two such 'bloodless' torture techniques were specified in the 1640 regulations: the *polé* and the *potro*. In the *polé*, also known as the *strappado* or *corda*, a prisoner's hands were tied together behind their back with a rope, and the prisoner was then suspended from the ceiling with that rope. In the *potro*, or 'rack', the prisoner was attached to a wooden frame and ropes were affixed around their arms and legs and progressively tightened. The *polé* was described as the 'ordinary' method of torture and clearly considered the more effective and brutal of the two. The regulations specified that the *potro* could be used only in specific cases. Such cases included those of male prisoners who were deemed by a doctor or surgeon to be too weak to endure the *polé* or when the inquisitors wanted to conceal the traces of torture on a prisoner who was about to be paraded during a public sentencing. In a strange manifestation of prudishness, the regulations specified that women should only be tortured with the *polé* method 'because of the great care that must be taken to protect their honesty'. Presumably, prisoners subjected to the *polé* could remain clothed, while those on the rack would have to be almost totally naked, so that ropes could be attached to their bare limbs.[15]

Another lengthy delay followed the General Council's authorization to use torture on Maria Duran. It was not until nearly six months later, on 15 April 1744, that Maria was tortured. In accordance with the strict procedures of the Inquisition, a series of legal rituals took place beforehand. In the morning, the jail warden led Maria before the inquisitors and she was officially 'admonished' before being tortured. When asked whether she had anything to confess, Maria declared that she had nothing to add or change to her previous declarations. Accordingly, at 9 o'clock in the morning, Maria was taken to the torture chamber (*casa do tormento*), which was located within the *Estaus* palace of the Inquisition.[16] A seventeenth-century plan of the *Estaus* palace shows that the torture chambers actually consisted of two, windowless rooms. One room, rectangular in shape, was the room in which torture would take place. The other room, smaller and square shaped, was adjacent to it and connected to the torture chamber by a doorway. A note on the plan described this second room as the place 'where the inquisitors stay while [torture] is happening'.[17] The Swiss prisoner John Coustos, arrested on suspicion of freemasonry, was tortured only ten days after Maria Duran and vividly remembered the torture chamber in the published account of his trial:

> I hereupon was instantly conveyed to the torture-room, built in form of a square tower, where no light appeared, but what two candles gave. And, to prevent the dreadful cries and shocking groans of the unhappy victims from reaching the ears of the other prisoners, the doors are lined with a sort of quilt.[18]

Despite the strict instruction in the 1640 regulations that women were not to be tortured with the *potro* or 'rack', this was the instrument used for Maria, in the presence of inquisitor Francisco Mendo Trigoso and two *deputados*. Maria was asked one last time whether she had anything to confess. When Maria answered negatively, she was read a legal disclaimer by an inquisitorial notary in which she was informed that 'should she suffer death, the breaking of bones or loss of feeling [in her limbs], the fault would be hers and not that of the inquisitors and their officials'. Having cleared his conscience, the inquisitor ordered the torture to begin. The notary recorded that Maria was tortured for 'circa half an hour, and screamed for help from Jesus and the Most Holy Virgin' (see Figure 6). If the inquisitors had hoped that torture would yield a confession or break Maria's resolve, they were disappointed. Maria did not break and no confession was forthcoming.

The inquisitorial notary did not provide a detailed description of Maria's torture or agony. John Coustos, however, wrote a detailed description of his

Figure 6 The notarial transcript of Maria Duran's torture session (*sessão de tormento*). Written as Maria was being tortured. (ANTT., *Inquisição de Lisboa, processo* no. 9,230, fol. 356r. (http://digitarq.arquivos.pt/viewer?id=2309369, PT-TT-TSO-IL-28–9230_m0711. TIF, CC BY-SA 4.0).

torture with the *potro*. Coustos's account is problematic not only because it was intended to serve as an anti-Catholic polemic but also because it does not match elements recorded in his surviving trial dossier. He claimed, for example, to have been tortured three times when the trial dossier only records a single torture session held on 25 April, that lasted a little more than a quarter of an hour. Doubtless exaggerated for the benefit of his Protestant readers, Coustos's account nonetheless conveys a sense of what Maria's experience with inquisitorial torture must have been:

> The reader will naturally suppose that I must be seized with horror, when, at my entering this infernal place, I saw myself, on a sudden, surrounded by six wretches, who, after preparing the tortures, striped me naked (all to linen drawers); when, laying me on my back, they began to lay hold of every part of my body. First, they put round my neck an iron collar, which was fastened to the scaffold; they then fixed a ring to each foot; and this being done, they stretched my limbs with all their might. They next wound two ropes round each arm, and two round each thigh, which ropes passed under the scaffold, through holes made for that purpose; and were all drawn tight, at the same time, by four men, upon a signal made for this purpose.
>
> The reader will believe that my pains must be intolerable, when I solemnly declare, that these ropes, which were of the size of one's little finger pierced through my flesh quite to the bone; making the blood gush out at the eight different places that were thus bound. As I persisted in refusing to discover any more than what has been seen in the interrogatories [related] above; the ropes were thus drawn together four different times. Side stood a physician and surgeon, who often felt my temples, to judge of the danger I might be in; by which means my tortures were suspended, at intervals, that I might have an opportunity of recovering myself a little. Whilst I was thus suffering, they were so barbarously unjust as to declare, that were I to die under the torture, I should be guilty, by my obstinacy, of self-murder. In fine, the last time the ropes were drawn tight, I grew so exceedingly weak, occasioned by the blood's circulation being stopped, and the pains I endured, that I fainted quite away; insomuch that I was carried back to my dungeon, without my once perceiving it.[19]

Unable to secure a confession from Maria through torture, the inquisitors and *deputados* gathered again on 11 May 1744 to consider a final verdict. Since the Inquisition was planning a grand public sentencing of heretics – or *auto-da-fé* – to take place in the presence of the King of Portugal on 21 June 1744, there was now considerable pressure to conclude the trial rapidly and determine whether Maria would be sentenced in that ceremony. Interestingly, there was no disagreement about the verdict this time. All the inquisitors and *deputados* agreed that Maria, 'being a true woman without a male sex organ committed repeated acts of consummated carnal copulation with a penis during which she ejaculated inside of the women with whom she had disgusting [sexual] relations'. These acts, they noted, 'exceed the powers of Nature and could only be achieved with help from the Devil, from which there results a presumption that the defendant lives outside of our holy faith and has made a pact with the Devil'.[20] The dossier does not explain why the inquisitor and *deputados* who had previously shown such scepticism and argued in favour of Maria's release without charge now supported her condemnation. Did they perceive that the General Council of the Portuguese Inquisition, which had supported the first group's desire to see Maria tortured, seemed to favour a harsh sentence? Were they frustrated by a seemingly baffling and interminable trial? Did they want to wash their hands of Maria Duran?

The only disagreement that persisted concerned the sentencing of Maria. Two of the inquisitors and the *deputados* agreed that Maria Duran should not be sentenced to abjure her crime in front of the public but rather in a private ceremony held within the *Estaus* palace of the Inquisition. Their main fear was that broadcasting the details of Maria's sexual relations in the *recolhimentos* in Lisbon and the Dominican convent in Évora during a public *auto-da-fé* would provoke ridicule and tarnish the reputations not just of those religious establishments but also of the Inquisition as well. The matter, they declared, was a 'sensitive and delicate one', especially since 'whispers and rumours' about the affair had already spread across Lisbon. The religious establishments affected risked losing social prestige and patronage if news of Maria's sexual escapades became public. Moreover, Father José Jofreu, a respected pillar of society and the church in Lisbon, would have to endure public ridicule given his prominent role in helping Maria enter various *recolhimentos* in that city.[21]

The one dissenting voice was that of inquisitor Manuel Varejão e Tavora, who argued that Maria Duran must be sentenced during a public *auto-da-fé*. The inquisitor stated that news of Maria's imprisonment was 'very public' in Lisbon and that, as his colleagues had noted, her crimes were already being discussed 'in one form or another'. Any attempt to hush up the condemnation of Maria would only encourage people to spread rumours about the case and help to tarnish the reputations of the religious institutions involved. Instead, the Inquisition must 'give satisfaction to the world' by having the sentence read out in public during the *auto-da-fé*. To forestall any possible scandal, the inquisitors must phrase the sentence in such a way that the only crime mentioned was the demonic pact and that it omitted the sexual details of the case. Inquisitor Manuel Varejão e Tavora concluded by noting that, however serious their crimes, the Inquisition had publicly sentenced many men and women from religious communities. Even Father Pedro Furtado, whose case the inquisitors considered the closest in character to Maria Duran's, was condemned at a public *auto-da-fé* held in Coimbra in 1701. If the Inquisition had been ready to treat an ordained priest in such a manner, 'there is no reason to act differently with a vagabond woman whose behaviour is so dissolute that it could be said without the least scruple that she has nothing to lose in relation to the way the world sees her'.[22]

The General Council of the Portuguese Inquisition reviewed the discussions of the inquisitors and *deputados* on 22 May 1744. Declaring the trial concluded, the members of the General Council sided with inquisitor Manuel Varejão e Tavora in determining that Maria Duran must be condemned in public at the next *auto-da-fé* because

> being a baptized Christian obliged to believe and hold [to be true] all that the Holy Mother Church of Rome teaches and to avoid communicating or dealing with the Devil, she has forgotten this and done the opposite. Without fear of God or the law, to the spiritual ruin of many souls, she has behaved in a way that is naturally repugnant and contrary to the common order of Nature.

They specified that her punishment was to be twofold. Maria would receive a flogging, administered whilst being paraded through the streets of Lisbon, and afterwards would be exiled from the Kingdom of Portugal. In accordance with inquisitorial procedure, they also noted that the flogging must take place 'without the spilling of blood'. This Latin formula (*citra sanguinis effusionem*) was a legal fiction more designed to safeguard the inquisitors' conscience than to actually protect the condemned. As churchmen, the inquisitors could not shed blood, but the punishment would be carried out by laymen (agents of the secular, royal authorities) not bound by such scruples. Moreover, Maria was also held liable for the cost of her trial. This too was just a standard legal procedure, given that her status as a destitute vagrant meant she was in no position to pay anything to the Inquisition.[23]

10

Maria on display: The *auto-da-fé* of 21 June 1744

On 21 June 1744, the inquisitorial tribunal of Lisbon held a public sentencing – known as an *auto-da-fé* – in the Portuguese capital.[1] While trials of prisoners like Maria Duran took place in strict secrecy behind the walls of the inquisitorial palace, the *auto-da-fé* was the only part of the Inquisition's proceedings that was public. In Portuguese, *auto* also means part of a theatrical performance and the *auto-da-fé* was indeed a carefully choreographed theatrical performance that featured a procession and public sentencing designed to remind those participating and the crowd of onlookers of the Day of Judgment, when God would judge the wicked from the righteous. The regulations of the Portuguese Inquisition set out in minute detail how the *auto-da-fé* was to be organized, stipulating such details as how the prisoners were to be dressed or in what order they were to appear in the procession.[2] The ceremony was also designed to publicize the Inquisition's mission to the rest of society and the French historian Bartolomé Bennassar has described inquisitorial *autos* as an essential part of a 'pedagogy of fear' whose objective was religious and social control.[3] It was not enough to prosecute those deemed to pose a threat to the church and society behind closed walls. Such dissenters must be exhibited in public in order to make examples of them and send a clear message to the population about the danger of heresy.

The event was widely publicized by the Inquisition in Lisbon and its surrounding district in the two weeks that preceded it. Eager to secure a large crowd of onlookers and avoid competition, the inquisitors of Lisbon issued a public proclamation that forbade other churchmen in Lisbon from preaching sermons in their churches on the same day. Moreover, they informed the inhabitants of Lisbon that not only the papacy had granted 'many indulgences to people who have observed similar *autos* in the past' but also warned them that they were forbidden from attacking the prisoners who were to be paraded, either through physical attacks or verbal insults 'such as calling them *sambenitados* or any other insulting name'. Instead, the crowd was encouraged to pray 'with a great deal of charity' for the prisoners' repentance.[4]

The news must have generated considerable excitement in Lisbon. Unlike other public religious rituals, the *autos-da-fé* did not follow a regular yearly schedule, and the last *auto* held in Lisbon had taken place in November 1742. Rumours circulating about the various prisoners, including the 'Catalan hermaphrodite', and the expected execution of some of the prisoners must have heightened public anticipation. Moreover, this *auto* would have a special observer alongside the Inquisitor General Nuno da Cunha de Athayde e Mello: King João V himself. The inquisitors must have been particularly pleased about the presence of the aging and infirm King João V, the royal family and the court. Arriving in the Portuguese capital on the previous day, João V stayed in the *Estaus* palace, the same building in which Maria was doubtless nervously awaiting the ordeal of her public sentencing in her cell. The royal visit was a particular mark of favour to the Inquisition, showing the populace that the Holy Office enjoyed the support of the Crown. On a more prosaic level, the balconies of the inquisitorial palace would give the king and the royal family a perfect vantage point from which to view the procession in safety and where the crowd of onlookers could clearly see them.[5]

Maria and her fellow prisoners were roused from sleep and taken from their cells in the early morning to prepare them for their public appearance. The forty-one prisoners whom the inquisitors selected to be sentenced on 21 June 1744 formed a motley collection of individuals arrested within the jurisdiction of the Inquisition of Lisbon. Since this jurisdiction extended to the colonies in Brazil, the list of prisoners also featured various Brazilians. The prisoners included blasphemers, alleged 'judaizers' or secret Jews, three 'members of the sect of the freemasons' (including John Coustos) as well as a number of men and women whom, like Maria, the inquisitors had prosecuted for witchcraft. The twenty-seven men and fourteen women came from a wide variety of social backgrounds and included both white and black individuals. The prisoners were mostly Portuguese subjects, but there were a few foreigners like Maria Duran. Eight of the prisoners – five men and three women – were condemned to be 'relaxed the secular arm'. The Inquisition used this expression to refer to the death sentence since, as a church court, it could not shed blood and carry out death sentences. Instead, the inquisitors would hand over the prisoners to the secular authorities for execution. Most of the 'relaxed' were repeat offenders or prisoners whose confessions were deemed incomplete by the inquisitors. Among the men condemned to death was the aged Pedro de Rates Henequim, whose unorthodox millenarian ideas were so feared by the government that he was forced to wear a gag (*mordaça*) out of fear that he would upset the ceremony by shouting to the crowd.[6] One of the women condemned to death was the 'witch' Mécia da Costa, a healer and midwife accused of worshipping the Devil. The Inquisition had already prosecuted and convicted Mécia once before. This led Mécia, unlike Maria, to be considered a relapsed heretic and therefore to receive an automatic death sentence.[7]

The prisoners wore penitential garments – the *sambenitos* – and were marshalled into order for the procession. One of those taking part in the procession, albeit not as a prisoner, was the Jesuit Father Miguel de Almeida, who wrote a detailed account of the *auto* in a private letter sent to a friend less than a week later. His role in the *auto* was to accompany Pedro de Rates Henequim and seek to persuade him to save his soul by recanting his heretical beliefs. Father Almeida records that the procession sallied forth from the *Estaus* at eleven o'clock in the morning and began to make its way around the *Rossio* Square amidst a 'horrible calm' (*uma horrivel calma*) (see Figure 7). The atmosphere

Figure 7 *Auto-da-fé* held in Lisbon's *Rossio* Square. Note the procession of prisoners sallying forth from the *Estaus* palace/jail of the Inquisition. Juan Alvarez de Colmenar, *Annales d'Espagne et de Portugal* (À Amsterdam: Chez François l'Honoré et Fils, 1741), Vol. IV, pp. 90–1. Biblioteca del Banco de España 2017. Signatura: FEV-SV-M-00199. Public Domain Mark 1.0.

was solemn, and the priest remembered that the heat of the sunny summer day was oppressive. Fortunately, the inquisitors had not scheduled the *auto* to take place in the open air but rather within the nearby Dominican church of São Domingos, located on the north-eastern corner of the square. Nevertheless, Father Almeida complained of the terrible heat that assailed him and the other members of the procession as they waited in the churchyard outside the church itself while the participants slowly filed in and inquisitorial officials directed them to their designated seating. Yet, even the inside of the church offered little respite. The ceremonial sentencing, during which the prisoners were called one by one to hear summaries of their trials and their sentences read aloud, lasted until midnight. Father Almeida complained of waiting for seemingly interminable hours amidst a suffocating heat generated by the 'innumerable people within the church' until the prisoner he was escorting was brought before the king and sentenced. This process took two and a half hours, just for this one individual.[8]

Once more, John Coustos provides us with an interesting prisoner's perspective of the procession and the *auto* in the church. Although tainted by his anti-Catholicism and a tendency to sensationalize his experiences, Coustos's account seems largely accurate:

> The procession opened with the Dominican Friars, preceded by the banner of their order. Afterwards came the banner and crucifix of the Inquisition, which was followed by the criminals, each whereof walked between two familiars, who were to be answerable for them, and [responsible] for bringing [them] back to prison, such as were not to be executed, after the procession was ended.
>
> The accompanying of prisoners on these dismal occasions is thought so great an honour, that such as attend, to execution, these unhappy victims, and even lean upon them, are always the first noblemen in the kingdom; who are so proud of acting in this character, that they would not resign that honour for any other that should be offered them, so cruelly blind is their zeal.
>
> Next came the Jewish converts, followed by such as were indicted for witchcraft and magic, and had confessed their crimes.
>
> The procession closed with the unhappy wretches who were sentenced to the flames.
>
> The march then began, when the whole procession walked round the court of the Chief Inquisitor's palace, in presence of the king, the royal family, and the whole court, who were come thither for this purpose. The prisoners being all gone through the court just mentioned, proceeded along one of the sides of

Rocio Square; and went down Odreiros Street; when, returning by Escudeiros Street, and up another side of Rocio Square, they came, at last, to St. Dominick's church, which was hung, from top to bottom, with red and yellow tapestry.

Before the high altar was built an amphitheatre, with a pretty considerable number of steps, in order to seat all the prisoners and their attendant familiars. Opposite was raised another greater altar, after the Romish fashion, on which was placed a crucifix surrounded with several lighted tapers, and mass books. To the right of this was a pulpit, and to the left, a gallery, magnificently adorned, for the king, the royal family, the great men of the kingdom, and the foreign ministers, to sit in. To the right of this gallery was a long one, for the inquisitors; and between these two galleries, a room, whither the inquisitors retire to hear the confessions of those who, terrified at the horrors of impending death, may be prompted to confess what they had before persisted in denying; they sometimes gladly snatching this last moment allowed them to escape a cruel exit.

Every person being thus seated in the church, the preacher ascended the pulpit, whence he made a panegyric on the Inquisition; exhorted such prisoners as were not sentenced to die, to make good use of the clemency indulged them, by sincerely renouncing that instant, the heresies, and crimes of which they stood convicted. Then directing himself to the prisoners who were to be burnt, he exhorted them to make a good use of the little time left them by making a sincere confession of their crimes, and thereby avoiding a cruel death.

During the sermon, the prisoners have some refreshments; the open air having a very strong effect on most, and the length of the march fatiguing them greatly. On this occasion, dry fruits are given them, and as much water as they can drink.

The preacher being come from the pulpit, some priests belonging to the Inquisition ascend it successively, to read the trial of each prisoner, who was standing all the time holding a lighted taper. Each prisoner, after hearing it returned to his place. This lasted till ten at night.[9]

Maria would thus have waited with her fellow prisoners until it was her turn to appear before the king and the crowd in the church. When summoned, Maria was required to approach the pulpit on her knees and with her head bowed to hear her sentence. Maria Duran's official sentence, read aloud within the church of São Domingos, presented a summary of her trial that simultaneously simplified the case and sought to protect the reputations of the *recolhimentos* in Lisbon and the Dominican convent in Évora. The sentence did not actually name these institutions. Maria's 'dishonest' sexual relations with women were presented as always coerced and achieved as a result of death threats. The inquisitors placed considerable emphasis on the evidence that had caused them to suspect Maria of making a pact with the Devil. Maria, however, had made a 'full and truthful' confession and could therefore be 'reconciled' or readmitted into Christian society.[10] After the sentence was read aloud, Maria was required to place a hand on the Gospels and repeat an official abjuration written in the first person singular (and presumably read out to her, line by line). The printed statement, with gaps left in it for Maria's name, was signed by Maria and included in the trial dossier. Maria swore that 'out of my own free will, I condemn all heretical beliefs that have arisen, both in the present and in the future, against our Holy Catholic Faith and Apostolic See, especially those that have been described in my sentence' (see Figure 8). Furthermore, Maria pledged to fulfil her penances, to be obedient to the present Pope, Benedict XIV, and his successors and recognized that she would be treated with the greatest of severity, should she reoffend.[11] Once this legal ritual was over, Maria kissed the crucifix and returned to her seat alongside the other prisoners.

Maria Duran's presence in the *auto* did not go unnoticed. A manuscript newsletter circulating that week highlighted the cases of three prisoners, including Maria:

> The famous D. Maria Christina was the one who was brought as a prisoner from the city of Évora, where she was a novice in the Dominican convent of Our Lady of Paradise. She also lived in Lisbon for a while and often assumed the role of a man through witchcraft.[12]

Likewise, Father Miguel de Almeida was aware of Maria's presence and told his correspondent about it, mixing his eyewitness testimony with rumours:

> The famous *donata* novice who served in the convent of [Our Lady of] Paradise in Évora also appeared, the third of the women sentenced. She was married and had two children. I did not get to listen to the summary of her trial when they read it out aloud because I was taking care of the prisoner entrusted to me at the time. They told me that her trial took place because she could become a man with the power to father children and achieved this through some artifice, although I do not understand how this can be.[13]

In another letter, Father Almeida reveals that people were still discussing Maria Duran in early July 1744. The Jesuit addresses his unknown correspondent as the 'Very Reverend Father Doctor', indicating a learned man who possessed a doctorate (almost certainly in theology):

> For a woman to have relations with another and to have the power to impregnate that woman by means of a demonic artifice does not surprise me as I have often

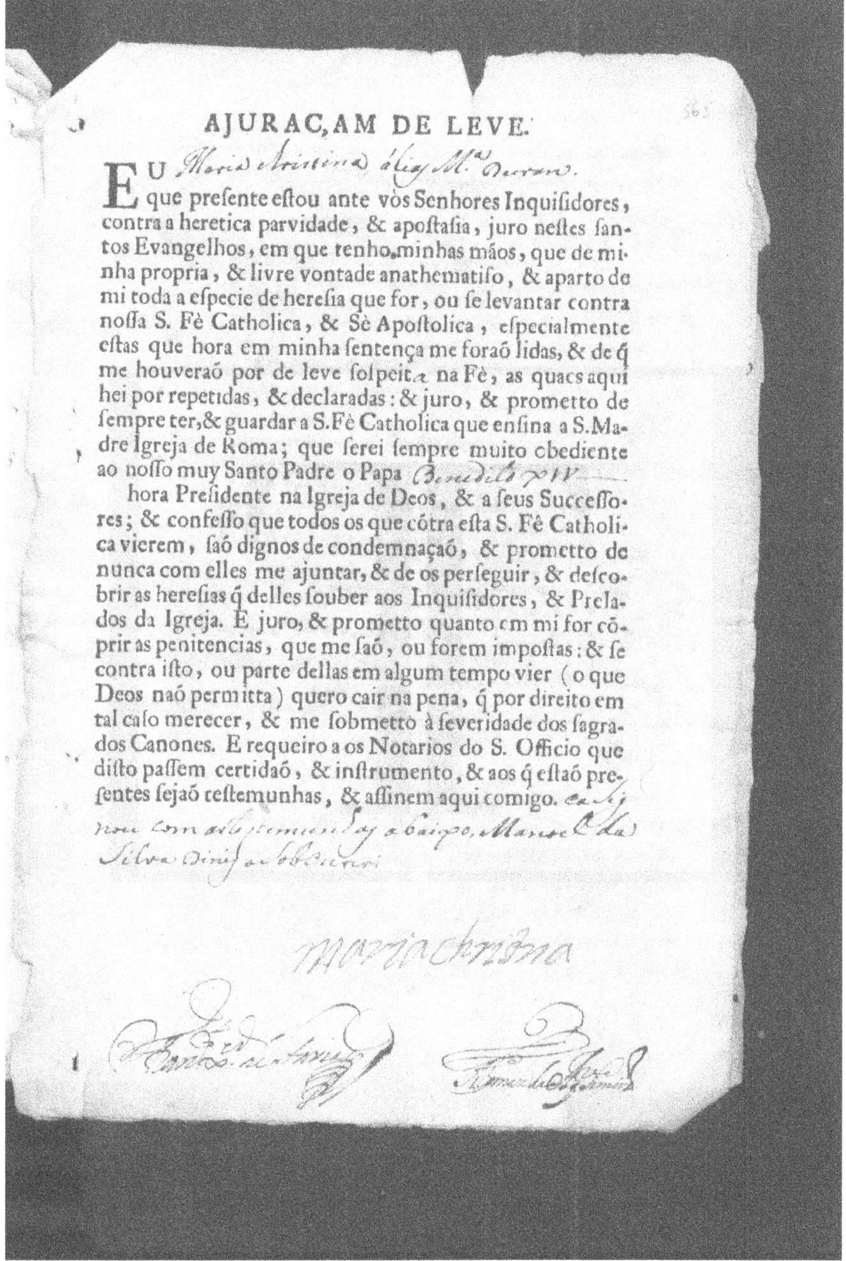

AJURAC,AM DE LEVE.

EU

que preſente eſtou ante vòs Senhores Inquiſidores, contra a heretica parvidade, & apoſtaſia, juro neſtes ſantos Evangelhos, em que tenho minhas mãos, que de minha propria, & livre vontade anathematiſo, & aparto de mi toda a eſpecie de hereſia que for, ou ſe levantar contra noſſa S. Fè Catholica, & Sè Apoſtolica, eſpecialmente eſtas que hora em minha ſentença me foraõ lidas, & de q̃ me houveraõ por de leve ſoſpeita na Fè, as quaes aqui hei por repetidas, & declaradas: & juro, & prometto de ſempre ter, & guardar a S.Fè Catholica que enſina a S.Madre Igreja de Roma; que ſerei ſempre muito obediente ao noſſo muy Santo Padre o Papa

hora Preſidente na Igreja de Deos, & a ſeus Succeſſores; & confeſſo que todos os que cõtra eſta S. Fè Catholica vierem, ſaõ dignos de condemnaçaõ, & prometto de nunca com elles me ajuntar, & de os perſeguir, & deſcobrir as hereſias q̃ delles ſouber aos Inquiſidores, & Prelados da Igreja. E juro, & prometto quanto em mi for cõprir as penitencias, que me ſaõ, ou forem impoſtas: & ſe contra iſto, ou parte dellas em algum tempo vier (o que Deos naõ permitta) quero cair na pena, q̃ por direito em tal caſo merecer, & me ſobmettò à ſeveridade dos ſagrados Canones. E requeiro aos Notarios do S. Officio que diſto paſſem certidaõ, & inſtrumento, & aos q̃ eſtaõ preſentes ſejaõ teſtemunhas, & aſſinem aqui comigo.

Figure 8 Printed abjuration, signed by Maria Duran as 'Maria Christina'. ANTT., *Inquisição de Lisboa*, *processo* no. 9,230, fol. 365r. (http://digitarq.arquivos.pt/viewer?id=2309369, PT-TT-TSO-IL-28-9230_m0729.TIF, CC BY-SA 4.0).

> heard of such occurrences and read about them in books. Beyond what you have told me, there are female (*succubus*) and male (*incubus*) demons who use human semen brought from another person [to impregnate a women]. What I said did not make sense is that she could do this except through some deception. When Maria Duran's sentence was read out (I was not able to listen to it as I was occupied with my charge) it was proclaimed that she did not exhibit any trace of being a man, and that she confessed to having had a son with another woman, by means of deception. I do not understand that she could have done this by means of a natural deception, but I am only able to believe that she accomplished this due to a demonic deception.[14]

Almeida states that the ceremony within the church lasted until midnight, when inquisitorial officials escorted the prisoners who were not condemned to death back to the *Estaus* palace. Those condemned to death, on the other hand, were executed in the early hours of the morning.[15] For Maria and those fortunate not to be condemned to death, the end of the *auto* must have brought a sense of relief. Indeed, Coustos notes that they were not led back to their cells but rather to 'several chambers, the doors of which were open'. The women were housed on a separate floor of the *Estaus* palace and they were all provided with rudimentary bedding. Once settled, Coustos recalled that 'we thought ourselves the happiest persons on earth, though we had little to boast of. However, we were now together and breathed the fresh air; we enjoyed the light of the sky, and had a view of the garden. In a word, we knew that we should not be put to death; all which circumstances proved a great consolation'. The Inquisition provided food and drink in the form of 'a loaf, a cake and water sufficient for the whole company' and the prisoners were allowed to 'divert themselves, provided we did not make a noise'.[16]

Keen to publicize the sentences read out at the *auto* beyond Lisbon to the other regions of the kingdom and elsewhere in the empire, the Portuguese Inquisition ordered the production of a printed list of the prisoners that listed them according to their place in the *auto*, offered very short summaries of their crimes and noted their sentences. In this document, Maria Duran is listed among the prisoners condemned to abjure *de levi* or deny and renounce heretical beliefs of which they were only 'lightly' suspected (see Figure 9):

> Number 3. Age 33. Maria Duran, alias D. Maria Christina de Escalhão e Pinos, married to Ignacio Solsona, labourer, a native of the place of Prullans, diocese of Urgel, Principality of Catalonia, being present in Lisbon; condemned for crimes of witchcraft, and the presumption of having made a pact with the Devil.

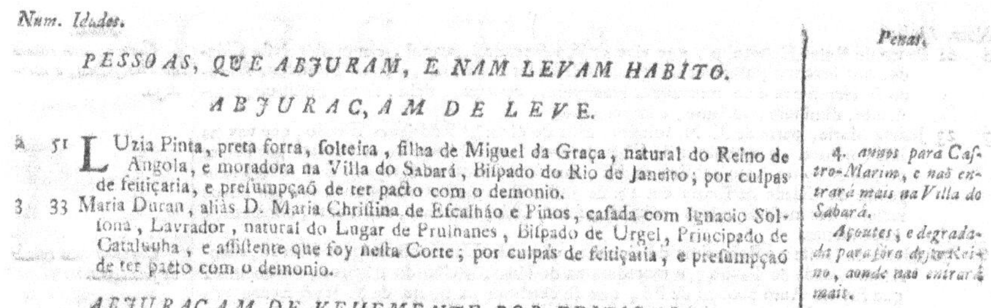

Num. Idades. | Penas.

PESSOAS, QUE ABJURAM, E NAM LEVAM HABITO.

ABJURAC,AM DE LEVE.

à 51 LUzia Pinta, preta forra, solteira, filha de Miguel da Graça, natural do Reino de Angola, e moradora na Villa do Sabará, Bispado do Rio de Janeiro; por culpas de feitiçaria, e presumpçaõ de ter pacto com o demonio. — *4. annos para Castro-Marim, e naõ entrará mais na Villa do Sabará.*

3 33 Maria Duran, aliàs D. Maria Christina de Escalhão e Pinos, casada com Ignacio Solsona, Lavrador, natural do Lugar de Pruinanes, Bispado de Urgel, Principado de Cataluuha, e assistente que foy nesta Corte; por culpas de feitiçaria, e presumpçaõ de ter pacto com o demonio. — *Açoutes, e degradada para fóra deste Reino, aonde naõ entrará mais.*

Figure 9 Detail of the printed list of the prisoners condemned at the *auto-da-fé* held in Lisbon on 21 June 1744. *Lista das Pessoas que Sahiraõ, Condenações, que tiveraõ, e sentenças, que se lêraõ no Auto publico da Fé, que se celebrou na Igreja do Convento de S. Domingos desta Cidade de Lisboa em 21 Junho de 1744* (s.n., s.l., s.d.). (BNP., RES-2487-A, https://purl.pt/26498, CCO 1.0).

> Sentence: a flogging and perpetual exile from this kingdom, into which she will never be admitted again.[17]

The desire to hush up an embarrassing case that could cause ridicule is clear. No mention is made of the sexual elements of Maria's trial: her sexual relations with women and claims that she possessed a penis, the institutions affected or the multiple anatomical examinations. The document circulated widely. John Coustos mentions that he acquired a copy in his book and the French Ambassador to Portugal sent a copy to his government to inform them of the condemnation of two Frenchmen in the *auto*. Moreover, a Spanish translation of the list appeared the same year.[18]

The regulations of the Inquisition stipulated that those condemned to be flogged through the streets must receive their punishment on the Tuesday following the *auto-da-fé*. The manuscript newsletter that mentions the *auto* also notes that Maria was 'sick' (*doente*) after the ceremony and thus did not receive her lashes on that day.[19] Exactly when the Inquisition paraded Maria through the streets of Lisbon and administered the flogging is unclear, but it is likely that the inquisitors only suspended this punishment until Maria's health improved. Regardless of the precise date of Maria's final, humiliating punishment, her dealings with the inquisitors only ended a month after the *auto-da-fé*. Maria Duran was forced to sign a *termo de segredo* or 'secrecy agreement' on 22 July 1744, before being released from custody. This would suggest that the public flogging occurred at some point in the month before that date.

The *termo de segredo* is a short, pre-printed document with gaps left for a notary to add the specific date and Maria's name as well as to properly gender pronouns and adjectives. By signing and swearing an oath on the Gospels, Maria

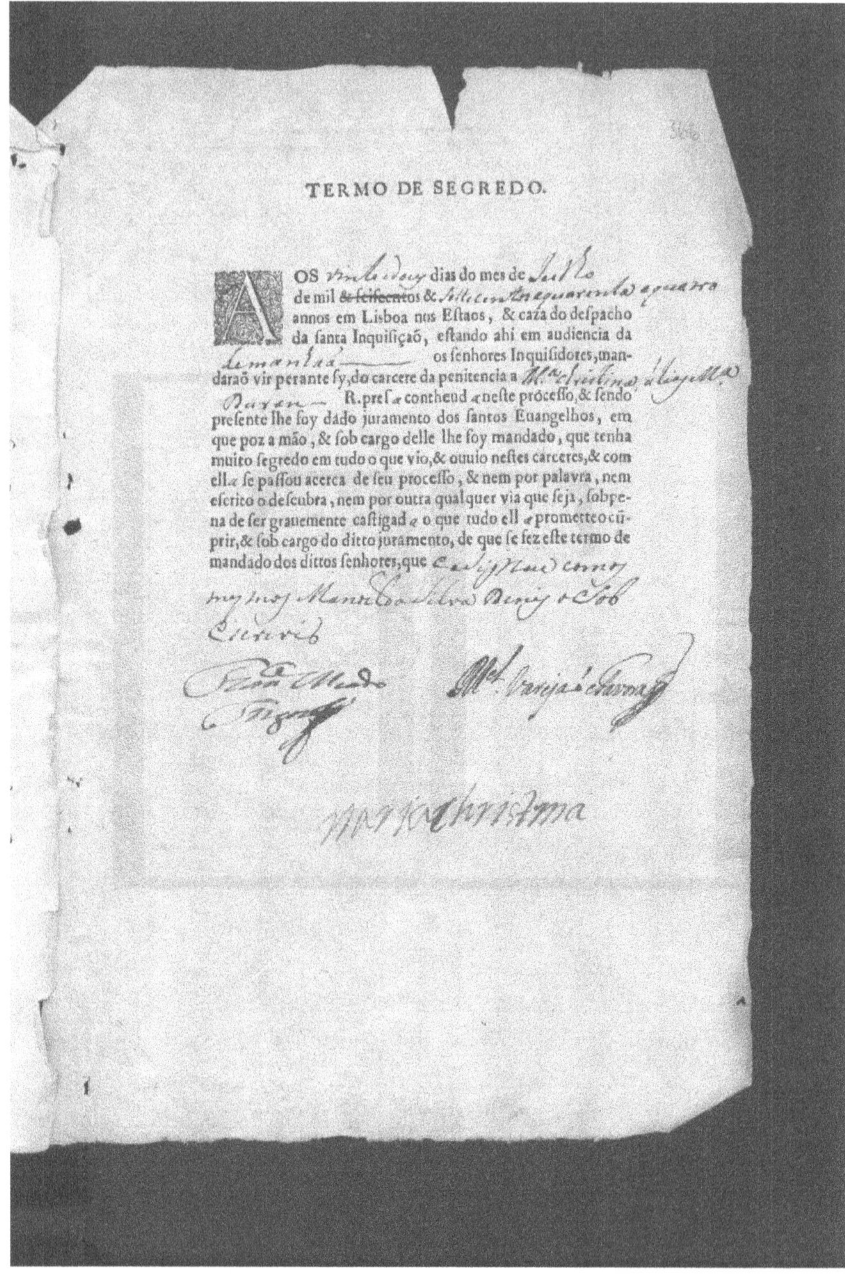

TERMO DE SEGREDO.

AOS [illegible] dias do mes de [illegible] de mil ~~& ſeiſcentos~~ & [illegible] annos em Lisboa nos Eſtaos, & caza do deſpacho da ſanta Inquiſiçaõ, eſtando ahi em audiencia da [illegible] os ſenhores Inquiſidores, mandaraõ vir perante ſy, do carcere da penitencia a [illegible] Duran R. preſa contheuda neſte proceſſo, & ſendo preſente lhe foy dado juramento dos ſantos Euangelhos, em que poz a mão, & ſob cargo delle lhe foy mandado, que tenha muito ſegredo em tudo o que vio, & ouuio neſtes carceres, & com ella ſe paſſou acerca de ſeu proceſſo, & nem por palavra, nem eſcrito o deſcubra, nem por outra qualquer via que ſeja, ſobpena de ſer grauemente caſtigada o que tudo ella prometteo cũprir, & ſob cargo do ditto juramento, de que ſe fez eſte termo de mandado dos dittos ſenhores, que [illegible]

[illegible]

Maria Christina

Figure 10 *Termo de Segredo* in Maria Duran's trial dossier. ANTT., *Inquisição de Lisboa, processo* no. 9,230, fol. 366r. (http://digitarq.arquivos.pt/viewer?id=2309369, PT-TT-TSO-IL-28–9230_m0731.TIF, CC BY-SA 4.0).

pledged never to reveal 'all that she saw and heard in this jail or during her trial, either by speaking [to other people] or writing about them, under pain of being severely punished' (see Figure 10). The final folio in the trial dossier consists of a page with part of its top-right corner torn, from which a considerable deal of the handwritten text is unfortunately missing. The text is dated the twenty-second, but the remainder of the date (month and year) is missing. The title is partly missing but contains the word '*Hida e* …' (Release and …), making it clear that the document was the official release form (*Hida e Penitencias*), signed by two inquisitors and Maria. It consists of a pledge by Maria never to return to Portugal or its colonies, to 'set a good example' through her conduct from then onward or suffer a serious (but unspecified) punishment, to confess her sins to a priest regularly and recite the Holy Rosary every Saturday. Maria signed the form 'Maria Christina' in her usually shaky hand that betrayed her poor literacy by the fact that the letter m of Maria is identical to the letter n of Christina. Why Maria chose Maria Christina instead of Maria Duran is unclear. Inquisitorial trial dossiers usually conclude with a short account of the costs of the trial – so that these could be deducted from the prisoner's property – but this is missing from Maria's dossier. Whether this is because Maria had no property or because the list became separated from the dossier and was lost is not clear.

Part II

The Maria Duran Mystery: Transgressive Sexuality, Transing Gender and Gender Performativity in the Trial of Maria Duran

Transgressive sexuality, transing gender and gender performativity in the trial of Maria Duran

For over three years, the inquisitors in Lisbon struggled to understand Maria Duran's behaviour and the accusations made against her. They floundered in the face of the baffling discrepancy between the seemingly credible testimony of multiple witnesses claiming that Maria was a man and the hard medical evidence that Maria possessed only female genitals. In their frustration, they resorted to torture, albeit without success since Maria Duran resolutely claimed to be a woman. In the mental world of the inquisitors, witchcraft and a demonic pact offered the only plausible way to rationalize the case, although even this explanation did not initially convince every inquisitor or *deputado* present when it was time to consider a verdict. In the end, the majority of the inquisitors and the members of the General Council of the Portuguese Inquisition accepted the explanation of a demonic pact as the most plausible way to account for the testimony against Maria Duran. Maria's trial ended with a conviction for witchcraft (*feitiçaria*) and the presumption of having made a pact with the Devil.

A modern historian cannot get into Maria's mind any more than an eighteenth-century inquisitor. When seeking to analyse Maria's sexuality and gender, a historian must approach the primary source of evidence, Maria's inquisitorial trial dossier, with considerable caution. Whilst rich in fascinating details, it ultimately offers evidence shaped by the preconceptions of the inquisitors, who formulated the questions put to Maria and all the witnesses. Neither can one accept at face value the claims Maria made in response to the questions of the inquisitors. Whilst she admitted to cross-dressing and having sexual relations with women, Maria Duran stubbornly insisted throughout the trial that she was a 'true woman' (*verdadeira mulher*) and that her relations with other women were therefore homosexual in nature, although she did not use that term since it did not exist in the eighteenth century. Of course, Maria Duran's claims could have been part of a defence strategy. Informed by her defence attorney, Maria may well have known that the Portuguese Inquisition had stopped prosecuting cases of sexual acts committed between women since the middle of the seventeenth century.

Trying to analyse Maria Duran's behaviour in light of the documentary evidence is, therefore, a challenging task. Nevertheless, it is impossible for a modern historian in the twenty-first century to read Maria's trial dossier without pondering a number of questions. Could Maria have been intersex? Is Maria's case that of a transgender ('trans') individual whose gender identity was the opposite of the one assigned at birth due to the possession of female sex organs? Alternatively, was Maria a female homosexual who cross-dressed as a man and who performed the behaviours expected of a man in eighteenth-century Iberia in order to convince women to have sex with her? As the Introduction of this book has noted, 'Intersex', 'transgender' and 'lesbian' are modern terms and the usage of such terminology in an eighteenth-century context might be questioned, or even attacked as an anachronism. It is worth emphasizing again the warning sounded by the cultural and linguistic anthropologist David Valentine that 'to imagine historical subjects as "gay", "lesbian" or as "transgender" ignores the radically different understandings of self and the contexts that underpinned the practices and lives of historical subjects.'[1]

In spite of such valid concerns about anachronism, it is possible to make a case for the usage of 'intersex', 'transgender' and 'lesbian' to analyse the behaviour and possible identity of individuals prior to the twentieth century. Insofar as the usage of the term 'lesbian' is concerned, scholars such as Judith Brown, Alison Oram, Annmarie Turnbull and Valerie Traub have argued in favour of a nuanced approach. They have proposed that using the term 'lesbian' in a premodern or early modern context can serve a useful purpose if the term is not employed in its modern sense. Instead, they maintain that its use as a discursive construct is helpful in a historical context.[2] Alison Oram and Annmarie Turnbull, in particular, have underlined not just the complexity of the dilemma regarding terminology but also the need for historians to exercise a degree of pragmatism:

> Nor can we simply apply our categories to the past. Until the mid-twentieth century, lesbians rarely identified themselves as such. 'Lesbian identity' is a late-twentieth-century concept and the historical past was a very different sexual place. In the past women who loved and/or had sex with other women, or who cross-dressed, or who resisted heterosexuality, did not necessarily have a language to describe themselves as lovers of women, or to claim any particular identity based on their sexuality. They could only understand their desires, behaviour and experiences within the social context of their own times. … If

> women leave evidence that they are conscious of the power of their feelings for and attractions to other women, we can be more confident in our attempts to identify, albeit partially, their lives as lesbian lives.[3]

Usage of the term 'transgender' raises many of the same potential problems, but historians should not treat the absence of a specific vocabulary in the eighteenth century as an insurmountable obstacle. Our understanding of the complexities of human sexuality and gender identity has evolved considerably since the 1740s.

This final chapter thus does not seek to make any categorical assertions about Maria Duran's sense of identity, which would be an entirely speculative endeavour. Rather, it examines Maria's behaviour and the reactions it provoked through the lens of modern understandings of gender and sexuality. It begins with an exploration of how and why so many witnesses could genuinely have believed that Maria was male and had a penis. The witnesses' reactions are analysed in the light of modern research on female-on-female sexual violence and recent legal cases involving 'rape-by-deception'. The chapter then proceeds from the witnesses' descriptions of and reactions to Maria's behaviour to consider Maria's own claims. Maria freely admitted to 'transing' gender by cross-dressing, imitating behaviour deemed to be 'male' and having sexual relations with women. What can we make of such claims? Is it possible to discern anything about Maria's gender and sexual identity from them? Does Maria Duran's story make more sense as a 'transgender' one in the sense that Maria's behaviour did not conform to social and cultural expectations about sex and gender? In order to supplement the evidence from Maria's testimony, this chapter ends with a comparative analysis between Maria Duran's case and other historical cases that have been described by historians as either 'transgender' or, at least, 'transing' gender. Dating from the eighteenth to the twentieth centuries, these cases present some striking similarities with that of Maria Duran. Despite the differences in place and time, these cases demonstrate the enduring power of gender stereotypes in Western culture and how those seeking to cross the man/woman gender binary can exploit such stereotypes.

Perceiving Maria as male: The witnesses' testimony

Maria's sexual relations with women in the convent of Our Lady of Paradise in Évora appear to have been consensual. In the *recolhimentos* of Lisbon, however, Maria admitting to using a mixture of psychological manipulation and even physical violence to coerce a number of women into having sex with her. In both places, female witnesses were willing to tell the inquisitors that they thought Maria was a man or, at the very least, possessed a penis. The reaction of these witnesses begs the obvious question: how could so many women have been so sure that Maria was male and possessed a penis? Indeed, they did so after having sworn an oath on the Gospels and having been warned of the dangers of perjury when questioned by the inquisitors or their officials. As the inquisitors themselves rapidly noted during their deliberations, many of the women who accused Maria came from different religious institutions. They could not possibly all have known each other or colluded to bring false accusations against Maria.

Some of the witnesses claimed that they initially believed that they were having sexual relations with a woman, but Maria Duran's behaviour during consensual sex led them to suspect, or even become convinced, that she was a man. This was the case of the nun Sister Teresa Maria Evangelista and the *recolhida* Veronica Maria, for example. Admittedly, not everyone was similarly convinced. The much older, and perhaps more experienced, Sister Isabel Elena confessed to having sexual relations with Maria Duran but asserted that Maria had used some sort of dildo. Other women maintained that Maria Duran had convinced them that she was male – sometimes even boasting about her virility – before sexual intercourse. Maria bragged about previous relationships with women, claimed to have fathered children and to possess extraordinary powers allowing her to seduce any woman to whom she was attracted. On some occasions, Maria Duran also appears to have exploited the confusion surrounding her sex. The *recolhidas* Agostinha Vitoria Rosa and Veronica Maria, for example, all maintained that Maria Duran had claimed to be a hermaphrodite with both male and female genitals. In addition to this, Maria showed one of her sexual partners, the *recolhida* Vitoria, a sharp knife, claiming that she used it to shave off her facial hair. This ploy was apparently successful in helping to persuade Vitoria that Maria was male since Victoria remembered it as one of the main reasons she always thought Maria 'was a man'.

Eighteenth-century Spain and Portugal were patriarchal and heteronormative cultures and societies, in which bodies were cultivated into discrete sexes assumed to be 'naturally' disposed to heterosexuality. It is therefore not surprising that Maria Duran's behaviour caused confusion or uncertainty. Dominant (even aggressive) sexual behaviour was assumed to be a male trait while females were perceived as sexually passive. Maria Duran's sexual behaviour appears to have confused her partners. She always initiated sex and then placed herself on top of her sexual partners (or victims). The *recolhida* Vitoria Rosa, for instance, was unambiguous in her recollection that Maria took off her robes and 'placed herself on top of her, like a man who wants to have carnal relations'. Even the *recolhida* Maria de Jesus – who was married and could be assumed to be reasonably familiar with heterosexual sex – maintained that she had felt a penis rub against her thigh or groin and that Maria Duran ejaculated on her body. The sexual position described by many of the witnesses – generally known today as the 'missionary position' – was obviously considered a characteristically heterosexual sexual position. Maria Duran appears to have been aware of such gendered norms and to have sought to exploit them.

The recurrent use of the phrase 'like a man' by witnesses describing Maria's actions during sexual relations echoes the testimony recorded in the investigations conducted in Italy by the papal nuncio in Florence into the conduct and beliefs of the 'Lesbian nun' and mystic Sister Benedetta Carlini (1590–1661), over a century earlier.

> This Sister Benedetta, then, for two continuous years, at least three times a week, in the evening after disrobing and going to bed would wait for her companion to disrobe, and pretending to need her, would call. When Bartolomea would come over, Benedetta would grab her by the arm and throw her by force on the bed. Embracing her, she would put her under herself and kissing her as if she were a man. She would speak words of love to her. And she would stir on top of her so much that both of them corrupted themselves. And thus by force she held her sometimes one, sometimes two, and sometimes three hours.[4]

Sister Benedetta's lover, Bartolomea, did not accuse her of being a man, but this description of her allegedly coerced sexual relations with Sister Benedetta is strikingly similar to those in Maria Duran's trial. The same perception of sexual agency as a male trait and of the 'missionary position' as a heterosexual position reveals the deeply ingrained nature of gendered sexual norms in early modern Europe. In addition to Maria's actions, her words were also conducive to leading various women to believe her to be male. The witnesses noted that Maria made no secret of her cross-dressing past, and claimed to be a man or a hermaphrodite in the presence of many women. Such statements could only add to the potential for confusion about Maria's identity and, when examined in context, it seems almost certain that Maria Duran deliberately made such claims to persuade women to have sex with her.

Another potential factor needs to be considered when seeking to understand the reaction of some of the women who accused Maria Duran of being male: the trauma of sexual violence. Indeed, if we are willing to accept the testimony of the *recolhidas* Agostinha, Vitoria Rosa and Maria de Jesus as trustworthy, Maria Duran's sexual behaviour strikes a modern observer as sexually predatory. Maria was ready to resort to verbal threats or even acts of physical violence to coerce a woman to have sex with her. After sex, Maria Duran sought to calm her victims by telling them that their sexual acts were heterosexual, and therefore 'normal'. By way of illustration, this is apparent in Vitoria Rosa's claim that Maria Duran had tried to comfort and reassure her after sex by stating that 'she had been deflowered by a man'. Maria also threatened physical violence if her sexual partners told anyone else, especially their confessors.

In a heteronormative culture that stereotypes male sexuality as dominant and aggressive and female sexuality as passive, sexual violence is easily perceived as a phenomenon that is, in essence, male and heterosexual. This stereotyping also affects the victims of violence in same-sex relationships, which has now begun to be the subject of research. A 2002 study of seventy women in the United States who were sexually assaulted by other women has highlighted the trauma and denial suffered by the victims of female-on-female sexual assault, with many of the victims associating rape with heterosexuality and male sexual violence and expressing disbelief that a woman could act in such a manner.[5] Studies published more recently have supported the finding that gender role stereotypes shape the responses of both victims and society to sexual violence and abuse perpetrated by a female offender.[6] There is no reason to believe that attitudes in eighteenth-century Portugal were different in this regard. Regardless of whether the *recolhidas* Agostinha, Vitoria Rosa and Maria de Jesus had a sexual preference for women or men, they had all grown up and lived in a society and culture that promoted the idea that aggressive sexual behaviour and violence were male traits. Indeed, Portuguese law at the time explicitly defined rape as a crime committed by men against women.[7] This highly gendered approach to sexual violence must therefore have compounded the trauma of Maria Duran's actions. Considering this context, it is perhaps easier to understand how many of the witnesses might have come to believe that Maria Duran possessed a penis and must be male.

Maria's sexual relationships suggest a clear sexual preference for women. Her marriage to Ignacio Sulsona in the village of Prullans is the only evidence of any sexual interaction with a man. Since Maria appears to have been a young teenage girl at the time, this may well have been an arranged marriage in which Maria had no say. All of Maria's other known sexual relationships were with women. More significant than that, however, is the fact that Maria both presented herself as a man to many of the women with whom she had sexual relations and that these women perceived her to behave as one. The *recolhidas* in Lisbon as well as many of the nuns in Évora offered clear testimony that Maria boasted about her previous life in male clothing and supposed sexual exploits with women. Moreover, as we have seen in the previous chapters, many of these women described Maria's behaviour during sex as being 'like that of a man' (*como homem*). Maria not only initiated sexual intercourse, sometimes aggressively, but also preferred to position herself on top of her partners in the so-called missionary position, a sexual position clearly associated with heterosexual intercourse. Finally, Maria also penetrated the vaginas of some of her partners. She admitted using either one of her fingers or a dildo, which she described as a pincushion (*agulheiro*) about *c.* 10 cm long and manufactured from cloth.

There are striking similarities between Maria Duran's reported behaviour and recent high profile and controversial court cases in the UK, especially the July 2017 conviction on appeal for rape-by-deceit of Gayle Newman. Newland met a female student online, using a male profile and the male alias of Kye Fortune. Media reports of the court case relate that Gayle and the student developed an online relationship before finally meeting in person. Gayle Newland pretended to be embarrassed by disfiguring injuries and insisted that the student wear a blindfold the entire time. Their relationship became a sexual one, with Newland wearing a prosthetic penis and body suit during intercourse. They had sexual relations for several months until at one point the student ripped off her blindfold during sex. Newland was charged with three counts of assault by penetration, and sentenced to six and a half years in prison. Widely reported as a case of 'gender fraud' in the media, Gayle Newland admitted to having trouble establishing a sexual identity as a teenager and a fear of rejection or embarrassment for being identified as a Lesbian.[8] Could this have been Maria Duran's case too? Even more recently, in May 2022, news outlets reported the case of Tarjit Singh, who was born a biological female, named Hannah Walters, and convicted of the assault by penetration of three women in the UK between 2010 and 2016. The three women claimed that Tarjit Singh fooled them into believing that Singh was biologically male. Singh used a prosthetic penis during sexual intercourse, which always occurred in the dark.[9] The similarities of both these cases with the story of Maria Duran are striking. Unfortunately, these high-profile legal cases have not yet been the focus of academic study. Sensationalized media reports are only of limited value to a historian, and it would be imprudent to seek to construct a comparative analysis on the sole basis of such problematic evidence.

Maria Duran's testimony: Transing gender

While Maria Duran consistently claimed to be a 'true woman' during her trial, straightforwardly accepting Maria's claims as evidence of a purported gender identity is not satisfactory. The subversion of gender through cross-dressing and the adoption of 'masculine' behaviour does not constitute proof of sexuality. Once more, a modern historian faces a major obstacle in the impossibility of separating Maria's own opinions from the voices of the inquisitors who moulded Maria's responses to their questions. There is the additional possibility that Maria was lying in the belief that any other answer would result in a harsher punishment. Finally, one cannot discount the possibility that Maria might simply not have known any other form of identity than the man/woman binary prevalent in her social and cultural environment. After reading the preceding chapters in this book, many modern readers will be tempted to ask the questions: Could Maria have been intersex? Was Maria transgender or 'trans'?

The first question raised – could Maria have been intersex? – can only remain the object of speculation. 'Intersex' is an umbrella term used to refer to individuals who, according to the definition of the Office of the High Commissioner of the United Nations for Human Rights, 'are born with sex characteristics (including genitals, gonads and chromosome patterns) that do not fit typical binary notions of male or female bodies'.[10] This includes a wide range of individuals with combinations of chromosomes that differ from XY (associated with male) and XX (associated with female) as well as those whose external genitals may physically conform to the male and female categories but whose internal organs and hormones do not. Repeated medical examinations in Spain and Portugal by physicians, surgeons, midwives and even an academic expert in human anatomy only identified female genitalia and found no evidence of male genitalia. Certainly, the medical practitioners commissioned by the inquisitors felt confident enough to declare at the end of the trial that Maria Duran was not a 'hermaphrodite', the generic term often used in the early modern period to describe individuals born with malformations of the genitalia. Of course, the medical practitioners who examined Maria were working within the limits of medical knowledge in the eighteenth century, in which hormones and chromosomes were unknown. They could not have accurately diagnosed a medical condition resulting from endocrine diseases and chromosome disorders. During the deliberations surrounding the verdict, one inquisitor and some of the deputies did not consider the anatomical examinations to be sufficient to declare Maria a 'perfect woman' beyond a shadow of a doubt. For the sceptics, the examinations had not discounted the possibility that Maria might have some male sexual organs concealed within her body. Like these sceptics, a modern historian can only speculate, without any positive proof, that Maria might have had a chromosomal or hormonal medical condition.

The second question – could Maria Duran have been 'transgender' (often shortened to 'trans')? – is no less problematic to answer. Like 'intersex', 'transgender' is also an umbrella term used to designate a person whose sense of identity and gender is not the one that was assigned to them at birth, or who does not conform to their society's cultural and social expectations about sex and gender. Susan Stryker has elaborated a simplified definition of transgender to mean 'people who move away from the gender they were assigned at birth'.[11] Stryker's definition is useful since it allows us to focus less on Maria's claims and more on her actions.

Maria's life story, as much as we can reconstruct it from the evidence in the inquisitorial trial dossier and taking into consideration the problems that such a source presents, can be interpreted as that of an individual transing gender. Indeed, Maria repeatedly transited between male and female identities. Maria was born a biological female in the village of Prullans around 1711, raised as a girl and married to a man. When the marriage fell apart, Maria fled from her village and started a new itinerant life. Dressed in male clothing, Maria travelled widely in southern France and eastern Spain, adopting a male identity and eventually joining the Spanish royal army. When Maria revealed her female body, supposedly because she wanted to avoid military service in Italy, the army expelled her and she was forced to dress as a woman. Nevertheless, dressing once more in male attire, Maria left eastern Spain and embarked upon a long and seemingly aimless journey via central Spain to Portugal and, ultimately, into the jails of the Inquisition in Lisbon. In Portugal, destitution forced Maria to resume a female identity and she gained admittance into a series of charitable institutions for destitute women in Lisbon before ending up in the convent of Our Lady of Paradise in Évora. Maria was wearing female clothing and claiming to be female by the time that she was facing the scrutiny of the inquisitors in February 1741. In total, Maria switched her public gender identity at least four times.

The inquisitors asked Maria Duran to explain why she had told women in Lisbon and Évora that she was a man. Maria did not seek to contradict the claims of the witnesses but rather readily admitted to falsely claiming a male identity. To explain this, Maria confessed that her 'principal motive' (*fundamento*) for claiming to be a man 'could have been as a joke' and her wish 'to have lascivious relations and obscene fondlings with some of the women'. Maria Duran, appears to have been keenly aware of the cultural and social expectations that could help an individual 'trans' gender and assume a male or female identity. Eighteenth-century Spain and Portugal were heteronormative cultures and societies, in which everyone was assumed to be heterosexual (attracted to males if female and attracted to females if male). To pass as male, Maria had to play the part and cater to the expectations of others. Not only did Maria conceal the two most revealing signs of having a female body: breasts and menstruation, she also took care to mimic 'male behaviour.' Indeed, it is striking that a number of Maria's female sexual partners in Portugal insisted on Maria Duran's ability to reproduce 'male behaviour' through words and deeds. Maria de Jesus' claim that Maria Duran was 'a man who dressed like a woman and who behaved like one in every action' (*era homem vestido em traje de mulher, assim porque em tudo o parecia nas acçoes*) is particularly interesting. Maria told the inquisitors that blending in with a crowd of rowdy soldiers necessarily involved conforming to cultural preconceptions of male behaviour. Thus, Maria acted the role of a boisterous male, joined in communal singing and played practical 'jokes' (*galhofas*) on her male companions. Despite her apparent skill at exploiting gender norms, Maria came perilously close to disaster. Maria confessed that during her time dressed in male clothing numerous men and women remarked, 'she had the face of a woman' or suggested, apparently in jest, that she must be a eunuch. Maria's transing of gender was not limited to adopting 'male behaviour'. Like any good actor, Maria also resorted to artifice. Maria Duran herself admitted to fashioning an artificial bladder from a gourd filled with water whilst serving in the Spanish army. Hidden in her breeches, this device allowed Maria to urinate in a standing position in the presence of onlookers, presumably facing away from them or not so close that they might notice the deception. Maria was, quite literally 'performing gender' for the benefit of others.

It is important to point out that Maria's 'transing' of identities went beyond gender norms to include the transgression of social status. Maria also knew how to take advantage of the obsession with social status and resulting prejudices in eighteenth-century Iberia. Born into a poor family in a remote Pyrenean village in Catalonia, Maria confessed to the inquisitors that her father was a 'labourer' (*lavrador*) and her husband, Ignacio Sulsona, a shepherd and labourer. Maria grew up in a village that was a fiefdom of the barons of Prullans, whose residence was the most significant building in the village after the parish church. She would have been aware of the significance of an aristocratic status from an early age. Once she had left her native village, Maria assumed a number of aristocratic identities that were always made explicit by the use of the all-important honorific titles *Don* (sir) or *Doña* (lady). In Catalonia, Maria adopted the name of Don Antonio Peretada when assuming a male identity in public and Doña Christina Bordas when female. Later, in Portugal, she adopted the pretentious title of Lady Maria Cristina de Escalhão e Pinos, similarly claiming a fictitious aristocratic status. When assuming a male identity in Portugal, Maria took on the name of Don Antonio de Escalhão Pinos. More than one nun in the convent of Our Lady of Paradise recalled that Maria boasted about being the daughter of a 'very noble and illustrious' couple named Don Raymundo Escalhão, Count of Pinos, and his wife Teresa. By claiming a fictitious aristocratic pedigree, Maria could exploit the greater degree of trust that people would confer upon the bearer of such a status. Aristocrats and those with 'blue blood' coursing through their veins – interestingly *sangre azul* is an expression that allegedly originates in Spain – were believed to inherit a proclivity to behave morally. Correspondingly, sumptuary laws and literary texts expressed anxiety about impostors like Maria Duran, who falsely claimed aristocratic ancestry.[12] Since inquisitorial regulations shrouded the trial in secrecy, the revelations about Maria's social background remained hushed and public gossip continued to report her fanciful aristocratic status even after her arrest. The sensational account of the case reported in the manuscript newsletter written on Saturday 4 March 1741, for instance, noted Maria's purported 'noble status'.

Maria's transing: A comparative approach

To gain a better understanding of Maria Duran's transing of gender, it may be helpful to consider what Maria Duran's story reveals not only about gender as a social construct and its distinction from biological sex but also about what can be described as the performativity of gender. From the moment of birth, society genders all human bodies. Assigned an identity (male/female), society constantly reinforces this gendered identity through cultural practices as well as the policing and enforcement of gendered norms, for example, legal prohibitions on cross-dressing or female military service. The performativity of gender, as Judith Butler notes, is rooted in daily behaviour:

> Significantly, if gender is instituted through acts which are internally discontinuous, then the *appearance of substance* is precisely that, a constructed identity, a performative accomplishment which the mundane social audience, including the actors themselves, come to believe and to perform in the mode of belief. [13]

Butler argues that 'a sedimentation of gender norms produces the peculiar phenomenon of a "natural sex" or a "real woman" or any number of prevalent and compelling social fictions'.[14] It is striking that Maria used exactly the same expression of 'real woman' (*verdadeira mulher*) when seeking to deny the claims of the Inquisition that she must have made a pact with the Devil to deceive women into believing she was male. Maria knew, whether consciously or not, the language that the inquisitors and wider society understood: one in which gender was defined by the sexual difference between 'true men' and 'true women'.

Yet Maria was also clearly aware that in order to successfully 'trans' gender, to pass as a man, it was necessary to 'perform' or 'act' male. To be accepted by others as male, Maria needed to perform the daily acts that would convince her 'mundane social audience' that she was male. The evidence from the trial indicates that Maria, unsurprisingly, took obvious steps like donning male clothing to good effect, binding her breasts and carefully hiding any signs of menstruation when passing as a soldier. Maria supplemented these subterfuges by the deliberate adoption of patterns of behaviour that were culturally deemed male, or as Maria put it in her own words to 'imitate male customs'. This included actively engaging in revelries and horseplay with fellow soldiers and others in taverns or through displays of aggressive sexuality with the women whom she wanted to seduce in the *recolhimentos* in Lisbon and the convent of Our Lady of Paradise in Évora. The firmest evidence that this was not an unconscious state of mind but rather that Maria was fully conscious of the need to 'perform gender' to successfully trans gender lies in her use of a hidden gourd filled with water to pretend to urinate whilst standing, with her breeches attached, 'just like a man'.

There exist interesting parallels on multiple levels between the life and behaviour of Maria Duran and those of a number of other individuals who 'transed gender' and faced the law in a variety of different contexts from the sixteenth to the twentieth centuries. These examples all involve individuals born female but who, later in life, cross-dressed and assumed a male identity. In all these cases, like that of Maria Duran, they engaged in sentimental (and sometimes sexual) relationships with women and came to the attention of the secular or religious authorities. The questions that these cases raise are often the same and it is possible to discern trends in the role played in them by the performativity of gender in the subversion of gender norms.

For many scholars of the early modern Iberian world, Maria Duran's story will evoke those of Catalina de Erauso (*c*.1585/92–*c*.1650) and Elena/o de Céspedes (1545 – after 1588). These two figures have become somewhat akin to celebrities in the fields of early modern Spanish history and literary studies.

The life of Catalina de Erauso, who became known as the 'lieutenant nun' (*la Monja Alférez*), has become famous in large part because of Catalina's published autobiography (though the identity of the actual author is still debated). Placed in a convent by her parents at a very young age, Catalina rebelled against the harsh discipline of the cloistered life. Escaping from her convent in the Basque port of San Sebastián at the age of fifteen, Catalina dressed in male attire, took a male name and assumed a male identity. Catalina sailed from Spain to the Americas, where she became a soldier and served with distinction against the indigenous Mapuche people in what is today Chile. Erauso claimed to have had a relationship with one woman in Lima (Peru) and to have been betrothed to various others, ending these engagements to avoid detection. When Catalina's female sex was finally discovered in 1623, she returned to Spain. King Philip IV granted her an audience and a pension as well as the right to keep her male name and military rank. Since the seventeenth century, Catalina has become the subject of plays, books and even films. Historians still debate the gender and sexual identity of Catalina de Erauso. Some argue that Catalina was transgender whilst others perceive her as a Lesbian.[15]

The superficial similarities between the lives of Catalina de Erauso and Maria Duran – the cross-dressing, military service and relationships with women – cannot hide the fact that the two were also quite different. Erauso was not accused of having a 'secret' penis concealed within her body. Moreover, the details about Erauso's claims of having relationships with women are very limited and it is quite possible that Erauso may have feigned such relationships to lend credibility to a male identity. Finally, the information about the life of Erauso comes from an alleged autobiography rather than from legal records. While legal records present problems of their own, Erauso's autobiography offers a perspective or version of events that does not provide evidence or testimony from the women with whom Erauso supposedly had sexual relations. A comparison with the famous trial of Elena/o de Céspedes, who was arrested and prosecuted by the Spanish Inquisition in 1587, would appear more logical.

Elena was born *c.* 1545 in the south of Spain to a Spanish father and an enslaved North African mother and raised as a girl.[16] Married at the age of sixteen to a stonemason, Elena ran away from her husband whilst pregnant. After giving birth to a son and entrusting the child to the care of an acquaintance, Elena adopted the masculine name of Eleno, began to wear male clothes and worked as a farmhand and shepherd. Despite having been exposed and admonished to wear female dress, Eleno continued to wear male clothing and assume a male identity. Eleno fought in the royal army during the Morisco rebellion of 1568–71 and eventually worked as an unlicensed surgeon in the region of Toledo. When Eleno sought to marry a woman in the village of Ciempozuelos, however, the couple ran into trouble. The Vicar General refused to grant them the necessary licence to marry, expressing doubts about Eleno's sex and accused Eleno of possibly being a eunuch. A physical examination found Eleno to be male but the parish priest and some villagers continued to oppose the marriage, claiming that it was 'public knowledge' that Eleno(a) was 'male and female' (*macho y hembra*) and possessed the genitalia of both sexes. A further medical examination, carried out by Francisco Díaz, a doctor and surgeon to King Philip II as well as a respected urologist, and a doctor from Madrid named Antonio Mantilla found that Eleno had male genitals and was not a 'hermaphrodite'. Eleno was declared male and thus eligible to marry.

Even though Eleno married, this was not the end of the story. Confusion reigned when a woman to whom Eleno had previously been betrothed made another complaint. This resulted in another physical examination conducted by four medical experts who examined Eleno's genitals. The examiners declared that Eleno did not possess any sign of a penis but only had a vagina and, as one of them declared, 'is not, nor has ever been, a man but rather a woman'. When doctor Antonio Mantilla was asked to account for his earlier finding that Eleno had a penis, he maintained that Eleno must have used 'some illusion created by the Devil' to fool him. Questioned, Eleno claimed that his penis and testicles had swollen and ulcerated after horse riding, forcing him to slice off pieces of his ulcerated penis 'little by little' (*poco a poco*).When questioned, Eleno's wife, Maria del Cano, asserted that her husband was a man and that they frequently had sexual intercourse 'like a man with a woman'. Nonetheless, like many of the female witnesses the later trial of Maria Duran, Maria del Cano admitted that she had never actually seen the 'member' that Eleno inserted into her vagina during sex although it felt 'smooth and hard'.

The tribunal of the Holy Office of the Inquisition in Toledo soon became aware of the case of Eleno and stepped in, since cases of suspected witchcraft fell within its jurisdiction. As a defence, Eleno claimed to be a hermaphrodite, possessing both male and female sexual organs, and that this allowed him to choose to marry a woman, citing Pliny, Cicero and St Augustine as authorities on the subject. The inquisitorial prosecutor, on the other hand, argued that Eleno's sex had always been female, that Eleno had never possessed a penis and that the doctors who had examined Eleno's genitals and declared him to be male must have been bribed to do so. Yet another physical examination of Eleno's genitals by two doctors and a surgeon found only a vagina and a clitoris but no evidence of a penis or even a scar that might confirm Eleno's claims about having removed his ulcerated penis with a knife. Convinced that Eleno was female, the inquisitors found Eleno guilty of the charge of sorcery and bringing the sacrament of marriage into ridicule. The sentence handed out during a public *auto* held in Toledo on 18 December 1588 ordered Eleno to revert to a female identity as Elena, to suffer 200 lashes and to work without salary for ten years in a charitable hospital in Toledo. Maria Duran and Elena/o's narratives do have clear and striking parallels. In both cases, they were born female and fled from husbands to whom they had borne a child, subsequently assuming a male identity. Both of them had sexual relations with women and were arrested and prosecuted by the Inquisition for witchcraft. In both cases, the Inquisition expended considerable effort to determine their biological sex through medical examinations. Ultimately, the Inquisition found them both guilty and condemned them to suffer a public flogging.

The early modern Iberian world did not have a monopoly on cases of 'gender transing'. Jen Manion has recently analysed numerous cases of so-called female husbands in Britain and North America during the eighteenth and nineteenth centuries: individuals who were assigned a female identity at birth and who chose to 'trans' to a male identity. One of these cases stands out: the trial of Charles Hamilton, born Mary Hamilton, prosecuted for marrying a woman in England in 1746, only two years after Maria Duran was sentenced by the Inquisition in Portugal.[17] Born in the early 1720s, Mary Hamilton began to pass as a boy from the age of fourteen, donning 'man's apparel' and using the first name of Charles. Charles/Mary became a travelling 'operator and oculist' who, without any formal medical training or licence, claimed to cure all manner of medical disorders. In July 1746, Charles/Mary married a woman named Mary Pierce, who denounced her husband to the authorities two months later and sought the annulment of the marriage because Charles/Mary was a woman. Described in 1746 as wearing breeches, ruffles and a periwig, Charles/Mary's character was described as 'very gay' (with none of the present associations of the word 'gay'), 'bold' and 'impudent'. Mary Price asserted during the proceedings that she did not immediately detect Charles/Mary 'was not a man but a woman' because her husband had 'entered her body several times' during their short marriage. The court's verdict was harsh and sought to be exemplary: six months of imprisonment, accompanied by a public whipping to be carried out in the four towns where Charles/Mary Hamilton had lived and worked.

Unsurprisingly, this unusual court case attracted attention and the novelist Henry Fielding wrote a fictionalized account of the life of Charles/Mary

Hamilton with the prolix title *The Female Husband: Or, the Surprising History of Mrs. Mary, Alias Mr George Hamilton, who was convicted of having married a young woman of Wells and lived with her as her husband, taken from her own mouth since her confinement.*[18] Sadly, the surviving evidence from the legal records of the Quarter Sessions held at Taunton, in Somersetshire, are nowhere near as detailed as Maria Duran's inquisitorial trial dossier. Interestingly, there is no evidence that the judge ordered a medical examination of Charles/Mary's body. Despite this dearth of detail, it is possible to find shared points between Charles/Mary Hamilton's life and that of Maria Duran. Just as in the Maria Duran case, we see a highly mobile individual, cross-dressing and travelling from one place to another where few would know them and question their sex or gender. The behaviour of Charles/Mary Hamilton and Maria Duran was described by witnesses as loud, boisterous, and thus considered to be 'male' in character. Moreover, the women who accused Charles/Mary and Maria Duran seemed convinced that they had a penis.

The story of another early modern 'female husband' that has only recently been brought to light from archival obscurity is that of Maria Leocadia Yta, also known as Antonio Yta, who was prosecuted in colonial South America in 1803 for having deceitfully married a woman whilst being female. Maria Leocadia Yta was born to upwardly mobile parents in Madrid in 1770. After being fostered by a wealthy duchess, Maria was placed in an Augustinian convent at the age of fourteen. Between 1783 and 1792, Maria was expelled from no less than four different convents. Although details are scant, these expulsions may have been the result of sexual relations with novices and nuns. When recalling the expulsion from the second institution, the convent of Santa Juana near the town of Illescas in central Spain, Maria/Antonio claimed that it was the result of the nuns 'catching her with a nun and because they were convinced she was a man'. Maria then claimed to have made a trip to Rome and received the permission of the papal penitentiary to take a male name and don male attire. With the new public identity of Antonio Yta, Maria crossed the Atlantic and moved to South America, where, in 1799, Antonio Yta married Martina Vilvado y Balverde. The marriage endured until 1803 when Martina denounced her husband as a woman to the ecclesiastical and secular authorities in Potosí (modern-day Bolivia). Martina asserted that Antonio had consistently refused sexual intimacy, claiming to have taken a vow of chastity, and that the deception was exposed when she noticed that her husband urinated 'the way that women are accustomed to' and she had seen evidence of menstruation as well as his 'very grown breasts'. Antonio/Maria was arrested and, contradicting Martina, claimed to have had sexual intercourse with Martina by means of 'a kind of fleshiness similar to the virile member' that 'protrudes over the pudenda'. A physician and a surgeon examined Antonio/Maria but only found evidence of female sexual organs, including a clitoris. The medical practitioners speculated that the 'fleshiness' might be an erect clitoris but they reserved their judgement, noting that they had not 'seen it in action'. Antonio/Maria escaped from prison in September 1804 and, unfortunately, the documentary trail ends at that point.[19]

Martina's claim that no sexual acts occurred during her marriage to Antonio/Maria Yta would appear to represent a fundamental difference between this case and that of Maria Duran. Indeed, in Maria Duran's trial, it was not one but a number of witnesses who accused Maria of possessing a penis or behaving 'like a man' during sexual intercourse. Maria Duran made no claim of possessing a penis or even a clitoris that might substitute for one. Of course, Martina's claim must be treated with caution, as Martina may well have wanted to avoid social ridicule and/or potential legal prosecution. The interesting point of convergence between these two trials is the contradictory testimonies of Martina and Maria/Antonio Yta and the inability of medical experts to find any evidence of male sexual organs. This mirrors the situation in Maria Duran's own trial, where a medical expert would not rule out the possibility that Maria might be 'some monstrosity of Nature until now never observed in a woman'. The reluctance of medical experts to pronounce themselves on the sex of the prisoner in both cases not only reflects the limits of early modern medical knowledge but also the hesitancy of these experts to expose themselves to ridicule and jeopardize their medical careers.

A final comparison can be made with two twentieth-century cases. The first is that of another remarkable individual who lived nearly two centuries later and on the other side of the planet. In 1920, Eugenia Falleni, who also used the aliases Harry Crawford and Jack Crawford, was put on trial in Sydney, Australia, and found guilty of the murder of Annie Birkett, to whom Eugenia was married. Eugenia was born with female genitalia in Italy in 1875 before moving as an infant with her family to New Zealand. Raised as a girl, at the age of nineteen Eugenia married (or was married by her family) to an older man, an Italian immigrant like her. Eugenia, however, left the marriage and her family and embarked upon an itinerant life in male clothing and with a male identity. The illiterate Eugenia took work on a ship and arrived in Sydney, Australia, in 1898. Pregnant, seemingly as a result of a sexual assault, Eugenia gave birth and entrusted her daughter to an Italian couple in Sydney before resuming a public male identity as Harry Crawford and earning a living from low-paid manual jobs as a gardener, an abattoir worker and a general 'useful' in hotels and drinking establishments. Harry Crawford married a widow named Annie Birkett in 1913, and the stormy relationship ended with Annie's death under suspicious circumstances. The police arrested Harry, who had remarried, in 1920. The police accused Harry of having murdered Annie when she discovered that her husband was, physically, female. The murder trial attracted sensational news coverage and the story of the 'man-woman Eugene Falleni' became a legal *cause célèbre* in Australia (although it remains little known elsewhere). Found guilty and condemned to death, although on appeal the verdict was commuted to a jail sentence, Eugenia/Harry was released in 1931 and lived as a woman until dying in a car accident in 1938.[20]

At first sight, the nature of two trials was, admittedly, very different. Whilst the trial of Eugenia Falleni was held in the very public forum of a Sydney law court, and in the full glare of journalists hungry for a sensational news story, Maria Duran's inquisitorial trial took place in secret and was shrouded in the secrecy of the Inquisition. Yet the lives of Maria and Eugenia bear striking similarities. Both of them were born with female sexual organs and assigned a female identity but ended up leaving their families to pursue a life that broke with social conventions in the most fundamental manner. Maria and Eugenia both transed gender. They dressed as men and, illiterate and without a trade, sought out any occupation they could get to earn a living. They both pursued sexual relationships with apparently heterosexual women, either making promises of marriage (Maria) or actually marrying (Eugenia). Furthermore, both of them pretended to have a penis (using fingers or a dildo to penetrate their partner's vagina in darkened rooms) and seemingly managed to convince their lovers that they were men.

The final comparative case study with remarkable echoes of Maria Duran's case is even more recent and brings us neatly back to Portugal. Maria Teresinha Gomes was born on the Portuguese Atlantic island of Madeira in 1933. After running away from her family as a teenager, Teresinha moved to Lisbon to find work as a seamstress. After the fall of the conservative dictatorship ruling Portugal in 1974, Teresinha cut her hair short and began to wear the uniform of a Portuguese general. Maria also used the name of an older brother who died in infancy, Tito Aníbal da Paixão Gomes. With this new male public identity, an immaculate military uniform and an easy demeanour, Teresinha Gomes was able to convince many neighbours not only that she was male but that she was also alternatively a diplomat, the director of the CIA in Portugal, the treasurer of the US embassy in Lisbon, a spy or a military lawyer. Taking advantage of their naivety, Teresinha persuaded her friends and neighbours to hand over their life savings to invest and promptly proceeded to embezzle them. As Tito Aníbal da Paixão Gomes, Teresinha shared a house with a nurse named Joaquina Conceição da Costa, although whether this relationship was sexual remains unclear.

Eventually, in 1992, Teresinha's financial frauds came to the attention of the police. Unsurprisingly, the trial of 'the she-general' (*A Generala*) attracted considerable media attention in a Portugal that remained religiously and socially conservative. Joaquina Conceição da Costa claimed during the trial that she had been utterly ignorant of Teresinha's real sex until the latter's arrest. The nurse explained that she did not share a bedroom with her companion, who always awoke early to complete morning ablutions privately and kept a man's shaving kit in the bathroom. To prove that Teresinha was in fact a woman, the police compelled Teresinha to attend the Institute of Forensic Medicine in Lisbon, where doctors conducted an examination of Teresinha's genitals and pronounced them female. The trial for fraud and use of a false identity led to a suspended sentence of three years in prison as well as considerable (but unwelcome) media exposure for Teresinha.[21] Like Maria Duran over two centuries before, Teresinha disappeared from the public gaze after the end of the sensational trial until a lonely death and a pauper's funeral in July 2007.[22] The case has not been forgotten, however. The Portuguese television network SIC produced and filmed a six episode series based on the life of Teresinha, though using a different name, under the title of *A Generala* in November-December 2020.[23]

The case studies outlined above align with the story of Maria Duran in demonstrating how the performativity of gender is crucial to the successful transing of gender. Maria Duran and all of these individuals were born with female sexual organs and do not appear to have been 'intersex' insofar as it is possible to know. Moreover, they all originated from more or less humble social backgrounds, many of them fled heterosexual marriages (and some had even borne children) to embark on a new, uncertain life as male individuals. They adopted whatever means of earning an income were available and became highly mobile, moving from town to town, sometimes from one country to another and even across oceans. Of course, they all cross-dressed, adopted a male name and in most cases, there appears to have been a conscious attempt to reproduce behaviour that was culturally associated with masculinity. They all had sexual or sentimental relationships with women who claimed to have believed that they were male, which is to say that they possessed male sexual organs. Such claims should not be taken at face value but neither should they be dismissed out of hand as incredible or false.

In some cases, the individuals claimed to have avoided sexual contact to prevent discovery, but in others, the women accusing them appear to have been fooled by the use of fingers or dildos during intercourse to simulate an aroused, erect penis. Sexual intercourse happened in the dark or obscurity and Maria Duran and the other individuals involved took great care to prevent their partners from touching or seeing their groin. It is indeed striking that Eugenia Falleni's two wives apparently had no idea that Eugenia possessed female genitalia and were content to have sexual relations in complete darkness, just as many of the witnesses against Maria who had sexual relations with her asserted that they had been convinced that Maria must have a penis and therefore was a man. Just as Maria Duran admitted to using a dildo or finger, the police discovered and seized a set of dildoes after Eugenie Falleni's arrest in Sydney.

All these case studies demonstrate the enduring power of deeply entrenched gendered expectations and norms of behaviour in modern Western society. Yet, paradoxically, gendered norms and the male/female binary also greatly facilitate the transing of gender. Social expectations of feminine and masculine behaviour in everyday life, interpersonal relations and sexual relations posit rigid boundaries. Failure to adhere to these boundaries in the early modern Iberian world did not go unnoticed. In 1637, the inquisitorial tribunal of Coimbra in Portugal arrested and prosecuted a cook named Manuel João for 'sodomy'. Witnesses highlighted how his failure to abide by gendered norms awoke their suspicious about his homosexuality. Indeed, they noted that Manuel João sifted wheat, kneaded dough, spun thread at the spinning wheel and carried out 'other occupations that belong to women'.[24] Likewise, the ambiguous sexuality and 'effeminate' behaviour of Pedro Furtado, the parish priest in northern Portugal whose case was discussed by inquisitors in relations to that of Maria Duran, led a number of men to denounce him to the Inquisition for being a woman in 1699–1701.[25]

By the 1730s, when Maria Duran fled from Prullans and began to cross-dress, Iberian churchmen had long debated the seriousness of cross-dressing as a threat to social order and the 'natural' distinction between sexes. They took their cue from prohibitions found in the Bible (Deut. 22.5) and medieval Canon Law (Gratian's Decretum, XXX, cause 6). In the thirteenth century, Saint Thomas Aquinas had condemned cross-dressing as sinful unless it was done 'either in order to hide oneself from enemies, or through lack of other clothes, or for some similar motive'.[26] Translations of Cardinal Thomas Cajetan's sixteenth-century commentary on Aquinas's work appeared in print in Spain and Portugal and included an elaboration that insisted that the blurring of gender identities required serious punishment. Cajetan pointed to theatrical cross-dressing as potentially problematic:

> It is clearly a sin if a man or a woman exchange their clothing because it is forbidden in chapter 22 of Deuteronomy as a thing that is abominable to God and the law states in chapter 30 of the Digest that the woman who dresses as a man should be excommunicated. We understand this to apply to cases in which it is done because of superstition or lust. If it takes place in comedies or masked balls it is tolerable except if [the cross-dressing] occurs continually, in which case it cannot be tolerated because it would be against the good government of the people and against the safeguard of chastity.[27]

Cross-dressing and the crossing of gender identities were certainly a recurrent feature of the early modern European theatre stage, including in the Iberian Peninsula where it provoked heated debates as well as moral panics. The famous Jesuit writer Juan de Mariana (1536–1624) argued in a treatise on spectacles that the sight of female actors dressed as men had the power 'to corrupt men' but that it was preferable to employ female actors than to have boys dressed as women. Objectors, however, feared the subversive example represented by women actors dressed as men.[28] Laws and edicts banning female cross-dressing or, curiously, only allowing female actors to wear male attire from the waist up and when the play absolutely required it, were promulgated in Spain in 1608, 1615, 1641, 1653, 1672 and 1675.[29] Their very frequency suggests a lack of enforcement and that these were responses to temporary moral panics, much like sumptuary laws. The fear of effeminacy and the decline of masculinity, especially among the nobility, was the regular subject of anxious diatribes by many Iberian authors writing not just about clothing but also hairstyles, use of cosmetics and behaviour. In 1609, the renowned Spanish man of letters Francisco de Quevedo pointed in a sardonic remark to the ease (disturbing in his eyes) with which 'natural' gendered identities could be blurred:

> What is most to be regretted is the manner in which men imitate women in their fine dress and anything effeminate so that now a man is less appealing to a woman than one woman to another. Some men appear through their finery to be sorry to have been born male and others presume to teach Nature how to turn a man into a woman. The result is that their sex is uncertain and [this practice has caused to appear] previously unknown vices, which has been the grounds for the promulgation of new laws.[30]

Another author bemoaned in 1619 that Spain was doomed if 'customs are so corrupted that men adorn themselves and treat themselves like women'.[31] Maria

Duran's story illustrates how gender could be 'transed' on the stage of real life. Maria's success, however, depended not just on cross-dressing or superficial markers as the previous writers claimed. Beyond gendering clothing, Maria had to exploit and usurp deeply entrenched cultural tropes and norms defining gender.

Conclusion

Between 1741 and 1744, Maria's sex and gender were on trial. The inquisitors sought to determine whether Maria was a 'man', a 'woman' or even a 'hermaphrodite' on the basis of the possession of male or female genitals and by seeking to rationalize the witnesses' testimony and Maria's failure to adhere to gendered norms of behaviour. Maria Duran's sense of identity, if she actually had a clear sense of it, must remain a mystery. Because of the nature of the evidence available to us, we can only accept that there are different ways in which we can interpret Maria's behaviour. In modern parlance, Maria may have been as Lesbian, butch, non-binary or transgender depending on the meaning and emphasis that one puts on the witness testimony or Maria's own claims. To focus on this aspect of Maria's story, however, is to lose sight of the wider significance of Maria's trial. An analysis of Maria's life and trial must also reflect on the wider social and cultural context of early modern Europe and what Maria and other, similar trials reveal about it.

In the eighteenth century, medical authorities in Europe gradually turned against the Galenic 'one-sex' model of Classical Antiquity and adopted a male/female binary. The existence of 'hermaphrodites' was, accordingly, increasingly rejected. The trial of Maria Duran demonstrates that some medical practitioners, churchmen and 'ordinary' women could still consider it as a possible explanation in the case of an individual whose sex and gender were ambiguous. Yet, following the idea of a male/female binary, the debate among the inquisitors judging Maria's case rapidly turned away from the possibility of 'hermaphroditism' to that of Maria possessing a clitoris that might substitute for a penis during sexual arousal. Notwithstanding this, Maria Duran's ability to 'trans' gender so successfully had little to do with changing medical models of human sex models.

Maria's successful transing of gender would have been impossible without the prevalence of social and cultural gender norms that created strongly gendered stereotypes of masculine and feminine behaviour. Beyond the debates among medical authorities, the male and female binary appears to have been a prevalent view in everyday life in eighteenth-century Spain and Portugal. This is evident in the witnesses' choice of the terms 'perfect man' (*homem perfeito*) and 'perfect woman' (*mulher perfeita*) when they described Maria's body. Maria was consistently described by witnesses as behaving 'like a man' during sexual intercourse. Likewise, Maria Duran employed similar language herself and claimed in her defence to be a 'true woman' (*verdadeira mulher*). Such expressions demonstrate that most individuals in eighteenth-century Portugal linked biological sex and gender. Even the inquisitors, in their final verdict, used the same expression. Maria was found guilty of having made a demonic pact based on the 'fact' that despite 'being a true woman without a male sex organ', she had 'exceed the powers of Nature' and 'ejaculated inside of the women with whom she had disgusting [sexual] relations'. It is clear that Maria was aware of these gendered norms of appearance and behaviour and of the performativity of gender. Maria deliberately exploited these norms to the full, whether it was to pass as a male soldier in Spain or to convince the women in Portugal to whom she was sexually attracted that she was male. Whatever Maria's sexuality or sense of gender identity was, the performativity of gender allowed Maria become a successful performer herself, transing gender until she ended up in the cells of the Inquisition.

Epilogue

What became of Maria Duran after her release from the Inquisition's jail in Lisbon and departure from Portugal in July 1744 remains a mystery. Maria Duran's shaky signature on the official release form and her pledge never to return to Portugal or its overseas colonies are both the last words written in the trial dossier and the last documentary evidence of Maria's existence. It is possible that documents in a Spanish archive will one day shed some light on Maria's later life. If such documents exist, historians have not yet found them. The inquisitorial tribunal in Lisbon archived Maria Duran's trial dossier, filing it away with thousands of other trial dossiers in the tribunal's secret archives. Fortunately for modern historians, the trial dossier survived a number of upheavals. The cataclysmic earthquake of 1 November 1755 that levelled much of Lisbon left the inquisitorial palace in ruins, but the secret archives mostly survived, including Maria's trial dossier. When the Portuguese Inquisition was abolished in 1821, one liberal parliamentarian proposed burning all of the Inquisition's archives but this suggestion was not adopted. Instead, the Portuguese government seized the archives and entered them into the official state archives of the *Torre do Tombo*.[1] Today, and following digitalization in 2009, the trial dossier is available online for any researcher or member of the public who wishes to read it.

Were it not for the survival of her trial dossier, Maria's extraordinary life and trial would have vanished into historical oblivion. The only traces of Maria's existence would be the vague, tantalizing references to the 'Catalan hermaphrodite' in the manuscript newsletters preserved in the public library of Évora and the extremely terse (and equally misleading) printed record of Maria's sentence in the *auto-da-fé*. The secrecy in which the trial took place and the inaccessibility of the trial dossier to those not working for the Inquisition meant that Maria Duran's story did not attract media interest at the time. The public may have whispered about the case and exchanged news in written letters and newsletters about the 'Catalan hermaphrodite' but not the official, censored press. The *Gazeta de Lisboa Occidental*, a printed newssheet circulating in Lisbon and the rest of Portugal, does not mention the case at all. This was not because the editors of the *Gazeta* recoiled from sensational stories about 'monsters' or the unusual. In October 1739, for instance, the *Gazeta de Lisboa Occidental* featured a report on the birth and death of an infant with 'two perfect faces' (craniofacial duplication) in the district of Chaves in northern Portugal.[2] The case of Maria Duran, however, was too scandalous and threatened the prestige of many religious institutions. It would never have passed official censorship.

So why does the story of Maria Duran's trial matter? Why does it deserve to be brought into the limelight by modern historical study? Modern moral panics about queer sexuality, gender theory and *LGBTQIA* rights frequently tend to associate them with an alleged recent moral decadence of Western countries and cultures and portrays them as a modern, liberal abandonment of age-old 'traditional values'.[3] They often harken back to a perceived 'Golden Age' of sexual binaries defined by cultural and sexual norms ('when men were men and women were women'). Moreover, the critics of gender theory often dismiss or attack it as a 'gender ideology' seeking to 'indoctrinate' the young and the gullible and to pervert society. This is just as much the case in modern Spain and Portugal as elsewhere. In Spain, the ultra-Catholic and far-right organization *HazteOir* ('Make Yourself Heard') gained publicity in 2017 by placing a large advertisement on the side of an orange bus that denied the existence of trans people through the message 'Boys have a penis. Girls have a vulva. Don't let them fool you. If you are born a man, you are a man. If you are a woman, you will continue to be so'.[4] More recently, in 2021, the Spanish far-right party Vox, which received over 15 per cent of the popular vote in the Spanish parliamentary election of November 2019, has used similar rhetoric. Jorge Buxadé, an elected member of the European Parliament for Vox, attacked a law allowing people to change their gender identity as constituting 'the destruction of the whole edifice of our civilization, in one fell swoop'.[5]

Maria's complicated story is an exemplary tale of how sexual and gender nonconformity as well as the 'transing' of gender are not new phenomena tied to modern, 'liberal' conceptions of society and gender. Studied alongside other cases, an analysis of Maria's life helps us to historicize 'trans' lives and attitudes towards gender. The vocabulary and concepts used by modern scholars to analyse transgressive sexuality and gender did not exist in the early modern period, but this cannot be taken as evidence that the 'transing' of gender did not exist either. The more stories like Maria's emerge from archives, the more we learn about the way that gender is a social and cultural construct.

Notes

Introduction

1 Carlo Ginzburg, *The Cheese and the Worms*, translated by John and Anne Tedeschi (Baltimore: Johns Hopkins University Press, 1980); Natalie Zemon Davis, *The Return of Martin Guerre* (Cambridge: Harvard University Press, 1983).

2 Judith Brown, *Immodest Acts: The Life of a Lesbian Nun in Renaissance Italy* (Oxford: Oxford University Press, 1986); Richard Kagan, *Lucrecia's Dreams: Politics and Prophecy in Sixteenth-Century Spain* (Berkeley: University of California Press, 1990); Ulinka Rublack, *The Astronomer and the Witch: Johannes Kepler's Fight for His Mother* (Oxford: Oxford University Press, 2015).

3 J. Arnold, 'The Historian as Inquisitor: The Ethics of Interrogating Subaltern Voices', *Rethinking History*, 2 (1998), pp. 379–86.

4 There is now an extensive literature on this subject. See Thomas Laqueur, *Making Sex: Body and Gender from the Greeks to Freud* (Cambridge: Harvard University Press, 1992); Ruth Gilbert, *Early Modern Hermaphrodites: Sex and Other Stories* (London: Palgrave Macmillan, 2002); Kathleen P. Long, *Hermaphrodites in Renaissance Europe* (Aldershot: Ashgate Publishing, 2006); Alice Domurat Dreger, *Hermaphrodites and the Medical Invention of Sex* (Cambridge: Harvard University Press, 1998); Richard Cleminson and Francisco Vázquez García, *Sex, Identity and Hermaphrodites in Iberia, 1500–1800* (London: Taylor & Francis, 2015); Victor Pueyo, *Cuerpos Plegables: Anatomías de La Excepción En España y En America Latina (Siglos XVI-XVIII)* (Woodbridge: Tamesis, 2016); Marta V. Vicente, *Debating Sex and Gender in Eighteenth-Century Spain* (Cambridge: Cambridge University Press, 2017) and Leah DeVun, *The Shape of Sex: Nonbinary Gender from Genesis to the Renaissance* (New York: Columbia University Press, 2021).

5 Michel Foucault, *The History of Sexuality: 1: The Will to Knowledge* (London: Penguin Books, 2019), Part II: The Repressive Hypothesis.

6 David Valentine, *Imagining Transgender: An Ethnography of a Category* (Durham: Duke University Press, 2007), p. 30.

7 François Soyer, *Ambiguous Gender in Early Modern Spain and Portugal. Inquisitors, Doctors and the Transgression of Gender Norms* (Leiden: Brill, 2012), pp. 210–85.

8 François Soyer, 'The Inquisitorial Trial of a Cross-Dressing Lesbian: Reactions and Responses to Female Homosexuality in 18th-Century Portugal', *Journal of Homosexuality*, 61 no. 11 (2014), pp. 1529–57.

9 John Huxtable Elliott, 'Preface', in *History in the Making* (New Haven: Yale University Press, 2012).
10 Clare Sears, 'All That Glitters: Tran-sing California's Gold Rush Migrations', *GLQ: A Journal in Lesbian and Gay Studies*, 14 (2–3) (2008), pp. 383–402 (quotation from page 384).
11 Jen Manion, *Female Husbands: A Trans History* (Cambridge: Cambridge University Press, 2020), p. 11.
12 Understanding Maria Duran as a homosexual or 'lesbian' is indeed a position I adopted in a brief survey of the case which I published in 2014 but which I would now describe as simplistic. See, Soyer, *The Inquisitorial Trial*, pp. 1529–57.
13 Hubert Wolf, *The Nuns of Sant' Ambrogio, the True Story of a Convent in Scandal* (Oxford: Oxford University Press, 2015).
14 The case of Eleno(a) de Céspedes has been discussed in numerous books and articles in French and English: Michèlle Escamilla, 'A propos d'un dossier inquisitorial des environs de 1590: les étranges amours d'un hermaphrodite', *Amours légitimes-amours illégitimes en Espagne, XVIe–XVIIe siècles*, edited by A. Redondo (Paris: Publ. de la Sorbonne, 1985), pp. 167–82; Israel Burshatin, 'Written on the Body: Slave or Hermaphrodite in Sixteenth-Century Spain', *Queer Iberia: Sexualities, Cultures and Crossings from the Middle Ages to the Renaissance* (Durham: Duke University Press, 1999), pp. 420–56 and 'Elena alias Eleno. Genders, Sexualities and "Race" in the Mirror of Natural History in Sixteenth-Century Spain', in *Gender Reversals and Gender Cultures. Anthropological and Historical perspectives*, edited by S. Ramet (London: Routledge, 1996), pp. 105–22; R. Kagan and Abigail Dyer, *Inquisitorial Inquiries: Brief Lives of Secret Jews and Other Heretics* (Baltimore: Johns Hopkins University Press, 2004), 36–59; Lisa Vollendorf, *The Lives of Women: A New History of Inquisitorial Spain* (Nashville: Vanderbilt University Press, 2005), 11–32.
15 See Sherry Velasco, *The Lieutenant Nun. Transgenderism, Lesbian Desire, and Catalina de Erauso* (Austin: University of Texas Press, 2000).
16 Thomas A. Abercrombie, *Passing to América. Antonio (Née María) Yta's Transgressive, Transatlantic Life in the Twilight of the Spanish Empire* (University Park: Penn State University Press, 2018).

1 The fugitive wife from a small village in the Pyrenees

1 Paul Aebischer and Joan Martí i Castell, *Estudis de toponímia catalana* (Barcelona: Institut d'Estudis Catalans, 2006), p. 126; *Els Castells. Catalans* (Barcelona: R. Dalmau, 1973), 1973, vol. 4, p. 677.

2 All the information about Maria's early life that is contained in this chapter is derived from her interrogation by the Inquisition and the testimony of witnesses interrogated in Catalonia by the inquisitors of Barcelona. ANTT, *Inquisição de Lisboa, processo* no. 9,230, fols. 86r–103v and 127r–138v.

3 Josep Iglésies, *Estadístiques de Població de Catalunya. El Primer Vicenni del Segle XVIII*, vol. III (Barcelona: Fundació Salvador Vives Casajuana, 1974), p. 1197.

4 Josep Albert Planes I Ball, *El general Moragues i la fortalesa de Castellciutat. La Guerra de Successió a la Seu d Urgell* (Barcelona: Farell Editors, 2011).

5 Enrique Giménez López, 'Conflicto armado con Francia y guerrilla austracista en Cataluña (1719–1720)', *Hispania: Revista española de historia* 65, no. 220 (2005), pp. 543–600; Henry Kamen, *Philip V of Spain* (New Haven: Yale University Press, 2001), pp. 112–17.

6 The name of 'chemin to Noailles' came from the Duc de Noailles, who established the route in 1691. For a detailed description see, Joseph Napoléon Fervel, *Campagnes de le révolution française dans les Pyrénées orientales, 1793–95* (Paris: Pillet fils aîné, 1853), vol. 2, p. 368.

7 Joan Mercader i Riba, 'El Valle de Arán, la Nueva Planta y la invasión anglo-francesa de 1719', *Actas del Primer Congreso Internacional de Estudios Pirenáicos, San Sebastián, 1950* (Zaragoza: Instituto de Estudios Pirenaicos, 1952), vol. 6, pp. 193–217; Enrique Giménez López (2005) 'Conflicto armado con Francia y guerrilla austracista en Cataluña (1719–1720)', *Hispania: Revista española de historia* 65, no. 220, pp. 543–600; Conde de Clonard, *Historia orgánica de las armas de Infanteria y Caballeria españolas desde la creacion del ejercito permanente hasta el dia* (Madrid: Imprenta a cargo de Don Francisco del Castillo, 1859), Tome XV, p. 77.

8 Socorro Sancho i Valverde and Carme Ros i Navarro, 'La població de catalunya en perspectiva històrica', in *La Societat Catalana*, edited by Salvador Giner (Barcelona: Generalitat de Catalunya, 1998), pp. 91–116.

9 The popular expression *morbo gallico* was adopted by early writers such as Ulrich von Hutten in his widely read 1519 treatise *De Guaiaci Medicina et morbo Gallico* (Mainz: In aedibus Joannis Scheffer 1519) and Niccolò Massa in his *Liber de morbo Gallico* (Venice: In aedibus Francisci Bindoni, ac Maphei Pasini, 1527).

10 Brenda J. Baker, George J. Armelagos, Marshall Joseph Becker, Don Brothwell, Andrea Drusini, Marie Clabeaux Geise, Marc A. Kelley, et al. 'The Origin and Antiquity of Syphilis: Paleopathological Diagnosis and Interpretation [and Comments and Reply]', *Current Anthropology* 29, no. 5 (1988), pp. 703–37.

11 Pedro de Torres, *Libro que trata de la enfermedad de las bubas* (Madrid: Por Luiz Sanchez, 1600), pp. 100–1.

12 On the medical and social history of syphilis in early modern Spain; see, Cristian Berco, *From Body to Community: Venereal Disease and Society in Baroque Spain* (Toronto: University of Toronto Press, 2016).

2 Maria becomes a soldier

1 This chapter is reconstructed from information that Maria Duran provided during her interrogations on 13 March 1741; 8 July 1741 and 11 July 1742 as well as the testimony from witnesses in Catalonia and collected by the Inquisition of Barcelona. ANTT, *Inquisição de Lisboa, Processo* no. 9,230, fols. 86r–94v; 96r–103v; 122r–138v and 329r–338v.

2 A. Roger Ekirch, 'Sleep We Have Lost: Pre-Industrial Slumber in the British Isles', *American Historical Review* 106, no. 2 (2001), pp. 343–86; Lawrence Wright, *Warm & Snug: The History of the Bed* (London: Routledge, 1962). For Spain, see, Juan Lafora, *Dormitorios. La historia del dormitorio* (Madrid: Cigüeña, 1950), p. 83.

3 *Novísima recopilación de las Leyes de España. Tomo V, Libro XII, Tit. XXX* (Madrid, s.n.: 1805), pp. 427–9.

4 F. Soyer, *Ambiguous Gender in Early Modern Spain and Portugal: Inquisitors, Doctors and the Transgression of Gender Norms* (Leiden: E. J. Brill, 2012), pp. 27–38.

5 Francisco Pasqual, *Sermon de la Concepcion de Maria Santissima Nuestra Señora, a quien con el amparo de S. Francisco Xavier venera por su tutelar el nobilissimo Regimiento de dragones de Villaviciosa, que predicò en la solene fiesta qve en sv primera formacion y obsequioso acto de bendicion de sus estandartes le dedicò dicho Regimiento siendo su coronel el muy ilustre señor Don Juan de Sentmenat, y de Oms, Cavallero del Orden de S. Juan de Jerusalen, &c. dia 21 de Mayo de 1735. Patente el Ssmo Sacramento, en el magnifico templo del colegio de N. Sra. de Belen de la Compañia de Jesus de Barcelona* (Barcelona: en la imprenta de Maria Marti viuda, n.d.).

6 Biblioteca Nacional de España (Madrid), Anon, *Soldados de diferentes cuerpos de Infantería y Caballería*, DIB/13/6/13.

7 ANTT, *Inquisição de Lisboa, processo* no. 9,230, fols. 101r–101v.

8 Rudolf Dekker and Lotte C. van de Pol, *The Tradition of Female Transvestism in Early Modern Europe* (London: St. Martin's Press, 1989), pp. 90–103.

9 Ibid.; Sherry Velasco, *The Lieutenant Nun. Transgenderism, Lesbian Desire, and Catalina de Erauso* (Austin: University of Texas Press, 2000).

10 *Novísima recopilación de las Leyes de España. Tomo V, Libro XII, Tit. XIX, Ley XV* (Madrid, s.n.: 1805), p. 389.

11 María F. Carbajo Isla, 'La población de la villa de Madrid desde finales del siglo XVI hasta mediados del siglo XIX', *Boletín de la Asociación de Demografía Histórica*, 2, no. 3 (1984), pp. 4–18.

12 María F. Carbajo Isla. 'La Inmigración a Madrid (1600–1850)', *Reis: Revista Española de Investigaciones Sociológicas* 32 (1985), pp. 67–100.

13 Julián de Sessé Broto y Coscojuela, *Comentario, epitome, equestre, origen, calidades, exercicios, jornadas, progressos, ò servicios de campaña, y prerrogativas del Real*

Cuerpo de Cavalleros Guardias de Corps, en el feliz reynado de nuestro Catholico Monarcha D. Phelipe V. (que Dios guarde.) en cinco manifiestos (Madrid: en la Imprenta de Joachin Sanchez, 1739), p. 46.

3 Maria Duran travels to Lisbon

1 Unless it is referenced separately, the information contained in this chapter is derived from Maria's claims during her various interrogations. ANTT, *Inquisição de Lisboa, Processo* no. 9,230, fols. 86r–103v.

2 See, Maria Beatriz Nizza da Silva, *D. João V* (Rio de Mouros: Temas e Debates: 2009).

3 Ibid., p. 214.

4 Thomas Cox, *Relação do Reino de Portugal. 1701*, edited by Maria Leonor Machado de Sousa (Lisbon: Biblioteca Nacional, 2007), p. 252.

5 Anon., *Description de la ville de Lisbonne* (Paris: Pierre Prault, 1730), pp. 8 and 13.

6 See Giuseppe Marcocci and José Pedro Paiva, *História da Inquisição Portuguesa (1536–1821)* (Lisbon: Esfera dos Livros, 2013).

7 Charles Dellon, *Relation de l'inquisition de Goa* (Leiden: chez Daniel Gaasbeek, 1687), p. 161.

8 Laurinda Abreu, 'Beggars, Vagrants and Romanies. Repression and Persecution in Portuguese Society (14th–18th Centuries)', *Hygiea Internationalis* 6, no. 1 (2007), pp. 41–66.

9 *Ordenações Manuelinas*, facsimile of the 1512–13 edition with an introduction by J. J. Alves Dias (Lisbon: Centro de Estudos Históricos. Universidade Nova de Lisboa, 2002), *Livro* V, *tit.* XXXI.

10 Nizza da Silva, *D. João V*, p. 220.

11 John Coustos, *The Sufferings of John Coustos for Free-Masonry and for His Refusing to Turn Roman Catholic in the Inquisition at Lisbon* (London: W. Strahan, 1746), p. 18.

12 BPE, *Códice* CIV, 1-10d (31 March 1742 and 28 November 1744).

13 João Luís Lisboa, Tiago C. P. dos Reis Miranda, and Fernanda Olival (eds), *Gazetas Manuscritas da Biblioteca Pública de Évora. Vol.* 3 (Lisbon: Edições Colibri, 2011), pp. 201 and 323.

14 BPE, Códice CIV, 1-10d (10 October 1744).

15 http://dbe.rah.es/biografias/40795/jose-jofreu (accessed 13 January 2021).

16 Rafael Bluteau, *Vocabulario Portuguez E Latino Q - S Volume 7* (Lisbon: Pascoal da Sylva, 1720), p. 157.

17 Laurinda Abreu, *The Political and Social Dynamics of Poverty, Poor Relief and Health Care in Early-Modern Portugal* (Oxford: Taylor & Francis, 2016), pp. 165–6.

18 Ibid., pp. 147–92.
19 Ibid.
20 Thomas Cox, *Relação do Reino de Portugal. 1701,* edited by Maria Leonor Machado de Sousa (Lisbon: Biblioteca Nacional, 2007), p. 116.
21 Marco Liberato, 'Trento, a Mulher e Controlo Social: O Recolhimento de S. Manços', in *Igreja, caridade e assistência na Península Ibérica (sécs. XVI-XVIII)*, edited by Laurinda Abreu (Évora: Publicações do Cidehus, 2004), pp. 275–89. http://books.openedition.org/cidehus/208.
22 Abreu, *The Political and Social Dynamics of Poverty*, pp. 174–5.
23 Cox, *Relação do Reino de Portugal*, p. 146.
24 Victor Ribeiro, *A Santa Casa da Misericórdia de Lisboa: subsidios para a sua historia, 1498–1898: instituição, vida historica, estado presente e seu futuro* (Lisbon: Academia Real das Sciencias, 1902), p. 55.
25 Nizza da Silva, *D. João V*, pp. 34–7; João Luís Lisboa; Tiago C. P. dos Reis Miranda, and Fernanda Olival (eds), *Gazetas Manuscritas da Biblioteca Pública de Évora* (Lisbon: Edições Colibri), vol. 1 (2002), pp. 111 and 128; vol. 2 (2005), pp. 58, 64, 119, 157, 167, 246 and 281; vol. 3 (2011), pp. 206, 210, 213, 292, 311, 335, 344, 354 and 358.

4 Sex and suspicion in the *recolhimentos* of Lisbon

1 Unless it is referenced separately, all the information contained in this chapter is derived from Maria's claims during her various interrogations as well as the interrogations of various women from the *recolhimentos* involved and Father Pedro de Santa Clara. ANTT, *Inquisição de Lisboa, Processo* no. 9,230, especially fols. 7r–52r; 86r–94v; 104r–116v; 202r–207r; 217r–230v; 236r–241r; 252r–261v; 329r–338v and 342r–345r.
2 João Bautista de Castro, *Mappa de Portugal Antigo, e Moderno* (Lisbon, 1763), Tome 2, parts 3 and 4, p. 237.
3 ANTT., *Inquisição de Lisboa, Processo* no. 9,230, fols. 50r–52v and 202r–207r.
4 ANTT., *Inquisição de Lisboa, Processo* no. 9,230, fols. 342r–345r.
5 BNP., *História da Fundação do Recolhimento de Nossa Senhora da Encarnação e Carmo, Instituído por Isabel Francisca, sob a Direcção do Padre Álvaro Cienfuegos, na Rua de São Bernardino, Rilhafoles* (Lisboa, *c.* 1749), MSS. 254, no. 51, fols. 1r–9v; See also http://patrimoniocultural.cm-lisboa.pt/lxconventos/ficha_imprimir.aspx?id=615 (accessed 11 December 2020).
6 ANTT., *Inquisição de Lisboa, Processo* no. 9,230, fols. 7r–10r and 217r–220v.
7 ANTT., *Inquisição de Lisboa, Processo* no. 9,230, fols. 11r–18r.
8 ANTT., *Inquisição de Lisboa, Processo* no. 9,230, fols. 13r–14v.
9 ANTT., *Inquisição de Lisboa, Processo* no. 9,230, fols. 15r–15v.

10 ANTT., *Inquisição, Conselho Geral, Habilitações*, António, *maço*. 76, doc. 1483; ANTT., *Registo Geral de Mercês, Mercês de D. João V, livro*. 23, fol. 293r; Adelaide Brochado, 'Relação dos oficiais de saúde na cidade de Lisboa (1504–1775)', *Cadernos do Arquivo Municipal*, 2ª Série No. 11 (janeiro-junho 2019), pp. 149–213 (see, pp. 170–5).

11 ANTT., *Inquisição de Lisboa, Processo* no. 9,230, fols. 35r–38r.

5 The nuns and novices of Our Lady of Paradise

1 William Dalrymple, *Travels through Spain and Portugal, in 1774; with a Short Account of the Spanish Expedition against Algiers, in 1775* (London: printed for J. Almon, opposite Burlington-House, Piccadilly, 1777), pp. 154–5.

2 José Vicente Serrão, 'População e rede urbana nos séculos XVI-XVIII', in *História dos municípios e do poder local*, edited by César Oliveira (Lisbon: Círculo de Leitores, 1996), p. 77.

3 Luis de Cacegas and Luis de Sousa, *Historia De S. Domingos: Particular Do Reino E Conquistas de Portugal* (Lisbon: Antonio Rodrigues Galhardo, 1767), pp. 48–55.

4 BNP., Manuscritos Reservados IL 152. *Regra e estatutos do Convento de Santa Maria do Paraíso de Évora, pertencente à Ordem de São Domingos* [1537].

5 ANTT, *Ministerio das Finanças, caixa* 1916, *capilha* 1.

6 ANTT., *Ministerio das Finanças, caixa* 1916, *capilha* 2; Inês Palma and Antónia Fialho Conde, 'Dos espaços que o tempo silencia: novos dados para a interpretação do conjunto edificado do convento dominicano de Nª Sr.ª do Paraíso (Évora)', *Almansor. Revista de Cultura* 3 (2017), pp. 71–98.

7 ANTT., *Mosteiro de Nossa Senhora do Paraiso de Evora, livro* 1.

8 Raphael Bluteau, *Vocabulario Portuguez e Latino, Vol. 3* (Coimbra: Real Collegio das Artes da Companhia de Jesu, 1713), p. 289.

9 ANTT., *Inquisição de Lisboa, processo* no. 9,230, fols. 171r–181v.

10 ANTT., *Inquisição de Lisboa, processo* no. 9,230, fols. 59r–66v and 277r–281v.

11 ANTT., *Inquisição de Lisboa, processo* no. 9,230, fols. 70r–74v and 282r–286r.

12 ANTT., *Inquisição de Lisboa, processo* no. 9,230, fols. 60r–70r; 75r–78r; 78r–79v and 82r–84r.

13 ANTT., *Inquisição de Lisboa, processo* no. 9,230, fols. 75r–78r and 80r–82v.

14 ANTT., *Inquisição de Lisboa, processo* no. 9,230, fols. 72r–72v.

15 ANTT., *Inquisição de Lisboa, processo* no. 9,230, fols. 4r–4v.

16 BPE., Cod. CIV/1-9 d., *Gazetas Manuscritas*, no. 10. Saturday 4 March 1741.

6 Enter the Inquisition

1 Unless referenced separately, the information in this chapter is derived from ANTT., *Inquisição de Lisboa, Processo* no. 9,230, fols. 1r and 86r–156v.

2 Giuseppe Marcocci and José Pedro Paiva, *História da Inquisição Portuguesa (1536–1821)* (Lisbon: Esfera dos Livros, 2013); for the number of trials for judaizing in Portugal, see Francisco Bethencourt, *The Inquisition. A Global History, 1478–1834* (Cambridge: Cambridge University Press, 2009), p. 345.

3 Luís da Cunha, *Instruções inéditas a Marco António de Azevedo Coutinho*, edited by Pedro de Azevedo (Coimbra: Imprensa da Universidade, 1929), p. 45.

4 Claude-Henri Frèches, *António José da Silva et l'Inquisition* (Lisbon: Fundação Calouste Gulbenkian, 1982).

5 José Eduardo Franco and Paulo de Assunção, *As Metamorfoses de um polvo: Religião e política nos Regimentos da Inquisição Portuguesa (séculos XVI-XIX)* (Lisboa: Prefácio, 2004).

6 Bethencourt, *The Inquisition*, pp. 341–2.

7 Franco and de Assunção, *As Metamorfoses de um polvo*, pp. 362–3.

8 Francisco Bethencourt, 'Portugal: A Scrupulous Inquisition', in *Early Modern European Witchcraft: Centres and Peripheries*, edited by B. Ankarloo and G. Henningsen (Oxford: Clarendon Press, 1990), pp. 403–22.

9 José Pedro Paiva, *Bruxaria e superstição num pais sem 'caça as bruxas' 1600–1774* (Lisbon: Notícias, 1997).

10 See, for instance, ANTT., *Inquisição de Lisboa, processo* no. 1,826 (1729–31, trial of Maria da Encarnação).

11 On the history of the *Estaus* palace, see Delminda Maria Miguéns Rijo, 'Palácio dos Estaus de Hospedaria Real a Palácio da Inquisição e Tribunal do Santo Ofício', *Cadernos do Arquivo Municipal*. ISSN 2183-3176. 2ª Série, 5 (2016), pp. 19–49.

12 ANTT., *Inquisição, Conselho Geral, livro* 470, fols. 3r–8r.

13 John Coustos, *The Sufferings of John Coustos for Freemasonry and for His Refusing to Turn Roman Catholic in the Inquisition at Lisbon* (London: W. Strahan, 1746), pp. 19–20.

14 See, Isabel Mendes Drumond Braga, *Viver e morrer nos cárceres do Santo Ofício* (Lisboa: Esfera dos livros, 2015).

15 BPE., Cod. CIV, 1–9 d., *Gazetas Manuscritas*, no. 9. Saturday 4 March 1741.

16 Ibid.

17 ANTT., *Inquisição de Lisboa, processo* no. 9,230, fols. 98v–99v.

18 François Soyer, 'Enforcing Religious Repression in an Age of World Empires: Assessing the Global Reach of the Spanish and Portuguese Inquisitions', *History: The Journal of the Historical Association* 100, no. 341 (2015), pp. 331–53.

7 Maria on trial

1 Unless referenced separately, the information in this chapter is derived from ANTT., *Inquisição de Lisboa, processo* no. 9,230, fols. 157r–316r.
2 Saint Thomas Aquinas, *Summa Theologiae: On Unnatural Sex* II-II, 154, 11. https://www.newadvent.org/summa/3154.htm#article11 (accessed 11 November 2022).
3 A. A. De Aguiar, 'Crimes e delitos sexuais em Portugal na época das Ordenações (sexualidade anormal)', *Archivo de Medicina Legal* 3 (1930), p. 15.
4 Gregorio López, *Las siete partidas del muy noble rey Don Alfonso el Sabio glosadas por el licenciado Gregorio Lopez* (Madrid: Compañía General de Impresores y Libreros del Reino, 1843–4), p. 476.
5 AHN., *Inquisición, libro* no. 962, fol. 8v. As cited by Sherry Velasco, *Lesbians in Early Modern Spain*, translated by Sherry Velasco (Nashville: Vanderbilt University Press, 2011), pp. 38–9.
6 D. Francisco de Castro, *Regimento do Santo Oficio da Inquisição dos Reinos de Portugal* (Lisbon: Manoel da Sylva, 1640), *Livro* III, *Título* 25, article 13.
7 See the handful of cases described in Paulo Drumond Braga, *Filhas de Safo. Uma história da homossexualidade feminina em Portugal* (Alfragide: Texto História, 2010).
8 ANTT., *Inquisição de Lisboa, Processos* nos. 1,942; 5,127; 11,458 and 11,459.
9 ANTT., *Inquisição de Lisboa, processo* no. 9,230, fol. 160v.
10 José Eduardo Franco and Paulo de Assunção, *As Metamorfoses de um polvo: Religião e política nos Regimentos da Inquisição Portuguesa (séculos XVI-XIX)* (Lisboa: Prefácio, 2004), pp. 308–9.
11 Franco and de Assunção, *As Metamorfoses de um polvo*, pp. 269–70.
12 L. M. Sinistrari d'Ameno, *De delictis, et poenis tractatus absolutissimus* (Venice: Albriccius, 1700). See also *Peccatum Mutum*, edited and translated by M. Summers (Paris: Collection Le Ballet de Muses, 1958).

8 'A real woman and not a hermaphrodite': The anatomical examination of Maria Duran

1 Unless referenced separately, the information in this chapter is derived from ANTT., *Inquisição de Lisboa, processo* no. 9,230, fols. 317r–328r.
2 Thomas Laqueur, *Making Sex: Body and Gender from the Greeks to Freud* (Cambridge: Harvard University Press, 1992).
3 Ambroise Paré, *On Monsters and Marvels*, translated and edited by Janis L. Pallister (Chicago: University of Chicago Press, 1982), pp. 31–3.

4 See, Helen King, *The One-Sex Body on Trial: The Classical and Early Modern Evidence* (London: Routledge, 2013) and Kathleen P. Long, *Hermaphrodites in Renaissance Europe* (London: Taylor & Francis, 2006).

5 See, Michael Stolberg, 'A Woman Down to Her Bones: The Anatomy of Sexual Difference in the Sixteenth and Early Seventeenth Centuries', *Isis* 94, no. 2 (2003), pp. 274–99. Translation by M. Stolberg.

6 Richard Cleminson and Francisco Vázquez García, *Sex, Identity, and Hermaphrodites in Iberia, 1500–1800* (London: Pickering & Chatto, 2013), pp. 17–19.

7 Amatus Lusitanus, *Curationum medicinalium centuriæ quatuor* (Venice: Apud Balthesarem Constantium, 1557), pp. 274–5.

8 See, Sherry Velasco, *Male Delivery. Reproduction, Effeminacy and Pregnant Men in Early Modern Spain* (Nashville: Vanderbilt University Press, 2006), 94–9.

9 For a detailed discussion of the differing opinions of Iberian medical authorities see Cleminson and Vázquez García, *Sex, Identity, and Hermaphrodites*, pp. 11–39 and 85–110.

10 Augustine of Hippo, *City of God*, book 16, chapter 8, translated by Henry Bettenson (London: Penguin, 1976), pp. 661–3.

11 Paré, *On Monsters and Marvels*, pp. 26–30.

12 François Soyer, 'The Inquisition and the "Priestess of Zafra": Hermaphroditism and Gender Transgression in Seventeenth-Century Spain', *Annali Della Scuola Normale Superiore di Pisa. Classe di Lettere E Filosofia, Serie* 5, 1, no. 2 (2009), pp. 535–62.

13 James Parsons, *A Mechanical and Critical Enquiry into the Nature of Hermaphrodites* (London: printed for J. Walthoe, 1741). See pages xvi–xvii.

14 Robert James, *A Medicinal Dictionary. Vol. II* (London: T. Osborne, 1745). *Hermaphroditus* (unpaginated).

15 Louis, Chevalier de Jaucourt, 'Hermaphrodite', in *The Encyclopedia of Diderot & d'Alembert Collaborative Translation Project*. Ann Arbor: Michigan, University of Michigan Library, 2003. http://hdl.handle.net/2027/spo.did2222.0000.208 (accessed 8 March 2021). Originally published as 'Hermaphrodite', *Encyclopédie ou Dictionnaire raisonné des sciences, des arts et des métiers*, 8:165–7 (Paris, 1765).

16 Julia J. Epstein, 'Either/Or—Neither/Both: Sexual Ambiguity and the Ideology of Gender', *Genders* 7 (1990), pp. 99–142.

17 Marta V. Vicente, *Debating Sex and Gender in Eighteenth-Century Spain*, translated by M. Vicente (Cambridge: Cambridge University Press, 2017), pp. 35–48.

18 Andrés Ferrer de Valdecebro, *El Por qué de todas las cosas* (Madrid: Antonio Delgado, 1727), pp. 22–3.

19 Ignacio Jordán de Assó y del Río and Miguel de Manuel y Rodríguez, *Instituciones del derecho civil de Castilla* (Madrid: Imp. de Francisco Xavier Garcia, 1771), book I, title I, chapter 3.

20 Joseph Jakob von Plenck, *Medicina y cirugia forense ó legal*, translated by Higino Antonio Lorente (Madrid: en la Imprenta de la Viuda e Hijo de Marín, 1796), pp. 135–7.

21 ANTT., *Inquisição de Lisboa, processo* no. 9,230, fols. 316r.

22 ANTT., *Inquisição de Lisboa, processo* no. 9,230, fols. 316r.

23 Bernardo Santucci, *Anatomia do corpo humano: recopilada com doutrinas medicas, chimicas, filosoficas, mathematicas: com indices e estampas, representantes todas as partes do corpo humano: dividida en tres libros* (Lisboa: Antonio Pedrozo Galram, 1739), chapters 11 and 12; On Santucci see, E. E. Franco, *Un anatomico italiano, professore a Lisbona nel secolo xviii, Bernardo Santucci da Cortona (1701–1764). Bio-bibliografijia documentata e illustrata da fijigure* (Arezzo: Viviani, 1925).

24 Philip Verheyen, *Corporis Humani Anatomia* (Louvain: Ægidium Denique, 1693), p. 105.

25 ANTT., *Inquisição de Lisboa, processo* no. 9,230, fols. 318r–320r.

26 ANTT., *Inquisição de Lisboa, processo* no. 9,230, fols. 321r–325v.

27 ANTT., *Inquisição de Lisboa, processo* no. 9,230, fols. 327r–328r.

9 Torture, verdict and punishment

1 ANTT., *Inquisição de Lisboa, processo* no. 9,230, fols. 347r–348r.

2 ANTT., *Inquisição de Lisboa, processo* no. 9,230, fols. 347r–348r.

3 Paolo Zacchia, *Quaestiones medico-legales* (Avignon: Apud Ionnem Piot, via Jacobea sub signo, 1655), pp. 503–4.

4 ANTT., *Inquisição de Lisboa, processo* no. 9,230, fols. 348r–348v.

5 ANTT., *Inquisição de Lisboa, processo* no. 9,230, fols. 348v–349r.

6 ANTT., *Inquisição de Lisboa, processo* no. 9,230, fol. 349r.

7 Christopher S. Mackay and Heinrich Institoris, *The Hammer of Witches: A Complete Translation of the Malleus Maleficarum* (Cambridge: Cambridge University Press, 2009), pp. 194–200 (part 1, question 9). For further details see F. Soyer, 'Androgyny and the Fear of Demonic Intervention in the Early Modern Iberian Peninsula: Ecclesiastical and Popular Responses', *Ordering Emotions in Europe, 1100–1800*, edited by Susan Broomhall (Leiden: E. J. Brill, 2015), pp. 245–62.

8 F. M. Guazzo, *Compendium Maleficarum* (Milan: Ex Collegii Ambrosiani typographia, 1626), book I, chapter 17, pp. 106–9.
9 ANTT., *Inquisição de Lisboa, processo* no. 9,230, fols. 349r–349v.
10 ANTT., *Inquisição de Lisboa, processo* no. 9,230, fols. 348r–349r.
11 AHN., *Sección Inquisición, legajo* 234, *exp*. 24; M. Escamilla, 'A propos d'un dossier inquisitorial des environs de 1590: les étranges amours d'un hermaphrodite', *Amours légitimes-amours illégitimes en Espagne, XVIe–XVIIe siècles*, edited by A. Redondo (Paris: Publications de la Sorbonne, 1985), pp. 167–82; I. Burshatin, 'Written on the Body: Slave or Hermaphrodite in Sixteenth-Century Spain', *Queer Iberia: Sexualities, Cultures and Crossings from the Middle Ages to the Renaissance* (Durham: Duke University Press, 1999), pp. 420–56 and 'Elena Alias Eleno. Genders, Sexualities and "Race" in the Mirror of Natural History in Sixteenth-Century Spain', *Gender Reversals and Gender Cultures: Anthropological and Historical Perspectives*, edited by S. Ramet (London: Routledge, 1996), pp. 105–22; R. Kagan and Abigail Dyer, *Inquisitorial Inquiries: Brief Lives of Secret Jews and Other Heretics* (Baltimore: Johns Hopkins University Press, 2004), pp. 36–59; L. Vollendorf, *The Lives of Women: A New History of Inquisitorial Spain* (Nashville: Vanderbilt University Press, 2005), pp. 11–32.
12 ANTT., *Inquisição de Coimbra, processo* no. 7,622; See F. Soyer, '"Father Paula": The Trial of Father Pedro Furtado (1698–1701)', in *Ambiguous Gender in Early Modern Spain and Portugal. Inquisitors, Doctors and the Transgression of Gender Norms* (Leiden: E. J. Brill, 2012), pp. 125–80.
13 ANTT., *Inquisição de Lisboa, processo* no. 9,230, fols. 348r and 350r.
14 For the various crimes of the convicted heretics, see the list published by the Inquisition in *Lista das Pessoas que Sahiraõ, Condenações, que tiveraõ, e sentenças, que se lêraõ no Auto publico da Fé, que se celebrou na Igreja do Convento de S. Domingos desta Cidade de Lisboa em 21 Junho de 1744* (s.n., s.l., s.d.).
15 D. Francisco de Castro, *Regimento do Santo Ofício da Inquisição dos Reinos de Portugal* (Lisbon: Manoel da Sylva, 1640), *Livro* II, *Título* 14.
16 ANTT., *Inquisição de Lisboa, processo* no. 9,230, fols. 356r–356v.
17 ANTT., *Tribunal do Santo Ofício, Conselho Geral, livro* 470, fol. 4r.
18 John Coustos, *The Sufferings of John Coustos for Freemasonry and for His Refusing to Turn Roman Catholic in the Inquisition at Lisbon* (London: W. Strahan, 1746), p. 62; for the torture session of Coustos in his trial dossier see ANTT., *Inquisição de Lisboa, processo* no. 10,115, fol. 88r.
19 Coustos, *The Sufferings of John Coustos*, pp. 62–3.
20 ANTT., *Inquisição de Lisboa, processo* no. 9,230, fols. 358r–359r.
21 ANTT., *Inquisição de Lisboa, processo* no. 9,230, fols. 358r–359r.
22 ANTT., *Inquisição de Lisboa, processo* no. 9,230, fols. 358r–359r.
23 ANTT., *Inquisição de Lisboa, processo* no. 9,230, fols. 363r–364v.

10 Maria on display: The *auto-da-fé* of 21 June 1744

1 Unless it is referenced separately, the information contained in this chapter is derived from Maria's trial, ANTT., *Inquisição de Lisboa, processo* no. 9,230, fols. 363r–367r.
2 D. Francisco de Castro, *Regimento do Santo Oficio da Inquisição dos Reinos de Portugal* (Lisbon: Manoel da Sylva, 1640), *Livro* II, *Título* 22.
3 On the use of the expression 'pedagogy of fear', see Bartolomé Bennassar, *L'Inquisition espagnole XVe-XIXe siècles* (Paris: Hachette, 1979), pp. 101–37 and Herman Roodenburg, *Social Control in Europe 1500–1800* (Columbus: Ohio State University Press, 2004), vol. 1, p. 126.
4 Maria Luísa Braga, *A Inquisição em Portugal; primeira metade do sec. XVIII: O Inquisidor Geral D. Nuno da Cunha de Athayde e Mello* (Lisbon: INIC, 1992), p. 285.
5 BPE., Cód. CIV, 1-13 d., *Gazetas Manuscritas*, no. 26. Saturday 27 June 1744.
6 ANTT., *Inquisição de Lisboa, processo* no. 4,864.
7 ANTT., *Inquisição de Lisboa, processos* nos. 6,973, 6,973-1 and 16,100.
8 Braga, *A Inquisição em Portugal*, pp. 286–7.
9 John Coustos, *The Sufferings of John Coustos for Freemasonry and for His Refusing to Turn Roman Catholic in the Inquisition at Lisbon* (London: W. Strahan, 1746), pp. 216–23.
10 ANTT., *Inquisição de Lisboa, processo* no. 9,230, fols. 363r–364r.
11 ANTT., *Inquisição de Lisboa, processo* no. 9,230, fol. 365r.
12 BPE., Cód. CIV, 1-13 d., *Gazetas Manuscritas*, no. 26, 27 June 1744.
13 Braga, *A Inquisição em Portugal*, p. 288.
14 Ibid., p. 289. There seems to be errors in the transcription, especially with the Latin passage '*demonios sucubus et incubus adducendo semen humanum ex alia parte*'.
15 Ibid., pp. 286–7.
16 Coustos, *The Sufferings of John Coustos*, pp. 225–8.
17 *Lista das Pessoas que Sahiraõ, Condenações, que tiveraõ, e sentenças, que se lêraõ no Auto publico da Fé, que se celebrou na Igreja do Convento de S. Domingos desta Cidade de Lisboa em 21 Junho de 1744* (s.n., s.l., s.d.).
18 José Antonio Ferrer Benimeli, *Masonería, Iglesia e Ilustración. (T.2): inquisición: procesos históricos (1739–1750)* (Madrid: Fundación Universitaria Española, 1976), p. 469; *Nueva relacion del auto de fe, que celebro en el Convento de Santo Domingo de la ciudad de Lisboa el dia 21. de junio de este año de 1744: en 41. judios penintenciados, penintenciadas, quemados, quemadas, hechiceros, y hechiceras: sendo inquisidor general el eminentissimo, y reverendissimo señor Nuño de Acuña* (Madrid: Juan Pérez, 1744).
19 BPE., Cód. CIV, 1–3 d., *Gazetas Manuscritas*, Num. 26, 27 June 1744.

Transgressive sexuality, transing gender and gender performativity in the trial of Maria Duran

1 David Valentine, *Imagining Transgender: An Ethnography of a Category* (Durham: Duke University Press, 2007), p. 30.
2 Judith C. Brown, *Immodest Acts: The Life of a Lesbian Nun in Renaissance Italy* (Oxford: Oxford University Press, 1986), pp. 172–4; Alison Oram and Annemarie Turnbull, *The Lesbian History Sourcebook: Love and Sex between Women in Britain from 1780 to 1970* (London: Routledge, 2001); Valerie Traub, *The Renaissance of Lesbianism in Early Modern England* (Cambridge: Cambridge University Press, 2002); Caroline Gonda and John C. Benyon, *Lesbian Dames: Sapphism in the Long Eighteenth Century* (Farnham: Ashgate, 2010), pp. 1–7.
3 Gonda and Benyon, *Lesbian Dames*, pp. 1–2.
4 Brown, *Immodest Acts*, pp. 117–18.
5 Lori B. Girshick, *Woman-to-Woman Sexual Violence: Does She Call It Rape?* (Boston: Northeastern University Press, 2002), pp. 63–99.
6 E. P. Seelau and S. M. Seelau, 'Gender-Role Stereotypes and Perceptions of Heterosexual, Gay and Lesbian Domestic Violence', *Journal of Family Violence*, 20 (2005), pp. 363–71; N. Glass and D. Hassouneh, 'The Influence of Gender Role Stereotyping on Women's Experiences of Female Same-Sex Intimate Partner Violence', *Violence Against Women*, 14 (2008), pp. 310–25; R. Barnes, '"Suffering in a Silent Vacuum": Woman-to-Woman Partner Abuse as a Challenge to the Lesbian Feminist Vision', *Feminism and Psychology* 21 (2010), pp. 233–9.
7 *Ordenações Manuelinas*, facsimile of the 1512–13 edition with an introduction by J. J. Alves Dias (Lisbon: Centro de Estudos Históricos. Universidade Nova de Lisboa, 2002), *Livro* V, *tit.* XIIII.
8 Alex Sharpe, *Sexual Intimacy and Gender Identity 'Fraud': Reframing the Legal and Ethical Debate* (London: Taylor & Francis, 2018). For some of the media coverage of the case see https://web.archive.org/save/https://www.bbc.com/news/uk-england-merseyside-34258993 (accessed 16 February 2022) and https://web.archive.org/save/https://www.huffingtonpost.co.uk/entry/prosthetic-penis-case-gayle-newland-convicted-of-sexual-assault_uk_59550a80e4b0da2c7321a71a (accessed 16 February 2022).
9 https://web.archive.org/web/20220525233245/https://news.sky.com/story/tarjit-singh-transgender-man-tricked-women-into-sexual-relationships-by-using-prosthetic-penis-12621386 and https://web.archive.org/save/https://www.standard.co.uk/news/crime/sexual-predator-hannah-walters-posed-as-man-trick-women-into-sex-london-crime-b1002373.html (accessed 26 May 2022).
10 https://www.ohchr.org/EN/Issues/LGBTI/Pages/IntersexPeople.aspx (accessed 5 May 2021).

11 Susan Stryker, *Transgender History* (Berkeley: Seal Press, 2009), p. 1.
12 Christina Lee, *The Anxiety of Sameness in Early Modern Spain* (Manchester: Manchester University Press, 2016), pp. 23–98.
13 Judith Butler, *Gender Trouble: Feminism and the Subversion of Identity* (New York: Routledge, 1990), p. 178.
14 Ibid.
15 See Michele and Gabriel Stepto, *Lieutenant Nun. Memoir of a Basque Transvestite in the New World* (Boston: Beacon, 1996); Mary Elizabeth Perry, 'From Convent to Battlefield: Cross-Dressing and Gendering the Self in the New World of Imperial Spain', in *Queer Iberia: Sexualities, Cultures, and Crossings from the Middle Ages to the Renaissance*, edited by J. Blackmore and G. S. Hutcheson (Durham: Duke University Press, 1999), pp. 394–419; S. Velasco, *The Lieutenant Nun. Transgenderism, Lesbian Desire, and Catalina de Erauso* (Austin: University of Texas Press, 2000); Eva Mendieta, *In Search of Catalina de Erauso: The National and Sexual Identity of the Lieutenant Nun*, translated by A. Prado (Reno: University of Nevada Press, 2009); Matthew Goldmark, 'Reading Habits: Catalina de Erauso and the Subjects of Early Modern Spanish Gender and Sexuality', *Colonial Latin American Review* 24, no. 2 (2015), pp. 215–35.
16 See the bibliography on Elena/o de Céspedes provided in footnote 14 of the Introduction to this book.
17 Jen Manion, *Female Husbands: A Trans History* (Cambridge: Cambridge University Press, 2020).
18 Henry Fielding, *The Female Husband: Or, the Surprising History of Mrs. Mary, Alias MR George Hamilton Who Was Convicted of Having Married a Young Woman of Wells and Lived with Her as Her Husband, Taken from Her Own Mouth since Her Confinement* (London: printed for M. Cooper, 1746).
19 Thomas A. Abercrombie, *Passing to América. Antonio (Née Maria) Yta's Transgressive, Transatlantic Life in the Twilight of the Spanish Empire* (University Park: Pennsylvania State University Press, 2018).
20 Suzanne Falkiner, *Eugenia: A Man* (Sydney: Xoum Publishing, 2014). For the archival records related to the case of Eugenia Falleni, see https://web.archive.org/web/20210507042721/https://www.records.nsw.gov.au/archives/magazine/galleries/eugenia-falleni-convicted-murderer (accessed 7 May 2021).
21 https://arquivos.rtp.pt/conteudos/caso-da-general-teresinha-gomes/ and https://web.archive.org/save/https://arquivos.rtp.pt/conteudos/julgamento-de-maria-teresinha-2/ (accessed 21 May 2021).
22 https://web.archive.org/save/https://www.publico.pt/2007/07/20/jornal/morte-duma--general-223056 (accessed 21 May 2021).
23 https://web.archive.org/save/https://www.imdb.com/title/tt12670228/ (accessed 21 May 2021).

24 ANTT., *Inquisição de Coimbra*, *processo* no. 7,083.
25 See, F. Soyer, *Ambiguous Gender in Early Modern Spain and Portugal. Inquisitors, Doctors and the Transgression of Gender Norms* (Leiden: E. J. Brill, 2012), pp. 125–80.
26 Thomas Aquinas, *Summa Theologiae* II, 2, Question 169, article 2, objection 3. https://www.newadvent.org/summa/3169.htm (accessed 15 March 2022).
27 Thomas Cajetan, *Summa caietana sacada en lenguaje Castellano, con annotaciones de muchas dubdas y casos de consciencia por el M. Paulo de Palacio – Segunda edicion en algunos passos acrecentada* (Lisbon en casa de Ioannes Blauio de Colonia, 1560), fols. 190v-191r.
28 Juan de Mariana, 'De spectaculis', in *De rege et regis institutione* (Toledo: P. Roderigo, 1599), pp. 406–19.
29 N. D. Shergold, *A History of the Spanish Stage: From Medieval Times until the End of the Seventeenth Century* (Oxford: Clarendon Press, 1967), p. 520; Ursula Heise, 'Transvestism and the Stage Controversy in Spain and England, 1580–1680', *Theatre Journal*, 44, no. 3 (1992), pp. 357–74.
30 F. de Quevedo, *España defendida y los tiempos de ahora, de las calumnias de los noveleros y sediciosos*, edited by Francisca Moya del Baño and José Carlos Miralles Maldonado (A Coruña: Universidade da Coruña, SIELAE, 2018), p. 170.
31 Juan de Santa María, *Tratado de república y policía Christiana* (Valencia: Pedro Patricio Mey, 1619), fols. 201r-201v.

Epilogue

1 *Diário das Cortes Geraes Extraordinárias e Constituintes da Nação Portugueza* (1821), 1, pp. 44–5, 63, 113, 354–9 and *Diário do Governo (1821), 6 de Fevereiro, 8 de Fevereiro, 19 de Fevereiro, 26 de Março.* On the abolition of the Portuguese Inquisition, see F. Bethencourt, 'Declínio e extinção do Santo Ofício', *Revista de História Económica e Social*, 20 (May–August 1987), pp. 77–85.
2 *Gazeta de Lisboa Occidental*, no.42, *Quinta feira*, 15 de Outubro de 1739, p. 504.
3 Emil Edenborg, '"Traditional Values" and the Narrative of Gay Rights as Modernity: Sexual Politics beyond Polarization'. *Sexualities* (April 2021). https://doi.org/10.1177/13634607211008067 (accessed 21 March 2022).
4 https://web.archive.org/save/https://english.elpais.com/elpais/2017/06/06/inenglish/1496762308_006073.html (accessed 21 March 2022) and https://web.archive.org/save/https://www.bbc.com/mundo/noticias-39133448 (accessed 21 March 2022).

5 Official Vox video, 'Rueda de prensa de Jorge Buxadé y Patricia Rueda', uploaded to Youtube: https://www.youtube.com/watch?v=rh-A3vUaJMk. Quotation at 35 minutes and 48 seconds (accessed 21 March 2022] and https://web.archive.org/save/https://www.europapress.es/eseuropa/noticia-vox-avisa-llevara-tc-ley-trans-denunciara-banderas-arcoiris-ayuntamientos-20210628143120.html (accessed 21 March 2022).

Bibliography

Primary sources

Manuscript sources

Archivo Histórico Nacional (Madrid).

Sección Inquisición, libro no. 962.

Sección Inquisición, legajo 234, *exp*. 24.

Arquivo Nacional da Torre do Tombo (Lisbon).

Inquisição, Inquisição de Coimbra, Processos 7,083 and 7,622.

Inquisição, Inquisição de Lisboa, Processos 1,826; 1,942; 5,127; 9,230; 10,115; 11,458 and 11,459.

Inquisição, Conselho Geral, Habilitações, António, *maço*. 76, doc. 1483.

Inquisição, Conselho Geral, livro 470.

Ministerio das Finanças, caixa 1916.

Mosteiro de Nossa Senhora do Paraiso de Evora, livro 1.

Registo Geral de Mercês, Mercês de D. João V, livro. 23, fol. 293r.

Biblioteca Nacional de España (Madrid).

Anon, *Soldados de diferentes cuerpos de Infantería y Caballería* (undated) DIB/13/6/13.

Biblioteca Nacional de Portugal (Lisbon).

Anon. MSS. 254, no. 51, *História da Fundação do Recolhimento de Nossa Senhora da Encarnação e Carmo, Instituído por Isabel Francisca, sob a Direcção do Padre Álvaro Cienfuegos, na Rua de São Bernardino, Rilhafoles*, Lisboa [*c*. 1749].

Impressos Reservados, RES-2487-A, *Lista das Pessoas que Sahiraõ, Condenações, que tiveraõ, e sentenças, que se lêraõ no Auto publico da Fé, que se celebrou na Igreja do Convento de S. Domingos desta Cidade de Lisboa em 21 Junho de 1744* (s.n., s.l., s.d.).

Manuscritos Reservados IL 152. *Regra e estatutos do Convento de Santa Maria do Paraíso de Évora, pertencente à Ordem de São Domingos* [1537].

Biblioteca Pública de Évora (Évora).

Códice CIV. *Gazetas Manuscritas.*

Printed sources

Anon., *Description de la ville de Lisbonne*, Paris: Pierre Prault, 1730.

Anon, *Novísima recopilación de las Leyes de España. Tomo V, Libro XII*, Madrid, s.n.: 1805).

Anon, *Nueva relacion del auto de fe, que celebro en el Convento de Santo Domingo de la ciudad de Lisboa el dia 21. de junio de este año de 1744: en 41. judios penintenciados, penintenciadas, quemados, quemadas, hechiceros, y hechiceras: sendo inquisidor general el eminentissimo, y reverendissimo señor Nuño de Acuña*, Madrid: Juan Pérez, 1744.

Anon, *Diário das Cortes Geraes Extraordinárias e Constituintes da Nação Portugueza* (1821), 1, pp. 44–5, 63, 113, 354–9 and *Diário do Governo (1821), 6 de Fevereiro, 8 de Fevereiro, 19 de Fevereiro, 26 de Março.*

Alvarez de Colmenar, Juan, *Annales d'Espagne et de Portugal*, Amsterdam: Chez François l'Honoré et Fils, 1741.

Aquinas, Saint Thomas, *Summa Theologiae*, Second and Revised Edition, 1920 Literally translated by Fathers of the English Dominican Province. Online Edition. https://www.newadvent.org/summa/ (accessed 11 November 2022).

Augustine of Hippo, *City of God*, translated by Henry Bettenson, London: Penguin, 1976.

Bluteau, Rafael, *Vocabulario Portuguez e Latino, Volume 3*, Coimbra: Real Collegio das Artes da Companhia de Jesu, 1713.

Bluteau, Rafael, *Vocabulario Portuguez E Latino Q–S, Volume 7*, Lisbon: Pascoal da Sylva, 1720.

Cacegas Luis de and Luis de Sousa, *Historia De S. Domingos: Particular Do Reino E Conquistas de Portugal*, Lisbon: Antonio Rodrigues Galhardo, 1767.

Cajetan, Thomas, *Summa caietana sacada en lenguaje Castellano, con annotaciones de muchas dubdas y casos de consciencia por el M. Paulo de Palacio -- Segunda edicion en algunos passos acrecentada*, Lisbon: en casa de Ioannes Blauio de Colonia, 1560.

Castro, D. Francisco de, *Regimento do Santo Ofício da Inquisição dos Reinos de Portugal*, Lisbon: Manoel da Sylva, 1640.

Castro, João Bautista de, *Mappa de Portugal Antigo, e Moderno*, Lisbon: Francisco Luiz Ameno, 1763.

Coustos, John, *The Sufferings of John Coustos for Free-Masonry and for His Refusing to Turn Roman Catholic in the Inquisition at Lisbon*, London: W. Strahan, 1746.

Cox, Thomas, *Relação do Reino de Portugal. 1701*. Edited by Maria Leonor Machado de Sousa, Lisbon: Biblioteca Nacional, 2007.

Dalrymple, William, *Travels through Spain and Portugal, in 1774; with a Short Account of the Spanish Expedition Against Algiers, in 1775*, London: printed for J. Almon, opposite Burlington-House, Piccadilly, 1777.

Dellon, Charles, *Relation de l'inquisition de Goa*, Leiden: chez Daniel Gaasbeek, 1687.

Ferrer de Valdecebro, Andrés, *El Por qué de todas las cosas*, Madrid: Antonio Delgado, 1727).

Fielding, Henry, *The Female Husband: Or, the Surprising History of Mrs. Mary, Alias Mr George Hamilton, Who Was Convicted of Having Married a Young Woman of*

Wells and Lived with Her as Her Husband, Taken from Her Own Mouth since Her Vonfinement, London: printed for M. Cooper, 1746.

Gazeta de Lisboa Occidental, no.42, *Quinta feira*, 15 de Outubro de 1739.

Guazzo, F. M., *Compendium Maleficarum*, Milan: Ex Collegii Ambrosiani typographia, 1626.

James, Robert, *A Medicinal Dictionary. Vol. II*, London: T. Osborne, 1745.

Jaucourt, Louis, Chevalier de, 'Hermaphrodite', *Encyclopédie ou Dictionnaire raisonné des sciences, des arts et des métiers*, edited by Denis Diderot and Jean-Baptiste le Rond D'Alembert (Paris, 1765), pp. 165–7.

Jordán de Assó y del Río, Ignacio; and Miguel de Manuel y Rodríguez, *Instituciones del derecho civil de Castilla*, Madrid: Imp. de Francisco Xavier Garcia, 1771.

Lisboa, João Luís, Tiago C. P. dos Reis Miranda, and Fernanda Olival (eds), *Gazetas Manuscritas da Biblioteca Pública de Évora. Vols. 1–3*, Lisbon: Edições Colibri, 2002, 2005 and 2011.

López, Gregorio, *Las siete partidas del muy noble rey Don Alfonso el Sabio glosadas por el licenciado Gregorio Lopez*, Madrid: Compañía General de Impresores y Libreros del Reino, 1843–4.

Lusitanus, Amatus, *Curationum medicinalium centuriæ quatuor*, Venice: Apud Balthesarem Constantium, 1557.

Mackay, Christopher S., and Heinrich Institoris, *The Hammer of Witches: A Complete Translation of the Malleus Maleficarum*, Cambridge: Cambridge University Press, 2009.

Manuel I of Portugal, *Ordenações Manuelinas*, facsimile of the 1512–3 edition with an introduction by J. J. Alves Dias, Lisbon: Centro de Estudos Históricos. Universidade Nova de *Lisboa*, 2002.

Mariana, Juan de, *De rege et regis institutione*, Toledo: P. Roderigo, 1599.

Massa, Niccolò, *Liber de morbo Gallico*, Venice: In aedibus Francisci Bindoni, ac Maphei Pasini, 1527.

Paré, Ambroise, *On Monsters and Marvels*, translated and edited by Janis L. Pallister, Chicago: University of Chicago Press, 1982.

Parsons, James, *A Mechanical and Critical Enquiry into the Nature of Hermaphrodites*, London: printed for J. Walthoe, 1741.

Pasqual, Francisco, *Sermon de la Concepcion de Maria Santissima Nuestra Señora, a quien con el amparo de S. Francisco Xavier venera por su tutelar el nobilissimo Regimiento de dragones de Villaviciosa, que predicò en la solene fiesta qve en sv primera formacion y obsequioso acto de bendicion de sus estandartes le dedicò dicho Regimiento siendo su coronel el muy ilustre señor Don Juan de Sentmenat, y de Oms, Cavallero del Orden de S. Juan de Jerusalen, &c. dia 21 de Mayo de 1735. Patente el Ssmo Sacramento, en el magnifico templo del colegio de N. Sra. de Belen de la Compañia de Jesus de Barcelona*, Barcelona: en la imprenta de Maria Marti viuda, n.d.

Quevedo, Francisco de, *España defendida y los tiempos de ahora, de las calumnias de los noveleros y sediciosos*, edited by Francisca Moya del Baño and José Carlos Miralles Maldonado, A Coruña: Universidade da Coruña, SIELAE, 2018.

Santa María, Juan de, *Tratado de república y policía Christiana*, Valencia: Pedro Patricio Mey, 1619.

Santucci, Bernardo, *Anatomia do corpo humano: recopilada com doutrinas medicas, chimicas, filosoficas, mathematicas: com indices e estampas, representantes todas as partes do corpo humano: dividida en tres libros*, Lisboa: Antonio Pedrozo Galram, 1739.

Sessé Broto y Coscojuela, Julián de, *Comentario, epitome, equestre, origen, calidades, exercicios, jornadas, progressos, ò servicios de campaña, y prerrogativas del Real Cuerpo de Cavalleros Guardias de Corps, en el feliz reynado de nuestro Catholico Monarcha D. Phelipe V. (que Dios guarde.) en cinco manifiestos*, Madrid: en la Imprenta de Joachin Sanchez, 1739.

Sinistrari d'Ameno, L. M., *De delictis, et poenis tractatus absolutissimus*, Venice: Albriccius, 1700.

Sinistrari d'Ameno, L. M., *Peccatum Mutum*, edited and translated by M. Summers Paris: Collection Le Ballet de Muses, 1958.

Torres, Pedro de, *Libro que trata de la enfermedad de las bubas*, Madrid: Por Luiz Sanchez, 1600.

Verheyen, Philip, *Corporis Humani Anatomia*, Louvain: Ægidium Denique, 1693.

Von Plenck, Joseph Jakob, *Medicina y cirugia forense ó legal*, translated by Higino Antonio Lorente, Madrid: en la Imprenta de la Viuda e Hijo de Marín, 1796.

Von Hutten, Ulrich, *De Guaiaci Medicina et morbo Gallico*, Mainz: In aedibus Joannis Scheffer, 1519.

Zacchia, Paolo, *Quaestiones medico-legales*, Avignon: Apud Ionnem Piot, via Jacobea sub signo, 1655.

Secondary sources

Abercrombie, Thomas A., *Passing to América. Antonio (Née María) Yta's Transgressive, Transatlantic Life in the Twilight of the Spanish Empire*, University Park: Penn State University Press, 2018.

Abreu, Laurinda, 'Beggars, Vagrants and Romanies. Repression and Persecution in Portuguese Society (14th–18th Centuries)', *Hygiea Internationalis*, 6, no. 1 (2007), pp. 41–66.

Abreu, Laurinda, *Political and Social Dynamics of Poverty, Poor Relief and Health Care in Early-Modern Portugal*, Oxford: Taylor & Francis, 2016.

Aebischer, Paul and Joan Martí i Castell, *Estudis de toponímia catalana*, Barcelona: Institut d'Estudis Catalans, 2006.

Aguiar, A. A. de, 'Crimes e delitos sexuais em Portugal na época das Ordenações (sexualidade anormal)', *Archivo de Medicina Legal*, 3 (1930), pp. 1–27.

Arnold, John, .The Historian as Inquisitor: The Ethics of Interrogating Subaltern Voices', *Rethinking History*, 2 (1998), pp. 379–86.

Baker, Brenda J., George J. Armelagos, Marshall Joseph Becker, Don Brothwell, Andrea Drusini, Marie Clabeaux Geise, Marc A. Kelley, et al. 'The Origin and Antiquity of Syphilis: Paleopathological Diagnosis and Interpretation [and Comments and Reply]', *Current Anthropology* 29, no. 5 (1988), pp. 703–37.

Barnes, R., '"Suffering in a Silent Vacuum": Woman-to-Woman Partner Abuse as a Challenge to the Lesbian Feminist Vision', *Feminism and Psychology*, 21 (2010), pp. 233–9.

Bennassar, Bartolomé, *L'Inquisition espagnole XVe-XIXe siècles*, Paris: Hachette, 1979.

Berco, Cristian, *From Body to Community: Venereal Disease and Society in Baroque Spain*, Toronto: University of Toronto Press, 2016.

Bethencourt, Francisco, 'Declínio e extinção do Santo Ofício', *Revista de História Económica e Social*, 20 (May–August 1987), pp. 77–85.

Bethencourt, Francisco, 'Portugal: A Scrupulous Inquisition', in *Early Modern European Witchcraft. Centres and Peripheries*, edited by B. Ankarloo and G. Henningsen, Oxford: Clarendon Press, 1990, pp. 403–22.

Bethencourt, Francisco, *The Inquisition: A Global History, 1478–1834*, Cambridge: Cambridge University Press, 2009.

Braga, Maria Luísa, *A Inquisição em Portugal; primeira metade do sec. XVIII: O Inquisidor Geral D. Nuno da Cunha de Athayde e Mello*, Lisbon: INIC, 1992.

Braga, Paulo Drumond, *Filhas de Safo. Uma história da homossexualidade feminina em Portugal*, Alfragide: Texto História, 2010.

Braga, Isabel Mendes Drumond, *Viver e morrer nos cárceres do Santo Ofício*, Lisboa: Esfera dos livros, 2015.

Brochado, Adelaide, 'Relação dos oficiais de saúde na cidade de Lisboa (1504–1775)', *Cadernos do Arquivo Municipal*, 2ª no. 11 (janeiro-junho 2019), pp. 149–213.

Brown, Judith, *Immodest Acts: The Life of a Lesbian Nun in Renaissance Italy*, Oxford: Oxford University Press, 1986.

Burshatin, Israel, 'Elena alias Eleno. Genders, Sexualities and "Race" in the Mirror of Natural History in Sixteenth-Century Spain', *Gender Reversals and Gender Cultures. Anthropological and Historical Perspectives*, edited by S. Ramet, London: Routledge, 1996, pp. 105–22.

Burshatin, Israel, 'Written on the Body: Slave or Hermaphrodite in Sixteenth-Century Spain', in *Queer Iberia: Sexualities, Cultures and Crossings from the Middle Ages to the Renaissance*, edited by Josiah Blackmore and Gregory S. Hutcheson, Durham: Duke University Press, 1999, pp. 420–56.

Butler, Judith, *Gender Trouble: Feminism and the Subversion of Identity*, New York: Routledge, 1990.

Carbajo Isla, María F., 'La población de la villa de Madrid desde finales del siglo XVI hasta mediados del siglo XIX', *Boletín de la Asociación de Demografía Histórica*, 2, no. 3 (1984), pp. 4–18.

Carbajo Isla, María F., 'La Inmigración a Madrid (1600–1850)' *Reis: Revista Española de Investigaciones Sociológicas*, no. 32 (1985), pp. 67–100.

Cleminson, Richard and Francisco Vázquez García, *Sex, Identity and Hermaphrodites in Iberia, 1500–1800*, London: Taylor & Francis, 2015.

Conde de Clonard, *Historia orgánica de las armas de Infanteria y Caballeria españolas desde la creacion del ejercito permanente hasta el dia*, Madrid: Imprenta a cargo de Don Francisco del Castillo, 1859.

Cunha, Luís da, *Instruções inéditas a Marco António de Azevedo Coutinho*, edited by Pedro de Azevedo, Coimbra: Imprensa da Universidade, 1929.

Dekker, Rudolf and Lotte C. van de Pol, *The Tradition of Female Transvestism in Early Modern Europe*, London: St. Martin's Press, 1989.

DeVun, Leah, *The Shape of Sex: Nonbinary Gender from Genesis to the Renaissance*, New York: Columbia University Press, 2021.

Dreger, Alice Domurat, *Hermaphrodites and the Medical Invention of Sex*, Cambridge: Harvard University Press, 1998.

Edenborg, Emil, '"Traditional Values" and the Narrative of Gay Rights as Modernity: Sexual Politics beyond Polarization'. *Sexualities* (April 2021). https://doi.org/10.1177/13634607211008067.

Ekirch, A. Roger, 'Sleep We Have Lost: Pre-Industrial Slumber in the British Isles', *American Historical Review* 106, no. 2 (2001), pp. 343–86.

Elliott, John Huxtable, *History in the Making*, New Haven: Yale University Press, 2012.

Epstein, Julia J., 'Either/Or – Neither/Both: Sexual Ambiguity and the Ideology of Gender', *Genders*, 7 (1990), pp. 99–142.

Escamilla, Michèlle, 'A propos d'un dossier inquisitorial des environs de 1590: les étranges amours d'un hermaphrodite', in *Amours légitimes-amours illégitimes en Espagne, XVIe–XVIIe siècles*, edited by A. Redondo, Paris: Publ. de la Sorbonne, 1985, pp. 167–82.

Falkiner, Suzanne, *Eugenia: A Man*, Sydney: Xoum Publishing, 2014.

Ferrer Benimeli, José Antonio, *Masonería, Iglesia e Ilustración. (T.2): inquisición: procesos históricos (1739–1750)*, Madrid: Fundación Universitaria Española, 1976.

Fervel, Joseph Napoléon, *Campagnes de le révolution française dans les Pyrénées orientales, 1793–95*, Paris: Pillet fils aîné, 1853.

Foucault, Michel, *The History of Sexuality: 1: The Will to Knowledge*, London: Penguin Books, 2019.

Franco, E. E., *Un anatomico italiano, professore a Lisbona nel secolo xviii, Bernardo Santucci da Cortona (1701–1764). Bio-bibliografijia documentata e illustrata da fijigure*, Arezzo: Viviani, 1925.

Franco, José Eduardo and Paulo de Assunção, *As Metamorfoses de um polvo: Religião e política nos Regimentos da Inquisição Portuguesa (séculos XVI-XIX)*, Lisboa, Prefácio, 2004.

Frèches, Claude-Henri, *António José da Silva et l'Inquisition*, Lisbon: Fundação Calouste Gulbenkian, 1982.

Gilbert, Ruth, *Early Modern Hermaphrodites: Sex and Other Stories*, London: Palgrave Macmillan, 2002.

Giménez López, Enrique, 'Conflicto armado con Francia y guerrilla austracista en Cataluña (1719–1720)', *Hispania: Revista española de historia*, 65, no. 220 (2005), pp. 543–600.

Ginzburg, Carlo, *The Cheese and the Worms*, translated by John and Anne Tedeschi, Baltimore: Johns Hopkins University Press, 1980.

Girshick, Lori B., *Woman-to-Woman Sexual Violence: Does She Call It Rape?* Boston: Northeastern University Press, 2002.

Glass, N., and D. Hassouneh, 'The Influence of Gender Role Stereotyping on Women's Experiences of Female Same-Sex Intimate Partner Violence', *Violence against Women*, 14 (2008), pp. 310–25.

Goldmark, Matthew, 'Reading Habits: Catalina de Erauso and the Subjects of Early Modern Spanish Gender and Sexuality', *Colonial Latin American Review*, 24, no. 2 (2015), pp. 215–35.

Gonda, Caroline and John C. Benyon, *Lesbian Dames: Sapphism in the Long Eighteenth Century*, Farnham: Ashgate, 2010.

Heise, Ursula, 'Transvestism and the Stage Controversy in Spain and England, 1580–1680', *Theatre Journal*, 44, no. 3 (1992), pp. 357–74.

Iglésies, Josep, *Estadístiques de Població de Catalunya. El Primer Vicenni del Segle XVIII, Vol. III*, Barcelona: Fundació Salvador Vives Casajuana, 1974.

Kagan, Richard, *Lucrecia's dreams. Politics and Prophecy in Sixteenth-Century Spain*, Berkeley: University of California Press, 1990.

Kagan, Richard and Abigail Dyer, *Inquisitorial Inquiries: Brief Lives of Secret Jews and Other Heretics*, Baltimore: Johns Hopkins University Press, 2004.

Kamen, Henry, *Philip V of Spain*, New Haven: Yale University Press, 2001.

King, Helen, *The One-Sex Body on Trial: The Classical and Early Modern Evidence*, London: Routledge, 2013.

Lafora, Juan, *Dormitorios. La historia del dormitorio*, Madrid: Cigüeña, 1950.

Laqueur, Thomas, *Making Sex: Body and Gender from the Greeks to Freud*, Cambridge: Harvard University Press, 1992.

Lee, Christina, *The Anxiety of Sameness in Early Modern Spain*, Manchester: Manchester University Press, 2016.

Liberato, Marco, 'Trento, a Mulher e Controlo Social: O Recolhimento de S. Manços', in *Igreja, caridade e assistência na Península Ibérica (sécs. XVI-XVIII)*, edited by Laurinda Abreu, Évora: Publicações do Cidehus, 2004, pp. 275–89.

Long, Kathleen P., *Hermaphrodites in Renaissance Europe*, Aldershot: Ashgate Publishing, 2016.

Manion, Jen, *Female Husbands: A Trans History*, Cambridge: Cambridge University Press, 2020.

Marcocci, Giuseppe and José Pedro Paiva, *História da Inquisição Portuguesa (1536–1821)*, Lisbon: Esfera dos Livros, 2013.

Mendieta, Eva, *In Search of Catalina de Erauso: The National and Sexual Identity of the Lieutenant Nun*, translated by A. Prado, Reno Nev: University of Nevada Press, 2009.

Mercader i Riba, Joan, 'El Valle de Arán, la Nueva Planta y la invasión anglo-francesa de 1719', in *Actas del Primer Congreso Internacional de Estudios Pirenáicos, San Sebastián, 1950*, Zaragoza: Instituto de Estudios Pirenaicos, 1952.

Oram, Alison and Annemarie Turnbull, *The Lesbian History Sourcebook: Love and Sex between Women in Britain from 1780 to 1970*, London: Routledge, 2001.

Paiva, José Pedro, *Bruxaria e superstição num pais sem 'caça as bruxas' 1600–1774*, Lisbon: Notícias, 1997.

Palma, Inês and Antónia Fialho Conde, 'Dos espaços que o tempo silencia: novos dados para a interpretação do conjunto edificado do convento dominicano de Nª Sr.ª do Paraíso (Évora)', *Almansor. Revista de Cultura*, 3 (2017), pp. 71–98.

Perry, Mary Elizabeth, 'From Convent to Battlefield: Cross-Dressing and Gendering the Self in the New World of Imperial Spain', *Queer Iberia. Sexualities, Cultures, and Crossings from the Middle Ages to the Renaissance*, edited by J. Blackmore and G. S. Hutcheson, Durham: Duke University Press, 1999, pp. 394–419.

Planes i Ball, Josep Albert, *El general Moragues i la fortalesa de Castellciutat. La Guerra de Successió a la Seu d'Urgell*, Barcelona: Farell Editors, 2011.

Pueyo, Victor, *Cuerpos Plegables: Anatomías de La Excepción En España y En America Latina (Siglos XVI-XVIII)*, Woodbridge: Tamesis, 2016.

Ribeiro, Victor, *A Santa Casa da Misericórdia de Lisboa: subsidios para a sua historia, 1498–1898: instituição, vida historica, estado presente e seu futuro*, Lisbon: Academia Real das Sciencias, 1902.

Rijo, Delminda Maria Miguéns, 'Palácio dos Estaus de Hospedaria Real a Palácio da Inquisição e Tribunal do Santo Ofício', *Cadernos do Arquivo Municipal*, 2ª, 5 (2016), pp. 19–49.

Roodenburg, Herman, *Social Control in Europe 1500–1800*, Columbus: Ohio State University Press, 2004.

Rublack, Ulinka, *The Astronomer and the Witch: Johannes Kepler's Fight for His Mother*, Oxford: Oxford University Press, 2015.

Sancho i Valverde, Socorro and Carme Ros i Navarro, 'La població de catalunya en perspectiva històrica', in *La Societat Catalana*, edited by Salvador Giner, Barcelona: Generalitat de Catalunya, 1998, pp. 91–116.

Sears, Clare, 'All that Glitters: Tran-sing California's Gold Rush Migrations', *GLQ: A Journal in Lesbian and Gay Studies*, 14 (2–3) (2008), pp. 383–402.

Seelau, E. P., and S. M. Seelau, 'Gender-Role Stereotypes and Perceptions of Heterosexual, Gay and Lesbian Domestic Violence', *Journal of Family Violence*, 20 (2005), pp. 363–71.

Serrão, José Vicente, 'População e rede urbana nos séculos XVI-XVIII,' in *História dos municípios e do poder local*, edited by César Oliveira, Lisbon: Círculo de Leitores, 1996, pp. 63–77.

Sharpe, Alex, *Sexual Intimacy and Gender Identity 'Fraud': Reframing the Legal and Ethical Debate*, London: Taylor & Francis, 2018.

Shergold, N. D., *A History of the Spanish Stage: From Medieval Times until the End of the Seventeenth Century*, Oxford: Clarendon Press, 1967.

Silva, Maria Beatriz Nizza da, *D. João V*, Rio de Mouros: Temas e Debates, 2009.

Soyer, François, 'The Inquisition and the "Priestess of Zafra": Hermaphroditism and Gender Transgression in Seventeenth-Century Spain', *Annali Della Scuola Normale Superiore di Pisa. Classe di Lettere E Filosofia, Serie* 5, 1, no. 2 (2009), pp. 535–62.

Soyer, François, *Ambiguous Gender in Early Modern Spain and Portugal. Inquisitors, Doctors and the Transgression of Gender Norms*, Leiden: Brill, 2012.

Soyer, François, 'The Inquisitorial Trial of a Cross-Dressing Lesbian: Reactions and Responses to Female Homosexuality in 18th-Century Portugal', *Journal of Homosexuality*, 61, no. 11 (2014), pp. 1529–57.

Soyer, François, 'Enforcing Religious Repression in an Age of World Empires: Assessing the Global Reach of the Spanish and Portuguese Inquisitions', *History: The Journal of the Historical Association*, 100, no. 341 (2015), pp. 331–53.

Soyer, François, 'Androgyny and the Fear of Demonic Intervention in the Early Modern Iberian Peninsula: Ecclesiastical and Popular Responses', *Ordering Emotions in Europe, 1100–1800*, edited by Susan Broomhall, Leiden: E. J. Brill, 2015, pp. 245–62.

Stolberg, Michael, 'A Woman Down to Her Bones: The Anatomy of Sexual Difference in the Sixteenth and Early Seventeenth Centuries', *Isis*, 94, no. 2 (2003), pp. 274–99.

Stepto, Michele and Gabriel, *Lieutenant Nun. Memoir of a Basque Transvestite in the New World*, Boston: Beacon, 1996.

Stryker, Susan, *Transgender History*, Berkeley: Seal Press, 2009.

Traub, Valerie, *The Renaissance of Lesbianism in Early Modern England*, Cambridge: Cambridge University Press, 2002.

Valentine, David, *Imagining Transgender: An Ethnography of a Category*, Durham: Duke University Press, 2007.

Velasco, Sherry, *The Lieutenant Nun: Transgenderism, Lesbian Desire, and Catalina de Erauso*, Austin: University of Texas Press, 2000.

Velasco, Sherry, *Male Delivery: Reproduction, Effeminacy and Pregnant Men in Early Modern Spain*, Nashville: Vanderbilt University Press, 2006.

Velasco, Sherry, *Lesbians in Early Modern Spain*, Nashville: Vanderbilt University Press, 2011.

Vicente, Marta V., *Debating Sex and Gender in Eighteenth-Century Spain*, Cambridge: Cambridge University Press, 2017.

Vollendorf, Lisa, *The Lives of Women: A New History of Inquisitorial Spain*, Nashville: Vanderbilt University Press, 2005.

Wolf, Hubert, *The Nuns of Sant' Ambrogio, The True Story of a Convent in Scandal*, Oxford: Oxford University Press, 2015.

Wright, Lawrence, *Warm & Snug: The History of the Bed*, London: Routledge, 1962.

Zemon Davis, Natalie, *The Return of Martin Guerre*, Cambridge: Harvard University Press, 1983.

Websites and online resources

Newspaper webpages

'Woman Who Posed as Man Guilty of Sexual Assault', *BBC News*, 15 September 2015: https://web.archive.org/save/https://www.bbc.com/news/uk-england-merseyside-34258993 (accessed 16 February 2022).

'Vox avisa que llevará al TC la Ley Trans y denunciará las banderas arcoiris en los ayuntamientos', *Europa Press*, 28 June 2021: https://web.archive.org/save/https://www.europapress.es/eseuropa/noticia-vox-avisa-llevara-tc-ley-trans-denunciara-banderas-arcoiris-ayuntamientos-20210628143120.html (accessed 21 March 2022).

'Sexual Predator Posed as a Man to Trick Women into Sex', Evening Standard, 25 May 2022: https://web.archive.org/save/https://www.standard.co.uk/news/crime/sexual-predator-hannah-walters-posed-as-man-trick-women-into-sex-london-crime-b1002373.html (accessed 26 May 2022).

'Prosthetic Penis Case: Gayle Newland Convicted Of Sexual Assault', *Huffington Post*, 29 June 2017: https://web.archive.org/save/https://www.huffingtonpost.co.uk/entry/prosthetic-penis-case-gayle-newland-convicted-of-sexual-assault_uk_59550a80e4b0da2c7321a71a (accessed 16 February 2022).

'Morte Duma General', *Público*, 20 July 2007: https://web.archive.org/save/https://www.imdb.com/title/tt12670228/ and https://web.archive.org/save/https://www.publico.pt/2007/07/20/jornal/morte-duma--general-223056 (accessed 21 May 2021).

'Julgamento de Maria Teresinha', *RTP Arquivos*, 31 March 1993: https://arquivos.rtp.pt/conteudos/caso-da-general-teresinha-gomes/ and https://web.archive.org/save/https://arquivos.rtp.pt/conteudos/julgamento-de-maria-teresinha-2/ (accessed 21 May 2021).

'Tarjit Singh: Transgender Man Who Tricked Women into Sexual Relationships with Fake Penis Is Convicted', *Sky News*, 25 May 2022: https://web.archive.org/

web/20220525233245/https://news.sky.com/story/tarjit-singh-transgender-man-tricked-women-into-sexual-relationships-by-using-prosthetic-penis-12621386 (accessed 26 May 2022).

Other websites

The Office of the High Commissioner of the United Nations for Human Rights, 'Intersex People. OHCHR and the Human Rights of LGBTI People': https://www.ohchr.org/EN/Issues/LGBTI/Pages/IntersexPeople.aspx (accessed 5 May 2021).

'Rueda de prensa de Jorge Buxadé y Patricia Rueda', uploaded to Youtube on 28 June 2021, *Official Vox Video*: https://www.youtube.com/watch?v=rh-A3vUaJMk (accessed 21 March 2022).

Municipality of Lisbon, Patrimonio Cultural, 'Recolhimento de Nossa Senhora da Encarnação e Carmo': http://patrimoniocultural.cm-lisboa.pt/lxconventos/ficha_imprimir.aspx?id=615 (accessed 11 December 2020).

NSW State Records and Archives, 'Eugenia Falleni – Convicted Murderer': https://web.archive.org/web/20210507042721/https://www.records.nsw.gov.au/archives/magazine/galleries/eugenia-falleni-convicted-murderer (accessed 7 May 2021).

Real Academia de la Historia. 'Biography of Father José Jofreu': http://dbe.rah.es/biografias/40795/jose-jofreu (accessed 14 November 2022).

Index

www.ingramcontent.com/pod-product-compliance
Lightning Source LLC
Chambersburg PA
CBHW062028270326
41929CB00014B/2355
9781350377639